Return

Return

A Palestinian Memoir

Ghada Karmi

VERSO

London • New York

First published by Verso 2015
© Ghada Karmi

The moral rights of the author have been asserted

1 3 5 7 9 10 8 6 4 2

Verso
UK: 6 Meard Street, London W1F 0EG
US: 20 Jay Street, Suite 1010, Brooklyn, NY 11201
www.versobooks.com

Verso is the imprint of New Left Books

ISBN-13: 978-1-78168-842-7 (HC)
eISBN-13: 978-1-78168-844-1 (US)
eISBN-13: 978-1-78168-843-4 (UK)

British Library Cataloguing in Publication Data
A catalogue record for this book is available from the British Library

Library of Congress Cataloging-in-Publication Data

Karmi, Ghada.
 Return : a Palestinian memoir / Ghada Karmi.
   pages cm
  ISBN 978-1-78168-842-7 (hardback)
 1. Karmi, Ghada. 2. Women, Palestinian Arab – Great Britain – Biography.
 3. Women, Palestinian Arab – West Bank–Biography. I. Title.
 HQ1728.5.Z75K37 2015
 305.48'89274 – dc23
                    2014045651

Typeset in Sabon by MJ & N Gavan, Truro, Cornwall
Printed and bound by
CPI Group (UK) Ltd, Croydon, CR0 4YY

For Lalla Salma

Contents

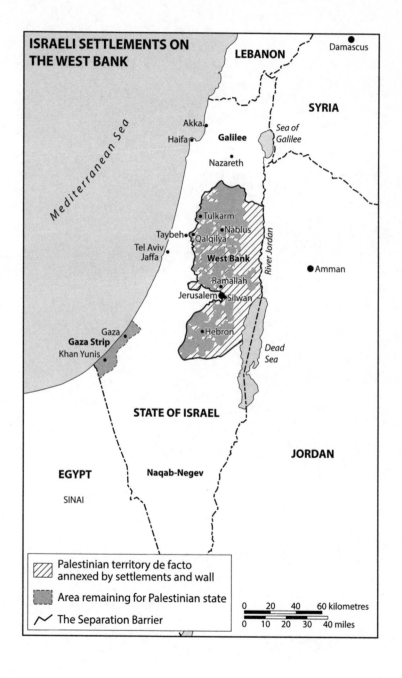

ISRAELI SETTLEMENTS ON
THE WEST BANK

LEBANON

Damascus

SYRIA

Akka
Haifa
Galilee
Sea of
Galilee
Nazareth

Mediterranean Sea

Tulkarm
Taybeh
Qalqilya
Nablus
Tel Aviv
Jaffa
West Bank
River Jordan
Ramallah
Jerusalem
Silwan
Amman

Gaza
Gaza Strip
Khan Yunis
Hebron
Dead
Sea

STATE OF ISRAEL

JORDAN

EGYPT
Naqab-Negev

SINAI

Palestinian territory de facto
annexed by settlements and wall

Area remaining for Palestinian state

The Separation Barrier

0   20   40   60 kilometres
0   10   20   30   40 miles

Acknowledgements

My thanks are principally due to Leo Hollis at Verso for his enthusiasm and support from the beginning, his unfailing encouragement while I was writing the book and his careful editing of the manuscript. I am grateful in equal measure to Adel Kamal who was invaluable in further editing the text with his usual thoroughness, insight and precision for linguistic and factual errors. His suggestions for how to resolve difficult passages in the narrative and move it on were essential to the completion of the book.

I wish also to thank the members of my writer's group, Zina Rohan, Martin Plaut, Christina Pribichevic, Roger von Zwanenburg and Sanjay Dasgupta who read various chapters and offered enormously helpful amendments, corrections and suggestions. I am likewise indebted to Tim Llewellyn who helped with information and suggestions for some sections of the book. I would also like to thank everyone at Verso who took *Return* through to its final stages.

My sister, Siham, provided important family details that I had not known or been mistaken about. My daughter and most exacting critic, Salma, was not slow to point out insensitivities and lapses of memory on my part in the personal sections of the book.

But the person I would most have wanted to acknowledge for having inspired and taught me ways of thinking that have informed this book, my late father, was not there for me to thank him.

Author's Note

All the characters in this book are real or based on real people, but a number of names have been changed to avoid embarrassment. That excludes well-known individuals whose original names have been preserved.

Prologue

As I sat at my father's bedside, listening to his irregular breathing and the sound of the pulse monitor attached to his finger, I thought how frightening it was to be brought up sharp against the awareness of one's own mortality. I feared death equally as much as I knew my father did. He was a very old man, but age had not dimmed his ardour for life and I imagined I would be the same. Like most people, I did not like to contemplate my dying and avoided thinking about it, but it was always there, waiting in the background to be attended to. An elderly doctor I knew once told me, 'I believe that people must prepare for death. Avoidance and denial are foolish. If we face up fair and square to the inevitability of death it will lose its terrors.'

I stroked my father's hand but his eyes remained closed and he made no motion to indicate he was aware of my presence. The male nurses checked him over and then left us alone. I stood and went to open the window of his room, not seeing out but thinking about his approaching death. It was not a time for reckonings and resentments, but I had a memory of how affectionate and indulgent he had been when I was very young and of how he changed later. I was never sure if that memory had been idealised by hindsight and wishful thinking. But that early childhood experience was never repeated, for when we went to England he changed into a stranger who never showed any emotion towards me except a keen interest in my academic progress. His view of me as a studious, clever

I

daughter, whose sole ambition in life was to gain professional success coloured my view of myself. I grew up uncertain of my femininity and wondering if I should model myself on him, to the detriment of many an emotional encounter I had subsequently. I never forgave him for that, nor for many other things, although I never said so.

Looking at his skeletal state now, pyjama jacket unbuttoned to show his bony ribcage, his sad hollow stomach with its overlying empty folds of skin, I put away those bitter thoughts. Whatever my disappointments about his personal relationship with me, I passionately did not want him to die, not just for *who* he was but for *what*. His final days would be drawn-out, overshadowed by family squabbles, as happens at such times. But hanging over that period was the haunting knowledge that an era, not just for his family, but for Palestinian history, was drawing to a close. My father was born in Palestine at the time of the Ottoman Empire, lived through its demise and its replacement by the British Mandate that ruled Palestine, endured the establishment of the State of Israel thereafter and was forced into exile. His life encompassed a century of conflict, a period of Palestinian history that demolished everything he knew and overturned the old order forever.

He had fallen ill a month before with what was diagnosed as pneumonia, malnutrition and severe anaemia and taken to the Palestine Hospital nearby. My sister Siham, who was living with him at the time, phoned me in London to say she thought he was dying. In the 1960s, when I was a medical student in England, we were taught to think of pneumonia as 'the old man's friend', a painless exit from this life which no one officiously strove to prevent. But in the late twentieth century and by the time my father fell ill, medical practice had changed. No one was allowed to die without energetic intervention, antibiotics, ventilators, intravenous fluids, even surgery. When I arrived I found my father in the hospital's intensive care unit, on antibiotics, a drip in his arm, being closely monitored. He was conscious and frightened. What rest he was afforded was constantly interrupted by a ceaseless flow of visitors inquiring after his health. The nurses' feeble efforts to stem the tide of people entering a supposedly sterile and quiet area collapsed completely after the first day. He felt constrained to respond when anyone came, and was exhausted and querulous.

When I arrived to see this situation, unheard of in such units in Britain, I did my best to stop visitors coming in. But this was Jordan, an Arab country, where relatives, however distant, and friends who might also be accompanied by people unknown to the patient, were expected to show their concern and respect for the sick. In my father's case, there was the additional factor of his public status as a scholar and foremost Arab savant, which drew admirers of his work to visit as well. My efforts to keep them out appeared ungracious, even offensive, and were in any case unsuccessful. In a while, the café area outside the wards became a meeting place for his visitors where they ran into acquaintances they had not seen for some time or met new people. The place became a focus for such gatherings, often chatty, social and light-hearted. Meanwhile, my father somehow improved enough to be returned to an ordinary hospital bed.

He was alert, but so weak that he needed help with every bodily function. He ate little because he could not swallow properly, and his weight kept going down. Many of our relatives, devout Muslims, prayed for his recovery. I would visit him with my brother's son, Omar, who had lived with my parents as a teenager and remained close to him. One afternoon, when I was alone with him, and thinking him asleep, he sat up and gripped my arm urgently. He looked at me almost desperately and whispered in a conspiratorial voice, 'What do you say to Omar, you and me going home now? We could just leave now, this afternoon. What do you say?' I could feel his urgency and desperate desire to go home. If only I could say yes, and we could all go together just as he wanted. 'No, father,' I shook my head gently. 'Not yet. But soon, soon.' He sank back and closed his eyes. This memory returns to me even now, because I know that passionate longing for normality, for life to resume as it has always been, and yet be powerless to make it happen. It took me back to an April morning long ago and to the child I was then, standing helplessly at the closed garden gates of our house in Jerusalem that my heart feared I would never see again.

Two weeks later, my father returned home as he had wished, but much altered and weaker. To make this return possible my sister and I had arranged twenty-four-hour nursing for him, and a hospital bed, suitably modified for home use, was set up in his bedroom. This had been no easy task, as the quality of nursing was not generally good, and there was little training in care of the dying at home. This situation was typical of many Arab and other underdeveloped countries. Nursing, indeed all medical services other than doctoring, was regarded as second-class. It had a low status, was poorly paid, and in general, most Arab parents would not wish for their daughters to join that profession, since it would involve immodest activities like nursing men, washing, dressing and undressing them. The result of this attitude was that it was hard for us to find a good nurse for my father. After trying and rejecting several candidates, we settled on two young men who seemed reasonably competent. Even so, they would take time off away from my father's bedside to perform their prayers at the prescribed times, a devotion well beyond the call of duty, since Islam allows for a postponement of prayer in special circumstances.

I went back to London where I was based, to cancel appointments and make arrangements for my absence, returning to Amman about a week later. The sight of my father in hospital, more shrunken and even thinner than before shocked me. His doctor, an amiable, efficient, youngish man, had pressed for a gastrostomy: an opening to be made directly into his stomach to enable the entry of adequate amounts of food. Up until then he had been maintained on a nasal tube, which did not allow sufficient nutrients to pass through and frequently got blocked. It also irritated his nose and the back of his throat. Removing it and feeding him in another way seemed to me the obvious course.

But not to the rest of the family, with whom there were heated discussions over the merits of the gastrostomy. They ignored the doctor's opinion and mine and consulted friends and relatives, including an elderly surgeon long out of practice, who was against it, and decided it would be cruel to subject an old man to an operation. He had lived a long life, they said, and his time had come. Muslims believe that to each of us there is a term of life appointed by God. When the end of that term arrives, none can advance or delay it even by one hour. There is a comforting fatalism in this belief, which I had often noted and envied. I remember when a cousin of mine lost her young daughter-in-law and two small grandchildren in a fatal car crash, leaving my cousin's eldest son suddenly widowed and alone, I went to give her my condolences. She met me with a calm, resigned face. 'It is as God wanted,' she said with a sigh, neither indifferent nor overly sorrowful.

As to my father, further argument with the family was useless, and he was in effect condemned to worse starvation. I urged the doctor to ignore the dissenting members of the family and proceed with the gastrostomy, but he declined, afraid to become embroiled in a family feud. It angered me that I could not overrule the family decision, despite its basic wrong-headedness. Though it was but one event, that disagreement underlined for me the difficulties in our relationships with each other, our common mistrust, disrespect and shifting affections. There were reasons not of our making for this, but it did not change the outcome. And in the end it was all for nothing. After two more futile weeks spent trying to feed my father through his nasal tube, he was readmitted to hospital and had his gastrostomy after all. Only now he was even more skeletal and starved, and it is doubtful that whatever happened at that point would make much difference.

I looked at him, lying in his bed, his eyes closed, and his breathing bubbling through the fluid in his lungs. The sound of the pulse monitor, clamped over his forefinger like a clothes peg, was sometimes the only evidence that he was alive. But yet at times he was aware of those around him, though he could not speak, and a slight nod indicated that he heard and understood what was said to him. When Salma, my daughter, whom he had asked about before he was so ill, came from London to see him, he smiled and seemed to know she was there. But most of the time, he half-slept, and I wondered what went through his mind as he lay attached to tubes, hardly able to breathe and with no hope of release.

It was as if he refused to let go of even this poor existence that he had. His hold on life had always been tenacious, and as death approached it grew even more so. My mother, then deceased for sixteen years, used to say to us, 'Mind my words, your father does not intend to die. Ever!'

CHAPTER I

Journey to Ramallah

'What the hell was I thinking of?'

I had sworn never to return to this torn-up, unhappy land after that first trip in 1991 when I broke a long-standing family taboo against ever visiting the place that had been Palestine and then became Israel. It had always been too painful to contemplate, too traumatic an acknowledgement of our loss and the triumph of those who had taken our place. In the two weeks I spent there on that first visit, I travelled up and down the country of my birth, looking at the remnants of the old Palestine and at what its new occupants had wrought in the years since our flight in 1948. I was barely able to comprehend the changed landscape of what had been an Arab place, its new inhabitants speaking an alien language, their looks a motley assortment of European, Asian, African, and any mixture of these.

It was a momentous journey that had filled me with bitterness and grief. I remember looking down on a night-time Tel Aviv from the windows of the plane taking me back to London and thinking hopelessly, 'Flotsam and jetsam, that's what we've become, scattered and divided. There's no room for us or our memories here. And it won't ever be reversed.'

As it transpired, I broke my resolve and returned to the same land several times after 1991, and here I was again. The white walls and white-tiled floor of the huge apartment I would be living in stared back at me silently. The man from the United Nations Development Programme office in Jerusalem, who had driven me to Ramallah, had left – it felt more like abandoned – me with affable expressions of welcome and reassurance that I would be very happy staying there. My footsteps echoed through the wide, tiled hall, the three large bedrooms, and spacious double reception room with its separate seating areas for men and women in the conventional Arab style. I wondered when on earth I would ever be inviting the hordes of people needed to fill them.

It was an early afternoon during the hot summer of 2005. I sank down on one of the armchairs, my case and computer still packed beside me, ready to leave at any minute. I was in one of the 'Gemzo Suites', an imposing white stone apartment hotel on a high point in al-Bireh, a large village just outside Ramallah that had been a separate place until 1994, when its administration was merged with Ramallah's. 'Gemzo' in fact stood for Jimzu, a village to the east of the town of al-Ramleh in pre-1948 Palestine, where the owner of the Suites' family had presumably originated. It must have been a pretty little place, built on a hillside and surrounded by cactus plants and olive trees, before it was demolished in September 1948 by Palestine's new owners. Commemorating place names in that now vanished Palestine was a common practice amongst Palestinians in exile, as if to defy history and recreate those lost towns and villages. Even when such people were not old enough to remember the places for themselves, their parents or other older relatives passed on their nostalgic memories. In the same way most Palestinian homes displayed pictures of Jerusalem in its Arab days, as if there had been no 1967 and no Israel.

I should have been grateful to be housed in such style, but all I felt that first day was a desire to cross the Allenby Bridge that separated Jordan from the Israeli-occupied Palestinian territories, and go back to my father's flat in Amman where I had been staying. Sitting in that large and echoing Gemzo suite, I tried to will myself back into the mood that had impelled me to leave England where I had lived for most of my life to come to a place which I knew more in theory than in practice, more as an abstract cause than a living reality. I thought back to the hurdles I had had to overcome in getting to this point: my own scruples, the difficulties of entering Palestine – even the visa application, a matter of banal routine when going anywhere but to the country I was headed for.

'Why is it so difficult for you to just give me the visa?' I asked the expressionless official behind the glass counter at the Israeli consulate in London. Visiting the consulate had been a novel experience. Up until then I had been nowhere near any Israeli official building except as part of a demonstration against Israel. I never even saw these places on such occasions, since a phalanx of policemen and a closed iron gate usually blocked the view. 'It's already been agreed by your people in Jerusalem. All I was supposed to do was collect it.'

'It's not so simple,' he answered wearily. He had fair hair and blue eyes; I could have taken him for a Swedish bank clerk. At my sceptical look, he threw up his hands. 'What can I tell you?' he exclaimed, 'computers down since two days, and we got no technician from Israel to repair them.' It seemed that for 'security' reasons, no computer expert from London would have been allowed to do the job. 'Anyway,' he said, trying to make light of it. 'What's the fuss already? You're a UK citizen. No problem. You get your visa when you arrive.'

In the event, no Israeli technician ever arrived, and I ended up travelling without the visa. 'Well, that's a good one!' snorted my Arab friends afterwards. 'Couldn't they think of anything better? You must know they've got a file on you for sure. You'll never get in! The Israelis know *everything*!' they added darkly. There was a widespread conviction amongst many Arabs that the Israeli secret services were fiendishly clever. Innocuous incidents involving Israelis became sinister until proved otherwise. But after my experience at the consulate, I remember wondering if Israelis were such super-efficient, Machiavellian geniuses after all. Perhaps they're just as bumbling and incompetent as we are, I thought. Had the same incident occurred at an Arab consulate, none of us would even have questioned it. 'Bloody useless Arabs,' we'd have said. 'Why don't they ever learn?'

The thought recurred on the next hurdle in my journey, as I stood before the Israeli immigration control at the Jordan–West Bank border. I had just arrived from Amman where I spent a few days with my father. The immigration officer, a young woman sitting behind the glass window of her booth, looked fed up and ready for her lunch break. She was dark and pimply with crinkly black hair and could have been Afro-Caribbean. She asked me a few questions in a listless sort of way, as if following a drill which she had learned by heart and which bored her stiff.

'Where are you going to in Israel? What is the purpose of your visit?' she intoned in a sing-song voice.

'I'm going to Jerusalem, where I'll be working for UNDP,' I answered, as I had been told to do. I doubted that she knew or cared to know what the UNDP was. Most Israelis regarded the UN as their enemy because of what they believed to be its inbuilt pro-Arab majority. They routinely dismissed any censure against them by the world body, usually voiced through its General Assembly, as plain and simple bias. But she did not question it any further.

'Do you intend to visit anyone in the West Bank?'

'I don't think so,' I answered untruthfully, but again as instructed, and added: 'Maybe.'

'Who do you know in Israel?'

I reeled off a list of Jewish Israeli friends, as it had been suggested I should. She eased herself off her stool and disappeared behind the booth. I could see her talking to another female immigration officer, this one blond and clearly Ashkenazi (of European extraction) and likely to be her superior on those grounds alone. There was a well-known but little publicised prejudice among Ashkenazi Jews in Israel against Arab or oriental Jews, which led to a variety of attitudes and practices that discriminated against them. The girl came back at a leisurely pace, taking her time studying my passport. 'It says here you were born in Israel.' She was looking at the page where my place of birth was recorded as Jerusalem.

'Not Israel,' I corrected, 'Palestine.' As indeed it was before 1948, but a grave error to mention in an interview which had been going well until then. 'OK,' she said, suddenly alert. 'Go there. You have to wait there,' pointing to a bench against the wall. The queue of people behind me pressed up to the window, glad of the space I had vacated.

It used to be routine for someone with a record of pro-Palestinian political activism like myself to be stopped for questioning each time I tried to enter Israel. But as I had grown older, and presumably less of a threat, it happened less often. A left-wing Israeli activist friend, Akiva Orr, who was regularly subjected to interrogation in the same way, used to say to me, 'Listen, Ghada, don't complain! If the day comes, God forbid, they don't stop me at the border any more, I'll know I'm finished!'

After an hour of waiting without an explanation from anyone, a man came over holding my passport. 'OK,' he said not without courtesy, 'you can go.' 'What was the problem?' I asked. He did not answer, and just waved me back to the same immigration officer. She looked at me without interest, and only mildly questioned my request to have the Israeli visa stamped on a paper separate from my passport. 'Why you don't want me to stamp the passport?' I explained that Arab countries like Saudi Arabia or Lebanon, having no diplomatic relations with Israel, would not allow me to enter if an Israeli visa were stamped on my passport. She shrugged and let me through. The relative ease with which I crossed the border, even given this incident, was probably due to my Western passport, although it was still no guarantee. British or European visitors whom Israel suspected of being Palestinian supporters could often be detained for hours, or even expelled.

However many times I made the bridge crossing in later years, I never got used to this exercise of Israeli control over what was not Israel's to police at all. Strictly speaking, only Jordanian and Palestinian immigration officers should have manned the border between Jordan and the West Bank, since Israel 'proper', as it was known within its pre-1967 borders, did not extend that far. Inside the Israeli terminal building a huge colour photograph of a smiling King Hussein of Jordan, lighting Yitzhak Rabin's cigarette in a show of friendship, paid lip service to the peace treaty signed between the two countries in 1994. In reality the only power in the vicinity was Israel, and the Israeli blue and white flag fluttering possessively at the Allenby Bridge emphasised the point.

Had I been a Palestinian West Bank 'resident', the scene at the bridge would have been very different: crowds, long queues, hold-ups, searches, interrogations and hours of waiting, with the ever-present possibility of rejection or arrest. In subsequent years, with Israel's increasing self-confidence in its occupation of Palestinian land, this distinction became less marked and crossing the bridge was easier. But whether it was a Western or a Palestinian traveller, the essence of all these measures was the unpredictability of Israeli behaviour. No one could be sure of entering the country, let alone getting anywhere inside it, and planning a journey in advance was something of a futile exercise.

I was not one of those people who found it exciting to live in other countries. Even when I was younger and supposedly more adventurous, I had never gone to summer camps or joined student groups on jaunts to foreign places. Aside from two years spent in the Arab countries at the end of the 1970s, when I had forced myself to go with much trepidation, I had never strayed far from England. That visit, first to Syria and then to Jordan, had been all about my quest for belonging, to find my roots and a credible identity. Perhaps I was too eager at the time, too intense in my search, but my journeys ended in failure on both counts. I felt no more a part of them than they did of me. I was not 'Arab' enough there, and too 'Arab' in England, despite being thoroughly anglicised and immersed in English culture.

I supposed my trip in 2005 was a search of the same kind, but it was more inchoate, not properly thought through, as if I were groping to find my way through a fog. My decision had been spurred on by a mixture of frustration and unhappiness, no basis for rational choices. I regarded my situation as a deeply unsatisfactory one. I had no settled personal life, something it seemed I was doomed to endure, and I felt that my professional life – the activism, the writing, the organisational work – was at a dead end too. In the past, when such feelings assailed me, I would find solace in a new political project or initiative. But this time I found none which I could pursue with any conviction. I felt stale and wrung out.

Like many Palestinians, my greatest pursuit, indeed obsession, for most of my adult life had been Palestine. There was no room in it for much else. I lived and breathed it, worried about its adversities which felt as urgent and immediate as if they were happening beside me. I kept abreast of all its news, read constantly, combed through the internet for more information, monitored the media, talked to other activists, attended and also organised meetings and conferences, and wrote endlessly about it – to such an extent that when anyone asked what I did for a living, I would answer, 'I'm a full-time Palestinian!' It was not really true, of course, since I had worked as a doctor of medicine, been a medical historian and later become an academic. But being a Palestinian was the only thing that felt real.

However, after years of activism I had begun to feel disconnected and irrelevant. The gap between what seemed like shadow-fencing with Israel in the security of London and the real fight taking place on the ground in Palestine was too great to ignore. After the Oslo Accords between Israel and the Palestinians were drawn up in 1993,[1] Yasser Arafat and the rest of the leadership returned to Palestinian soil from forty years of exile. And with them, the centre of gravity of the Palestinian cause and the real political action shifted inside. This made the rest of us still promoting the cause outside Palestine feel left behind, like people trying to catch a train that has long departed.

Until that happened, the cause had been with us in exile. Since the late 1960s when the Palestine Liberation Organisation (PLO) was at its zenith, internationally known and a magnet for idealists from all over the world who flocked to join its ranks, our ideas and decisions were the ones that mattered. For the first time since the Nakba – the cataclysmic event of 1948, when most of us were dispersed out of Palestine – we felt ourselves connected to one another in an unprecedented national project that promised liberation from the Israeli grip on our homeland. It was the PLO, formed in exile, its fighters drawn from the refugee camps of exile, that gave us those feelings of relevance and value, even of importance. It brought our case, previously forgotten or scornfully dismissed, before the world's attention. Our compatriots inside Palestine, living under either Jordanian or Israeli rule, were often sidelined in this national awakening. As its power grew, the PLO acquired, however unconsciously, the status of a substitute homeland for the refugees in their camps and most of us in exile, even of signifying Palestine itself.

This was not universally acknowledged at the time, and it was only when the PLO departed our midst that we realised

---

1 This agreement between the Israeli government and the Palestine Liberation Organisation under the auspices of the US gave the Palestinians under Israeli occupation a degree of autonomy and held out an implicit promise of future statehood for them.

how central its existence had been for a scattered people like us. It had given us an identity and a focus. That last act of return from exile, trumpeted as a triumph, was for us outside an abandonment. 1994, the year in which Arafat and his men moved to Gaza, deprived the diaspora, especially the refugees in the camps, of their backbone support and signalled the end of our relevance as political actors. This was not as drastic as it seemed when it first happened, for there was still a PLO representative office in London which to some degree maintained our connection with each other.

In its heyday, the PLO had functioned as a virtual government-in-exile, with a parliament in the shape of the Palestine National Council (PNC), the PLO's highest legislative body. The PNC aimed to represent the whole Palestinian people and brought together delegates from all the Palestinian communities inside and outside Palestine. Various PLO unions of workers, writers, students and women were established, and a host of welfare services was set up for Palestinian refugees, chiefly those in Jordan and Lebanon. These refugees had hitherto subsisted on international aid from the UN and other charitable sources. But after 1971, the PLO developed its own welfare, medical and social programmes for them, created work opportunities, and adopted the children of fighters killed during operations against Israel.

Most crucially, the organisation provided armed protection for the refugee camps. Supposedly safe places under international law, these had been a target for Israeli military operations from the 1950s onwards. They were also subject to in-fighting among groups with different political affiliations. The loss of PLO protection in 1982, when the fighters were withdrawn from the camps and forced into exile in the wake of the Israeli siege of Beirut, leaving them defenceless, had tragic consequences. A short while later, in September 1982, two Beirut refugee camps, Sabra and Shatila, were overrun by fiercely anti-Palestinian Lebanese Phalangist

forces, their entry facilitated by Israel's army, which had surrounded the camps. Up to 2,000 people, mostly old men,
women and children, were massacred in a killing spree lasting
two days.

After 1974, when Yasser Arafat, the PLO chairman, gave
his famous address to the UN General Assembly signalling
the organisation's international acceptance, PLO representatives, acting as quasi-ambassadors, were appointed to most
world capitals. The first PLO representative in London, Said
Hammami, arrived in 1975. We were soon drawn to his office,
which became a centre for meetings, engagement and activism. Many of us aspired to visit the PLO's headquarters in
West Beirut and meet Arafat in person. I remember making
such a trip in 1976, and the sense of wonderment I felt on
seeing the huge map of Palestine on the wall outside his office,
and the young men in kufiyyas (the black-and-white check
headdress that has become Palestine's national symbol), chatting in Palestinian Arabic. I felt connected with my origins as
never before, and thrilled to be at the centre of the cause.

Looking back years later, the PLO had been far from
perfect. Its guerrilla factions were frequently disunited, disagreed on strategy, and as a result made serious mistakes.
Many Palestinians were quick to condemn and criticise. But
for all that, it was undeniable that the PLO achieved a seismic
shift in their political fortunes. Forgotten for two decades as
'Arab refugees' living on handouts, their cause returned to the
world stage with the PLO. In the exceptional circumstances of
exile, with a displaced people, most of whom lived outside the
homeland, the PLO managed to bring Palestinians together
under its umbrella and restore their sense of themselves as a
community fighting for a common cause. The institutions it
established had never existed before and, had things gone differently, they could have been adapted to form the basis of a
new Palestinian state.

But now all that was over, part of another world, and

Arafat and his men had gone. In the vacuum of leadership left behind, everyone was looking for a role, uncertain how to go forward or what to do. I remember writing comments and articles about these events until it dawned on me that in this changed world I was likely to end up a kind of second-hand Palestinian, an armchair windbag, whom no one listened to because of my distance from the real thing.

The thought was galling, especially when I found myself with people who had gone to work or live in my homeland. Although most of them were not Palestinian, when they came back they often regarded themselves as authorities on the country. I had noticed that Palestine frequently brought out such feelings in people because they saw it as a friendless orphan, and no one seemed to be in overall charge. I would listen to their experiences with something like envy that it was they and not I who was recounting those stories. They created in me a sense of distance and irrelevance that became intolerable, until I realised there was only one way to end it. I would have to go there myself and re-establish my connection with the people who lived there, my people, whose lives I would share, even if only for a while.

Although I had sworn in 1991 never to return, I had gone back on my oath within two years of that visit, and several times afterwards. But those trips were often brief and work-related. Living there would be different, and as the thought became more insistent, I found myself eager to try. It was a daring decision for someone so averse to foreign travel as I was, but the moment it was taken I discovered a longing in myself, not just to reverse my sense of irrelevance by going there, but to draw from the experience the sense of purpose I had so lost. Whether those wishes would be fulfilled I had no idea, but I was determined to go.

In 2005, 'Palestine' was usually taken to mean the Israeli-occupied West Bank and Gaza. If I decided to go I would be living in Ramallah, the West Bank city that functioned as the capital of this small Palestine. Ramallah was a landlocked place six miles north of Jerusalem with a population of some 300,000 people. Before 1948, its main attraction was the cool climate that made it a popular summer resort for well-to-do Palestinians. But by the time I went there it was the seat of the Palestinian Authority (PA), which enjoyed a quasi-official status as the headquarters of 'Palestine', and had become a destination for visitors from all over the world. It also provided an address for those, like me, who wanted to come and help out in some way.

My decision was not just motivated by fears of political irrelevance, but also by the old, unresolved conflicts that still haunted me and which my abortive trips to Syria and Jordan had done nothing to resolve: the desire to belong, to be part of the community, to fit into my skin. By 2005 I had lived in England for more than fifty years, and was fairly integrated and at ease in my adopted country. It was my home as much as anywhere could be. But I was of that generation of Palestinians who still retained a memory of the homeland, however fragmented and shadowy, and still knew it as their real country. Nowhere else could take its place, and by definition could only be a temporary stop, standing in for the real thing. And living in such a stopover place, was I not also temporary, a stand-in, no more than a good actress so long as I did not find my real self, placed in its real setting?

I suspected that these feelings were in part a reflection of my mother's. She never got over the loss of Palestine in 1948, and after our arrival in England eighteen months later, she did her best to instil in us her own sense of impermanence. It was for that reason that she was against making any improvements to the house we lived in; she did not want central heating, for example, or a washing machine or a new fridge, and would tell us not to think of settling down, as we were 'not staying for long'. I remember growing up with a sense that life in

England was temporary, and there would come a time when we would all be going 'home'.

I did not fool myself into believing that I would find this 'home' in modern-day Ramallah, anomalous and artificial as it was, distorted by four decades of Israeli military occupation; nor that it could re-create the lost childhood of long ago. But it was still a Palestinian place, and the towns and villages nearby still retained the old ways, the food, the customs and traditions that defined them as Arab. Israel had taken much of their lands and livelihoods, but could not stamp out their deep-rooted underlying culture, instead appropriating some of it, like hummus and falafel, traditional Arab dishes that were subsequently called 'Israeli'. Whether what I found in this denuded Palestine would be enough to restore my sense of self and heal the other rifts in my life, I did not know, but would soon discover.

My journey to this Promised Land began in London, from where I had applied for a job at the Palestinian Authority. This was no accident; I was determined not to join the host of marginal 'researchers', foreign 'experts' and hangers-on who cluttered the numerous non-governmental organisations in the West Bank. By contrast, at the Palestinian Authority I reasoned that I would be at the heart of things, and would learn the inner workings of the institution that organised life in the Occupied Territories, although they were under Israeli rule. What an anomaly, I remember thinking. Where else in the world would such a government-within-a-government exist, operating as if it were sovereign over its own lands, while in reality subservient to someone else in every sense? How this contradiction played out in practice was something I was fascinated to explore.

At the time, in 2005, the PA was in charge of both the West Bank and Gaza, a unique moment in a short history. I could not know that I would be witnessing the dying days of an arrangement that had lasted, in all its complexities and contradictions, since the PA's beginnings in 1994. It was a period when the fruits of the 1993 Oslo Accords had fully ripened, indeed were overripe, as was evident in every so-called peace-building institution and organisation that international aid had set up since then. Despite these efforts, no peace had ever been built, and soon afterwards a Hamas-dominated government would be elected. The break-up of the PA, with Gaza split off under Hamas and the West Bank under Fateh, would follow. But at the time of my arrival in Ramallah that summer, none of this was even envisaged.

I remember the delight I felt when my application for work there was successful. I would be attached as a consultant to the PA's Ministry of Media and Communications, to work with its minister, whom I had known for many years and liked. My real employer was of course not the PA but the United Nations. The PA had no independent means, and survived on donated funds from a variety of sources. Its entire attached staff was paid for by international organisations. The UNDP had devised a special initiative to attract diaspora Palestinians like myself to return and work as consultants in various specialties. Once appointed we were expected to relate to the department or ministry we worked at, and resort to the UNDP only in emergencies.

Before Mounir Kleibo, the UNDP man, left, he took me to the Ministry of Media and Communications building, the place of my coming employment. There was little time to investigate this in detail, but my first view of it filled me with gloom. It had something about it that, oddly enough, reminded me of those miserable old London buildings belonging to the British National Health Service, the NHS, where I had worked for many years. The minister whom I knew and thought would be there to welcome me was not around, and, to my dismay, they said he hardly ever was. That first glimpse gave me a sense of foreboding about the time that lay ahead.

Alone in my flat and having finally unpacked my cases with resignation, I decided to walk to where I was told the nearest shops were. The general look of that part of Ramallah was closely reminiscent of Amman which was also hilly, with white stone buildings and builders' rubble here and there, investing the occasional tree that survived with a coating of fine dust. The houses were mostly whitewashed, with flat roofs and front balconies or verandas. But unlike Amman's equivalent so-called better areas, this looked like more of a third-world place: its shabbiness showed in every large rubbish dump and cracked pavement.

I soon reached the shopping centre, a square with an assortment of dry-cleaners, hair salons and fabric shops, dominated on one side by a large supermarket. This had been built by a Palestinian entrepreneur in the heady early Oslo years, when wealthy Palestinian businessmen were keen to invest in what was shaping up to be the capital city of the Palestinian Authority. I discovered that people were proud of this supermarket, which was remarkable for its size and range of products. In Ramallah, as in other Arab cities, small convenience stores which called themselves supermarkets were a common feature, dotted about everywhere but usually containing limited stock. They were a popular form of private enterprise, an easy source of livelihood for small businessmen, especially in the Palestinian territories, whose economic situation did not allow for many other forms of work.

Inside it was spacious and structured on the lines of supermarkets I was familiar with in the West – large counters of fresh produce, fruit and vegetables, and roomy refrigerators for perishables. I took a basket and wandered round, looking for basic foods I would need. The profusion of Israeli goods on the shelves, almost all labelled in Hebrew and usually in no other language, immediately struck me. I often had to guess at their contents from the pictures on the packaging. Only in the dairy section could one find local, Palestinian produce like cream cheese, *labaneh* or salty Nablus white cheese. The young people who served in the shop all looked at ease with their surroundings, unaware of my discomfiture. But of course the Israeli occupation had been there for all their lives, and they had no experience of anything different.

Back at the Gemzo Suites I ran into a small dark-haired Danish woman called Annetta, who was also living there. She was genial and self-confident, knowledgeable about Ramallah and the PA. Inviting me to her flat which, unlike mine, was nicely furnished with rugs, pictures and indoor plants, she made us coffee. To my surprise, this was Arabic coffee (variously claimed as Turkish or Greek, but essentially the same strong brew, traditionally sweet, and served in small cups). 'I learned how to make this here,' she explained.

'I heard from Mounir that you were coming,' she said. 'Sorry I wasn't here to help you shop. I've got a car.' I could see she was comfortably at home here. 'Who're you working for? The Media and Communications Ministry?' She laughed. 'Good luck!'

She told me that she had been in Ramallah for two years and was now working on a cultural project, funded by a Japanese government grant.

'I started off working for the PA,' she said, 'but after a year I couldn't take it any more.' She saw alarm on my face. 'They may treat you better, you're one of them. I mean, you're Palestinian, at least. But with me, they constantly ignored what I said, ordered me about, and generally behaved as if I wasn't there.' She shook her head at the memory. 'The desk they gave me was in an office shared with a load of men who ignored me as well. They spent their time on the phone or talking to each other in Arabic, which of course excluded me more. It was dark and unheated and really cold in winter. I was glad to get out of there, and quite frankly, I don't think they even noticed I'd gone.'

'How awful,' I said. 'I don't understand, Palestinians are

normally courteous people, and especially to Western foreigners. I'm surprised.'

'Well, maybe, but not in my case. Probably because I'm a woman. They don't think much of women around here. At the beginning I used to complain to Mounir all the time. But there was really nothing he could do. You know, once they've assigned you to a ministry they don't like to interfere.'

'Terrific!' I said. 'So if I do as badly with them as you did, it means I've got no one to turn to?'

'Oh, but I mustn't put you off.' She leaned forward and touched my arm. 'Not when you've just arrived. Try it out. You never know, you may well get on far better than I did.'

Seeing me so crestfallen, she said, 'Come on! I'll take you out to dinner with a few friends. We'll go to Darna, Ramallah's best restaurant. It's very lively and you'll see there's more to this place than the PA!'

CHAPTER 2

The Ministry of Media and Communications

The next day dawned as sunny and warm as the last. I got up and made tea in the unfamiliar kitchen with its massive fridge, in which the few items of food I had bought the day before huddled pathetically in a corner. It was quiet: the sounds of those Arab mornings I had become so familiar with in Amman and found comforting, a medley of car horns, street vendors calling out, neighbours chatting and children shouting, could not be heard here. It emphasised the sense of isolation I already felt. But I hurried on, dressed and had my breakfast watching Al Jazeera's morning news. When I walked out it felt fresh and pleasant in the morning air, and the gardener working on the front flower beds greeted me. Atallah was an odd-job man as well, and did repairs for people in the flats. Later, when I got to know him better, it turned out he had a sad story. Still single at the age of thirty-seven in a society where people were almost uniformly married much sooner, he longed to be married too. But he could not afford a wife, and accepted sorrowfully that he probably never would.

I said goodbye to Ahmad, the gatekeeper, who had also befriended me, and set out on my walk to what would be my first day at the office. This took about twenty minutes, until I learned to take the shorter cut through the back of the Gemzo Suites via the car park. At the top of the road was a busy highway, where cars and yellow minibuses called *servisses*, a sort of public people-carrier that could take about a dozen passengers, went by at frequent intervals. I crossed at what I learned were called the 'ramzone', the Hebrew name for traffic lights and one of the few in Ramallah at the time, and turned into quieter roads. Here most street lamps were festooned with stickers proclaiming various religious messages: 'Fear God!', 'Remember God!', 'There is no God but God and Muhammad is his Prophet!', or just simply 'Muhammad' or 'Allah'. These irritated me every time I passed them after that. Who looked at such things, I wondered, and what purpose did they serve?

The houses I walked by were occasionally interspersed with strips of wild, open patches, seemingly unclaimed by anyone. One such that I would pass every day must have once been part of someone's farmland. It had been planted with fig and olive trees, which were now growing amidst rubble and tufts of yellowing grass littered with discarded black plastic bags and cans. A herd of goats often grazed there freely, and once or twice I saw a few men sitting on low stools under the trees, smoking and chatting. In this, too, Ramallah resembled Amman, where such open spaces were also to be found. Usually those in Amman did not stay that way for long, as a developer was soon found to invest in building on them. In the case of Ramallah, this same drive to use every available space for housing was not so much the result of entrepreneurship as of Israeli settlement-building. The settlements were set up on Ramallah's agricultural land and hemmed in the town on all sides, making its expansion impossible. So what land was left in the city was at a premium.

One could see these giant settlements high up on the hills, their houses cascading down towards the town's outskirts and almost merging with them. There were even houses stuck virtually on top of each other, one Palestinian, the other Israeli. 'Do they become friends?' I asked someone when I first saw this strange sight. 'No, not friends,' he said, shaking his head vigorously, 'but they're sort of neighbours. What else can they do?'

Further along, I passed by at least three ministries, each in new-looking white buildings and grandly named: Ministry of

Transport, Ministry of Foreign Affairs, Ministry of Sports. All in all, there were some twenty ministries in Ramallah, excluding the presidential and prime-ministerial offices, cabinet and associated buildings and the Palestinian Legislative Council, which stood close together in the Masyoun area of town. All the ministries bore the imposing insignia of the 'Palestinian National Authority' above their entrances.

As I walked, I found the road had opened into a large triangle bordered by shops. Here were parked one or two police jeeps full of cheerful-looking lads in uniform, lounging in the seats, drinking coffee, and passing the time of day with the shopkeepers. Everyone looked relaxed, and I could not imagine what circumstance might end this bonhomie which had obviously become a way of life. A few days later Israeli soldiers, presumably following what was their way of life, raided several Ramallah homes in search of 'terrorists' and left, unimpeded by anyone.

The Ministry of Media and Communications was not a new building, unlike the others I had seen. It stood on several floors and was shabby and dark inside. I wondered what it had been before it was appropriated by the PA. The walls needed a coat of paint and what furniture I could see was old and much used. The doorman, who also doubled up as telephonist and porter when required, did not know who I was and directed me towards an office on the ground floor. I passed a small kitchen and some young women in headscarves chatting to a boy making coffee. There were several other rooms on this floor, one of which was the deputy minister's office.

The chief administrator was a middle-aged woman called Esperance, an old-fashioned French name which, like Violette, Clemence and Marie, was still used amongst Catholic Palestinians. She had an ample figure and dyed red hair.

'Are you expecting me?' I asked.

'Of course. Welcome, Doctora,' she said without warmth, 'how are you? I hope all is well. Please come this way.' She took me to a room at the back of the building which, apart from a few chairs stacked against the window, was empty. 'Oh!' she tutted. 'I told them to sort this out, and to move a desk in for you. Mahmoud!' she called out sharply, and the doorman I had just seen at the entrance came hurriedly over. 'What happened about the Doctora's office? Where's the furniture I asked to be moved?'

He looked mystified, and shrugged his shoulders. 'Sort this out at once!' she ordered. 'I apologise,' she said unapologetically. 'Please come to my office while yours is being prepared.'

Before long I was invited back to the same room, which was now furnished with a faded and stained wooden desk, a desk lamp, and a bin, but looked just as dingy as before. From its window could be seen a small square of scrubland and a wall. Later I would find that this 'garden' was where some of the office workers hung out, chatting and laughing. After another wait, a desktop computer was found, and the phone was connected to the ministry's operator.

'If you need anything else,' said Esperance, surveying the room with satisfaction, 'please let me or Hanan here know.' This was one of the young women in headscarves, who I presumed was her assistant. She looked friendly and smiled at me. 'But for now, when you're ready, I've arranged for the staff to meet you.'

It did not take me long to 'settle in'; I had brought nothing with me but my handbag, since I had little idea of what to expect. I found Hanan hovering outside the office door and followed her to a large meeting room on a lower level. About six people sat round a large table, with Esperance, who had preceded us, at its head. She rose to introduce me.

'This is Doctora Ghada, who has joined us as a media consultant to Dr Farid' (the minister who had as yet not appeared). 'She's actually a medical doctor and has come all the way from England to tell us what to do here.' She attempted a smile in my direction. The others, two men and four women, murmured a welcome. It turned out that one of the men was an English–Arabic translator, the other was in charge of online work, and the women had various functions as press reviewer, meetings organiser and secretary. I took a chair and smiled at them uncertainly. I was unsure of what they expected of me and felt I had been thrown into something I did not understand.

'Hello, *marhaba*,' I said. 'It's nice to meet you all, and really I haven't come here to tell you what to do. If anything it's the other way around. I mean, I need to know from you what the situation is like here and what issues you identify as being problems, to see how I can help.' I went on to say something about myself and my activist work in London, all the time aware of Esperance's cold eye on me. The women looked from her to me, but we managed to have a discussion about the problems of presenting the Palestine case to the outside world. I said that this was an area I could help with, and asked if they already had a strategy and what were their ideas about how to put out the message.

A ten-page document in Arabic was produced, entitled 'The Plan for Communication to the Media on the Palestine Cause'. It looked well-thumbed and some of the text was faded. I scanned it rapidly and, seeing them waiting expectantly, I decided that the only way was to ignore Esperance and behave as if she were not there. I could not divine the reason for her hostility, but that would have to wait till later. I thought, what would I do now if I were at a National Health Service planning meeting back in England? In my latter years as a medical practitioner I had taken up the specialty of public health, which by the 1990s had little in common with the pioneering field of a previous age. Those public health champions had fought for clean water, child vaccination and public hygiene. The excitement of their early discoveries that the environment caused infectious and other diseases had, by my day, given way to something quite different. Public health medicine, as it was known, was little more than a bureaucratic branch of the NHS, mostly taken up with committee meetings, wrangling over health budgets, and chiefly concerned with planning and strategy-making for health service provision. As a specialist in this field I had gained some experience of organisational work, and the task at hand seemed a familiar one.

'Look, I think we're going to have to start all over again with this,' I said, pointing to the document. 'I'm sure this paper is fine, but it looks old to me, and almost certainly needs updating. So I would like to suggest that we work on a new media strategy that deals with the way we present the facts to the Western media, and also the Israeli media.' Warming to my theme, and oblivious of the effect on Esperance, I asked if each of them could come to my office afterwards so that I could get to know them better. All assented readily, and I had the impression that no one had ever talked to them individually before. I said that we could start that very morning, and agreed times for each one, half an hour apart.

Esperance cleared her throat loudly. 'They have other duties, Doctora,' she objected. 'They will not be able to talk to you for long.' She shot them each a look, and I could see that she disliked the whole plan. 'Never mind,' I responded firmly, 'however much time they can afford would be good.'

The men were intrigued but guarded at first. The women were more forthcoming, but it was clear that they all feared Esperance. I wondered how much of what they said was already censored. Not that it seemed to matter a great deal, for I could see that any interest in or commitment to the content of their work was secondary to the need to remain in work, no matter what it was. Their lives were governed by the overriding imperative to go on drawing their salaries, whatever the quality of the work they produced. This reflected a general situation for all PA employees, since there was no system of national insurance or social benefits of any kind in the Palestinian territories. As a result of Israel's seizure of much of their agricultural land for its settlements, and the restrictions on trade imposed by the occupation, working for the PA was often the only available source of livelihood. The monthly salary became a means of daily survival for thousands of people and their dependants.

They told me something of their personal stories, and described how long it took for those who lived outside Ramallah to get to work. The journey from Nablus, which before the occupation would have meant no more than a forty-minute drive along the Nablus–Ramallah road, now took two hours or more. The old direct route had been closed in order to divert Palestinian traffic away from the huge Beit El settlement near Ramallah, with the result that cars had to use various circuitous roads instead, skirting other settlements. The hold-ups at the Israeli army checkpoints on these roads could be short or take up several hours. A few of the girls came in from outlying villages and could also face unexpected delays, when the army might suddenly and inexplicably put up so-called flying checkpoints on the road and as suddenly and inexplicably remove them.

When I subsequently passed a few of these checkpoints outside Ramallah I would marvel at the disruption that they caused, even though they often consisted of no more than a couple of soldiers and an army jeep, and looked as if they had been put up on a whim because the soldiers felt like it. People waited obediently in long queues to have their papers checked by these soldiers, who were often no more than youths. When I asked why people allowed such a puny army presence to so obstruct their journey, they told me that the soldiers, few as they were, could summon massive military back-up from the nearest army depot at a moment's notice.

After my meetings with the staff, I felt I had established a distinct rapport with the six workers, which pleased me. And to my surprise they all seemed to be under the impression that

I had come to be their new manager, which pleased me too. Later I decided to walk around the ministry and get to know other members of staff. On the upper floors were more offices, all presumably carrying out some function, though I never discovered what it was exactly. An air of relaxed camaraderie reigned here, some men on the telephone, others reading the papers. Offices in the Arab world had an important social dimension. Friends and relatives often dropped in to exchange news and gossip over coffee, frequently joined by other office workers, and a large part of the working day could pass by in this way. In that respect Ramallah was no different. I even heard a rumour that one man came into the ministry every morning, scanned the internet for press articles he was interested in, and after a coffee and a chat, went home again. No one took any notice.

Office hours were eight in the morning to two in the afternoon, but in practice all work ceased by half-past one as the workers prepared to leave for the day. By two o'clock sharp, Mahmoud, the doorman, stood in the front hall with his keys, waiting to lock up. Outside, the sun was at its hottest as I walked back to the Gemzo Suites, regretting that I had decided to go on foot while the ministry employees sped past in cars and taxis. I arrived back thirsty and tired. Eating my simple lunch in the sitting room with the TV on, I wondered how long I would be able to survive like this.

The next day, Dr Sabah, the deputy minister, appeared at the ministry. He had been away on a visit to Abu Dhabi on PA business, we were told, and was back in his office. Towards mid-morning his secretary, a pretty girl without a headscarf, came to invite me to meet him. I noticed that she looked at me with curiosity and, as she reached her desk outside the deputy minister's office, I heard her whispering to another girl sitting nearby.

'Ah, Doctora!' cried the deputy minister affably as I entered, standing up and coming forward to greet me. He was a dapper, shortish man with a smooth face and thick-lensed glasses. 'Please sit down. Let me get you some coffee.' Another man, who had been lolling on a chair behind the door, got up and left, presumably to order the coffee. Two others were sitting in the office. 'Let me introduce our brother, Tayseer, and the other brother, Abdullah,' Dr Sabah said, pointing to the two men, both bearded and playing with their worry beads. 'This is Doctora Ghada, who has come here from England – which we appreciate very much, of course – to advise us on our work.' Turning to me, he went on, 'The brothers are visitors from Gaza, and I'm sure you won't mind if they listen in on our conversation.'

'Of course not,' I responded. But I had been expecting to be alone with him for a discussion among equals, to get a better idea about my work and what was expected of me. I also wanted to discuss Esperance and her unhelpful attitude towards me. I certainly had not anticipated this line-up of what were clearly the deputy minister's cronies. There was a knock on the door and Esperance walked in. 'Welcome, Miss Esperance,' said Dr Sabah. And turning to me, 'I have invited her to join us. She's an indispensable part of our office. We couldn't do without her, could we?' he beamed. She walked past me, her head held high, and put several files on Dr Sabah's desk before taking a seat near him and facing me.

'Well, now,' he continued, pushing his swivel chair back from the desk and crossing his legs. He too had worry beads which he now started to roll with his fingers. 'Can I ask first of all what you, Doctora Ghada, a doctor of medicine as I understand it, are doing offering advice on a field which is not your own? I mean, you come all the way from London, leaving your great medical practice I presume, to be here in this place to work on media and communications of all things with us. What has this to do with you? I simply don't understand.' He affected a look of genuine puzzlement, drawing the others in, and especially Esperance.

'I thought you knew all about me,' I said. 'Dr Farid had all the information before I came, and it was agreed with him.'

'Ah, Dr Farid. Ah yes, I see. But,' he leaned forward, 'Dr Farid is one thing and we are another.' He smiled triumphantly, clearly enjoying himself. 'As you see, Dr Farid isn't here.'

I looked puzzled, but he ignored me. 'I gather from Esperance that you've been taking charge of some of our staff here.'

'Well, not taking charge exactly,' I countered. 'It's just normal practice to get to know people one will be working with.'

'Working with? Hmm.' He paused as if mulling over this strange idea. 'Esperance also tells me that you want to rewrite our media strategy,' he continued, smiling at the others. 'What's wrong with the present one?'

But then his manner grew serious and he frowned. 'Doctora, this will not do for us. We have practices and procedures in place, very successful ones, and it's best for you to learn about these before rushing in to make changes. Isn't it the same in England?' He stressed the last word. Esperance, who had until then been looking straight ahead with a detached air, could not suppress a smile of pleasure at this.

'I didn't intend to offend you or anyone, Dr Sabah,' I said, feeling wrong-footed and defensive. 'I merely thought to start working as soon as I could on updating what I am sure is a very good media strategy. That is part of what I am here for.'

'Esperance?' He turned towards her. 'What do you say?'

She responded with alacrity. 'The Doctora was only trying to help, I think, but she's new and doesn't understand what we do here. She asked the staff to talk to her in her office, each one by themselves ...' She left the rest to her listeners' imagination.

Dr Sabah laughed in exaggerated disbelief. I realised that he already knew all this. He cleared his throat and addressed me. 'Doctora, we don't do such things here. Our people aren't used to it and may tell you whatever comes into their heads.

You should leave the staff to Esperance. She's very good at handling them, and you should stick to whatever it is you're here for.'

I had grown exasperated, by him, by the gleeful Esperance, and the bearded men who stared vacantly at me all the time. 'Dr Sabah,' I said. 'I don't know why you know so little about why I am here, or what goes on between you and Dr Farid. I was appointed to this ministry through the UNDP and with Dr Farid's knowledge and consent. He should have briefed you before I came. He's the person you should talk to.'

Dr Sabah was not a bit put out. But the affability he had shown earlier was now gone. 'Dr Farid doesn't work here. We weren't told anything about you or that you were coming until a few days ago. It's a wonder, and only thanks to Esperance, that we found you an office.' He could barely disguise his irritation and scorn.

I was stunned and humiliated. I didn't know what he meant about Dr Farid, but I could see that I had mishandled the situation badly when I should have known better. Years of working as a doctor within the labyrinthine NHS system of office politics and rivalry had apparently taught me nothing. I could only think that, outside that familiar British setting, I had lost my bearings. Yet there was nothing inherently different about this ministry from the head offices of many an English health authority, where staff formed cliques and chiefs had favourites and everyone worked towards maintaining the status quo. I had blundered into Esperance's little empire at the ministry and imagined I could go over her head to the boss, forgetting that, apart from anything else, I was transient while she was permanent.

I walked back to my office, leaving Dr Sabah with his gathering, and wondered what I should do. I would tell Mounir at UNDP, I thought; he must surely be able to help. The phone on my desk, however, was not all it seemed. Every time I tried to use it, I found myself connected to a conversation between two other people. No amount of banging or clicking cleared the line. Eventually, Bilal, the coffee boy, was despatched to see what was wrong, to find the ministry's operator overwhelmed and unable to cope with the number of people trying to make outside calls. I could hear shouting and doors banging, Mahmoud being summoned and harangued and him shouting back, until there was a sudden hush. I looked out to see Dr Sabah, briefcase in hand and escorted by two or three young men I had not seen before, striding past with the bearded visitors from Gaza on his way out of the building. The hush lasted until the ministerial car drove off.

When I finally got through to Mounir he explained that UNDP didn't like to interfere once a consultant like myself had been appointed to a ministry. 'They're very sensitive about any suggestion of being told what to do,' he said. But I persisted, and he promised he would speak to Dr Farid. 'Where *is* Dr Farid, by the way?' I asked. 'His deputy said he didn't work here. Isn't he supposed to be at this ministry?' 'Of course,' Mounir replied, but would not be drawn further.

As I prepared to leave for the day, uneasy and apprehensive about the time to come, Hanan, Esperance's assistant, came into my office. She closed the door behind her and sat in one of the chairs.

'Doctora,' she said. 'I hope you don't mind my coming to talk to you.' I thought she probably had an unpleasant message from Esperance. But I shook my head and smiled encouragingly. Her voice dropped to a whisper.

'I know it's not been a nice day for you. Someone should explain to you what's going on here. It's not right.' She kept looking behind her at the door. 'I don't live far from the Gemzo Suites where I think you're staying. Would you like to pay me a visit, or I can come over to you?'

I had not expected this. 'By all means,' I said, 'I'd be very happy to talk to you. When?'

We arranged for her to visit me on the evening of the next

day, but she would telephone later to confirm. At least it seemed I had one friend in that place.

Back at the Gemzo Suites, I went to see my neighbour, Annetta, who asked how I was getting on. I told her something of my first day at work, wanting to say more, indeed to pour out my misgivings and dismay at my experience of the ministry. But to my surprise she made no comment except to sigh. I could see she did not want to be drawn out, and I was disappointed. Perhaps seeing my gloomy expression, she asked if I would like to accompany her to the Cultural Palace that evening for an event. It seemed there was an active programme of music, dancing and shows at this place, which had become a central part of Ramallah's cultural life. A glossy booklet called 'This Week in Palestine', copies of which I had seen lying about in the reception area of the Gemzo Suites, had listings of events taking place throughout the Palestinian territories, amongst which the Cultural Palace featured prominently. I remember being astonished at the number and variety of activities in the Palestinian towns, and the accounts in the booklet of local crafts and village life.

People in Ramallah were very proud of the Cultural Palace, showed it off to visitors and boasted of its uniqueness in the Occupied Territories. It had become the first address for visiting foreign delegations, political conferences and meetings with dignitaries. And no wonder, I thought when I saw it: a handsome, imposing building, with a wide forecourt, a spacious atrium and a sweeping staircase up to the huge auditorium on the first floor that could seat over 700 people. There were exhibition halls and lecture rooms, and studios for film screenings.

Without doubt it was a Palestinian success story, the culmination of sustained effort by a partnership between the PA, the UNDP and the Japanese government. A generous grant from the latter had funded the design and construction which took eight years to complete, frequently held up by Israeli restrictions on the movement of workers and the importation of building materials. Those obstacles finally overcome, it stood proudly, a monument to perseverance and defiance, and more than that, I thought, a passionate desire for normality in an abnormal world. As I looked at the teeming crowds inside, most of them young people, chattering and eager, in jeans and T-shirts, some with such incongruous labels as 'I love San Francisco' and 'USA Inc', I was reminded of similar young people in London, indeed anywhere in the West. Only if one looked out towards the Israeli settlements framing the horizon with their twinkling yellow night-time lights, and the huge dark shadows they cast on the hillsides, did the outside reality intrude.

Annetta had also invited a French water engineer named René, a fellow resident at the Gemzo Suites. He was a quiet, middle-aged man who said little throughout the evening, but I discovered when I got to know him better that he was in fact quite garrulous and excitable. Over tea in my flat a few days later, he told me of his passionate attachment to the Palestinian people. He had left his job in Toulouse some years before to come to the West Bank, and was on a contract with the PA for work in irrigation and water conservation. René was one of a type of foreigner I was to come across many times in Ramallah. Something of a loner in his native country, he had found acceptance and warmth amongst the Palestinians. Their natural friendliness had won his heart, and he could not imagine ever having to give it up. He regarded Palestinians as his brothers and sisters. 'I love them,' he cried. 'They are my friends, my family!' Even so, and despite having lived in Ramallah for three years, he had learned no Arabic and had only the haziest notion of Arab culture, history and religion, and I doubted that would ever change.

When, a few weeks after I got to know him, the French company which had seconded him to the occupied territories lost out on a tender for a major water project, depriving him of a job, he was devastated. For a while it looked as if he had lost his mind.

'I know why this happened,' he went around muttering. 'I never liked the minister, and I know he gave the contract to the other company because they bribed him with a big handout.'

'How can you be sure?'

'I know it! I know it!' he asserted vigorously. 'It's a big danger here. All of them, these ministers and PA officials, they're all on the take. Sometimes it's a relative of theirs who needs a helping hand, or someone promises them a big promotion or something like that. But my friend at the ministry told me, he assured me I'd be OK, he would put in a good word for me with the minister. I can't believe it. He must have been bribed as well!'

The concert consisted of music and dancing. A Palestinian dance group performed the *dabka*, a traditional folk dance, with young men and women lining up opposite each other and performing the steps with great verve and energy. It was invigorating to watch and largely unspoiled by the logistics: loudspeakers pitched too high so that an ear-splitting whistle would shoot through from time to time, the curtain starting to come down once or twice before the interval and being hauled up again, and similar mishaps. However, the audience was good-humoured, and no one minded; many were in any event chatting to each other and walking in and out during the performance. The hubbub of conversations outside the auditorium sometimes threatened to drown out the sounds inside. But the singers continued undaunted, and the oud player, whose delicate fingering on that fine instrument was quite exceptional but needed quiet to be heard, also carried on.

After the performance, with people still greeting those they had not spotted at the beginning, Annetta introduced me to several of her friends who were there, including Mary, an elderly American woman, and Samir, a young Palestinian businessman with brilliant blue eyes who also sounded American. Annetta took us all to a café in the town centre, where we had drinks. Ramallah was full of restaurants and bistro-style cafés, crowded with people enjoying themselves. Mary was another like René, attached to the Arab way of life. After living in the Gulf for twenty years, she chose on her retirement to come to Ramallah. She had no residency there, as was the case for all foreigners, and was forced to leave the territories every three months to renew her visitor's visa.

'Why do you do that?' I asked. 'It must be very annoying to have to leave in order to come back.'

'What else can I do?'

'You could return to America, surely?'

She shook her head vehemently. 'I couldn't possibly live there again, not after being in the Arab world. So many friendly people here, such kindness. What on earth would I do back in Denver: go to the food store and watch TV? No, thank you.'

CHAPTER 3

The Separation Wall

The next morning, as I sat in my office unsure where to begin, there was a knock on the door and Esperance walked in. I was surprised to see her so early, but braced myself for whatever might come.

'Good morning, Doctora,' she said pleasantly enough. 'Dr Sabah and I have been discussing things, and I would be grateful if you could let me have a plan of the work you intend to do here.' She smiled at me.

'How do you mean?'

'You know. Your work plan. Haven't you done one of those before?' Her tone was patronising and I thought of the lowly workers in her charge, no doubt frequently exposed to the same thing.

'No, no,' I retorted, 'I think you've got it wrong. *I* don't draw up a work plan. I help *you* all with yours, as I said at the meeting yesterday, if you remember.' I knew this was unwise and would antagonise her further, but I didn't care.

'All right, if that's how you feel.' She pursed her lips, paused for a moment as if about to say more, then left. It did not take long for a reaction to this exchange to develop. Passing by the desks of the girl who had invited me to see Dr Sabah the day before and her colleagues, I noticed them smirking to one another, and shortly afterwards a note from Dr Sabah was handed to me. It said that the work protocol at the ministry required all employees to present their work plans to Esperance, and he would be grateful for my compliance in the matter.

I asked about Hanan, whom I had not seen that day, and was told she was not coming in. There was no message for me, and I thought about our evening meeting which I had been eagerly waiting for, and wondered when I would see her again. None of the workers of the day before came to see me, but a young computer engineer called Thabit arrived to work on my desktop, which he said needed upgrading. He was quiet and courteous and I warmed to him. Though he spent some time working on the computer, I could detect no improvement in its aged performance after he left, and spent the rest of the morning trying to read the ministry's dreary Media Strategy and avoiding Esperance.

Towards the end of the day Thabit came back and to my surprise asked if I would like a lift to my residence. 'My wife and I – she works upstairs – saw you walking in the heat yesterday, and we thought it wasn't right.'

I thanked him and took up the offer. When we arrived at the Gemzo Suites they came up to the flat and stayed for a short while. I learned that they lived in Beitunia, a large village of some 20,000 people about two miles west of Ramallah. The name stirred a faint memory, and I asked them about it. Beitunia used to be a wonderful place of rich agriculture and ample grazing land, they said. But Israel had come the year before and built its separation wall which cut off two-thirds of the village land, leaving them to manage on what was left. Even so, they told me proudly, they were not cowed by the barrier or by the huge settlement of Giv'at Ze'ev that towered over the nearby countryside. 'God sees what they do, and He is above everything.' I then remembered hearing about Beitunia's fierce demonstrations against the wall, against the settlements, and in solidarity with the Palestinian prisoners in Israel's jails. Later, when Gaza was besieged and subsequently assaulted, they demonstrated against that too, undeterred by the Israeli army's tear gas and 'rubber' bullets – live ammunition in reality, encased in a rubber coating which made it no less lethal.

Thabit told me he and his wife had recently married. She was young, with an open, fresh face nicely framed by her white headscarf, and was already pregnant. 'Twins,' she said proudly. 'I love them so much already just from seeing the hospital scan!' It was the norm in Arab society for a couple, once married, to make no attempt to delay pregnancy but 'leave things to God'. Marriage was virtually synonymous with procreation, and in most cases the wife fell pregnant within the first month. Thabit's wife looked utterly contented with her life, as if there were no occupation and no hardship, and I was touched. I should not have disturbed their evident happiness, but I could not resist asking for their views of the ministry. They would not be drawn out, however, and said they were not unhappy there. It was a job, and they did not interfere in what went on around them. When we parted, they insisted I visit them for lunch one Friday when the ministry was closed, the equivalent to an English Sunday. Their circumstances were modest but I knew they meant it, such was the easy hospitality of Arab society. I never did visit them in the end, although they renewed their invitation several times.

That afternoon, Annetta – who had become an indispensable guide to life in Ramallah – called on me in the company of a woman named Reema. They were on their way to pick up other activists and drive to join a demonstration against the separation wall at Abu Dis, a village on the outskirts of Jerusalem. This was apparently a regular weekly occurrence that drew activists from around the area and also from Israel. Samir, Annetta's blue-eyed friend whom I had met the evening before at the café in Ramallah, was no less an activist than any of the women accompanying Annetta, but he could not join us, since he had no permit to enter Jerusalem. I was not certain that I could go either, as I had arranged to see Hanan that same evening. Interested in the trip with Annetta and her friend, I telephoend Hanan to postpone our meeting. But repeated attempts to contact her at home and on her mobile phone failed to find her. I decided to phone her later on.

As we drove away from Ramallah, we picked up the Jerusalem road without having to go through the Qalandia checkpoint that guarded its entrance. This checkpoint was unpleasant and difficult to cross even then, in 2005, but it would become quite formidable a few years later, when it came to resemble a border terminal between states rather than simply a barrier to shut Ramallah off from Jerusalem. People queued here for hours while they and their vehicles were checked and re-checked.

Annetta's car had a yellow Israeli number plate, so we could avoid Qalandia and use another exit out of Ramallah with an easier checkpoint. It meant a longer and more circuitous drive until we reached the Hizma crossing, where many settler cars passed through on their way to Jerusalem. Hizma was another Palestinian village which had lost its land to the surrounding Jewish settlements, including the land on which the check-point stood. On our immediate right was the large settlement of Pisgat Ze'ev, whose modern-built houses were so close we could almost touch them, and on the opposite side was dusty and impoverished Hizma. The soldiers at this checkpoint were chatty and relaxed with us in our Israeli car. When I took this route afterwards, I found them especially friendly whenever I wore my cream linen hat, which I had brought from London. This was because, as I later discovered, many Jewish settlers' wives wore similar hats.

We drove through, leaving behind a long queue of white-number-plated Palestinian cars, whose drivers waited patiently to have their papers examined. It was a fine afternoon and the heat of the day was beginning to give way to cooler air. There were five of us in the car by now, all talking. The wide highway ran past the rest of Pisgat Ze'ev and wound around hilly country from which I could see the unfinished separation wall dividing up the West Bank. The skyline on the approach to Jerusalem was dominated by massive settlements with row upon row of identical red-roofed houses, each built on top of the hills surrounding the city. In the valleys below were white, flat-roofed Palestinian villages, some with minarets.

'Look, there's the settlement of Neve Yaakov,' my companions explained, pointing at these red-roofed excrescences. 'And that is Givat Binyamin, there is Almon, and in the distance you can see the French Hill settlement.' I didn't know how they distinguished one from the other; to me, they all had identical-looking European-style houses sprawling along hillsides which had never before been built up, as incongruous in that landscape as if they had dropped out of the sky. They had been so expanded that they were almost contiguous, approaching the city boundaries in an unnatural urban continuity. I stared at this ungainly carve-up of what had been a harmonious, gentle landscape with its wide spaces and open skyline, its huddles of old villages and mosques in the valleys, and wondered what my father, who had known Jerusalem and its unfettered hills long before there was an Israel, would think of this sight.

We entered a city of wide highways and modern buildings that I scarcely recognised as Jerusalem, and drove through to our destination. Although I had visited the city before, each time I went it seemed more built-up and more unrecognisable as the Arab place of my childhood. When we arrived at Abu Dis, now part of Jerusalem, Annetta parked and I got out of the car to see the separation wall right in front of me, so close that I could touch it. We were in the 'Israeli part' of Abu Dis, separated from the 'West Bank part' by the wall. The Israeli section had been annexed from Abu Dis along with a quarter of its most fertile farmland, and included within Jerusalem's municipal boundaries.

The place looked deserted, unnaturally quiet, like a ghost town. There were about fifteen demonstrators already there, some of them chalking slogans on to the wall about freedom for Palestinians and chatting to each other. Why so few, I wondered? Did this infamous place not deserve many more? Should there not have been armies of protestors against this wanton incision into the heart of a little farming village? But then perhaps there had been in the past, only to give up in the face of Israel's implacable will and the granite hardness of its wall. I saw a mixed bunch of people, among them liberal Jewish Israelis and some local Palestinians, but most were foreigners from various countries, involved in human rights. They wore old T-shirts, faded jeans, sandals or casual shoes, the uniform of activists everywhere.

As we joined them, Annetta introduced me but soon wandered off to see her friends. I found myself among filmmakers, foreign journalists and activists, obviously familiar with each other and with the routine of meeting here to protest. They had been on similar demonstrations, they said, in other parts of the West Bank where the wall was being erected. The section I was looking at was but a small part of an extensive, winding wall weaving its way in and out of West Bank territory. If Israel's building programme proceeded unhindered, the wall would end up spanning more than 400 miles of land.

But that afternoon, no one was talking about the future. People were good-humoured and chatty, and it reminded me nostalgically of the camaraderie such protests used to create between us activists in London. I felt at home and among friends.

'You should go to Bil'in on Friday,' said one of the Palestinian filmmakers. 'Annetta will probably go too, she'll take you. There are lots of people there every week.' Bil'in was a village to the west of Ramallah which, like Beitunia, had fallen victim to the route of the wall being built just adjacent to it. When completed it would cut off two-thirds of Bil'in's lands and attach them to the nearby settlement of Mod'in Illit. Early that year the villagers had started to hold regular Friday demonstrations against the wall's construction. Unarmed, they faced Israeli soldiers trying to force them back with tear gas and rubber bullets each time, and each Friday their numbers only swelled. This heroic resistance soon became a cause célèbre, and scores of Israeli peace activists and members of international solidarity movements began to join the weekly protests.[1]

'Are you talking about Bil'in?' asked one of the Israelis, joining us. 'It's tremendous. I go every week. But I warn you, it can be dangerous. The army has orders to stop anyone getting close to the construction site. And they shoot live ammunition if you ignore them. But it hasn't stopped me, and I think you should come.'

I noticed a couple of women in headscarves making their way down the hill by the wall. They stared at us curiously and laughed when we greeted them. One of the protestors wanted to take a photo of them, but they covered their faces, shook their heads and hurried on. After a while I broke away and left the activists chatting. I walked right up to the wall on my own, staring at it. It wound along the side of the street all the way up to the top where it curved sideways to form a complete shield that shut off the light and everything else behind it. Higher up along its course and inserted into its side was a huge cylindrical watchtower, with sinister-looking apertures for windows all around the top, where I imagined armed soldiers to be monitoring what went on below. The wall here was at least eight metres or twenty-six feet high, and I thought how impossible it would be to scale its slate-grey slabs of solid concrete. Here and there the monotony of the stone was broken up by slogans and other graffiti supporting the Palestinians. These could be highly imaginative, like the drawings on the wall at the Qalandia checkpoint, some of which looked deceptively realistic. One of the most striking

---

1 In 2012 a film of this struggle against the wall, *Five Broken Cameras*, was made by Emad Burnat, a Palestinian from Bil'in, with the Israeli Guy Davidi, and went on to be nominated for an Oscar.

portrayed a 'hole' as if cut out of the wall, depicting blue sky and a patch of green field on the 'other side', so skilfully done one could almost believe it was real.

I stood close up against the wall and pressed my palms against its surface. The concrete felt cold and smooth against my skin and I had to crane my head backwards to see up to the top. It felt powerfully solid and immovable. Someone came and stood beside me. 'Behind that wall is my husband.' The speaker was a tall Palestinian woman, Naila, I had just been introduced to. She startled me. 'He's there because we're not allowed to live together any more,' she explained. Everyone in the group must have known her story, but I was new to it.

They had owned a house in Abu Dis which had been their home until the wall was built, putting the house on the Israeli side of the village. They were instantly separated, for she was a 'resident' of East Jerusalem – the quaint Israeli designation for the native Arab population of the city – and held a blue Israeli ID, but her husband was a 'West Bank resident' with an orange ID, which meant that he could not enter the Israeli side thereafter without a special permit. Using this, he was able to visit his wife and children in the Israeli part of Abu Dis, but only during the day; he had to leave by seven every evening, and even this access ceased during Jewish holidays, when the whole of the West Bank was sealed off.

'I'm so sorry,' I said, thinking how inadequate that sounded. 'Why don't you move from here and join him?'

'How can I? If I did that, they'd take away my Jerusalem ID and I wouldn't be able to get it back.' She would lose much else, no longer able to use Israel's airport, or take her children to Jerusalem's schools, or use its hospitals. Residents of the West Bank and Gaza were not allowed to travel from Ben Gurion airport; they had to travel from Amman or Cairo, and could only enter Jerusalem with permits which were usually difficult to obtain. So the couple were condemned to a forced separation with what consequences for their relationship I could only guess at, not to speak of the effect on the children's contact with their father. 'It's all right,' Naila said, seeing my concerned expression. 'I'm not the worst case of what this wall has done to us, believe me. I could tell you so many stories of other families split up, disruptions and all sorts of terrible things. By and large, we still manage.'

We talked some more and agreed to meet again. The demonstration straggled on for another hour, with nothing much happening beyond an exchange of pleasantries with the man who sold cigarettes and sweets in the kiosk by the car park. The group broke up and people dispersed, leaving the truncated village to its walled silence. Annetta got into the car, and I followed her slowly, haunted by what I had just seen. I wondered why I felt so disturbed by it. After all, Israel's transgressions against the Palestinians were nothing new to me. I had been campaigning against them since 1971, and was familiar with the long catalogue of its attacks and misdemeanours over the years. Surely the wall was but another addition to a long, unsavoury list. But yet it wasn't. It was in a different league, a symbol of something indefinably cruel, a brutal expression of Israeli entitlement. What else could explain these mighty fortifications, as if wild beasts and ravening wolves roamed the other side and had to be kept out at all costs?

Of course the wall was not everywhere the same high structure as at Abu Dis; in parts, it was an electrified fence with deep ditches on either side. But wherever there were Palestinian urban areas it assumed the shape before me now and, fence or wall, it was impossible to cross. A glance at its route on the map showed its real purpose. It wound in and out of Palestinian territory in such a way as to enclose the best farming land and water sources within the Israeli side – a plain and simple seizure of other people's property. But for me, the wall signified much more; for behind its huge bulk was blotted out, and deliberately so, the physical presence, the very thought even, of another people who walked and breathed there, as if they had no right even to be alive. Its brazen message to the world was that this country was Israel's and Israel's alone, to settle, loot, divide, carve up, refashion, rename, and do with whatever it pleased.

Preoccupied with these thoughts, I said nothing for a while as she drove. But then I turned to her. 'Tell me, Annetta. What made you come to this miserable place? Why do you choose to stay here?' I knew that her husband was a diplomat in Copenhagen, and although they visited each other regularly, she travelling to Copenhagen more frequently than the reverse, her main residence was in Ramallah.

She did not answer straight away. 'I find it interesting, you know. In Europe, we've solved everything, all the major things, and it's so boring. OK, I know there are problems there too, but they're humdrum, not really serious like here. I don't know what I would do without the vibrancy of this place, the variety, the struggle. I love it. And I can do so much here, which would mean nothing in Denmark.' She was animated. 'You saw the Cultural Palace, didn't you? Well, I worked on that, and now Samir and I will be putting on an exhibition of children's drawings. You'll like it.'

'How long do you intend to stay?' I asked.

'A very, very long time, I hope. Until there's no more money for our projects, I suppose!' She laughed. 'We're going to dinner with Maher, and you'll see what I mean about variety,' she continued, unaware of my mood. 'You'll like him, and I tell you, he's one businessman who's spent his money on art, Palestinian art, things maybe you've not seen before, not big cars and silly things. I hope he shows you his collection. It's huge and so varied.'

It was quite dark by the time we arrived, and the air was balmy. I could make out neat, clean streets, and it felt cosy here. We were in Beit Hanina, an ancient village to the north of Jerusalem which used to be the largest in the West Bank. But when Israel built a highway linking to the centre of Jerusalem, the village was bisected: half became 'Old Beit Hanina' in the West Bank, and the rest was annexed as a suburb of East Jerusalem. The residents of this part all had blue Jerusalem IDs and so were permitted to stay.

Maher's house was large and luxuriously furnished, tastefully decorated with beautiful tiled floors and fine Persian rugs. Paintings hung on every wall, oil originals softly lit up. A servant ushered us into a wide hallway where our host hastened out to greet us. He was a small, neatly dressed man in his forties with a warm handshake and an expansive manner. He hugged Annetta and welcomed us into a large and elegant reception room where his other guests were sitting over drinks. Everyone there knew Annetta, and waved at her enthusiastically as she introduced me. This group, in marked contrast to the activists we had just been with, was in evening wear, and included the head of UNDP – an affable, friendly American whom I'd met when I first arrived in Jerusalem – several young Palestinian members of UNDP's staff, a couple of European consuls and their wives,[2] and a Palestinian gynaecologist and his wife.

None of the Palestinian women wore headscarves and there was wine in abundance here, served in large crystal glasses. The conversation was urbane, mainly about various art exhibitions coming up, and little was said about politics, as if in an unspoken agreement to eschew anything unpleasant. In all ways I could have been back at a smart dinner party in London. I wondered how our host made his money, but, as Annetta had said, he had clearly used it to good effect in this beautiful house with its profusion of paintings. When his wife called us in to dinner, the table was lavishly laid with Palestinian dishes, exquisitely cooked and prepared. I had not

2 Jerusalem was not internationally recognised as Israel's capital. In consequence, foreign representatives in Jerusalem were known as consul-generals, while ambassadors were based in Tel Aviv, the legally accepted capital of Israel.

eaten so well since leaving Amman. The teenage son and two daughters of our hosts now joined us, polite, well-brought-up young people, all bound for US universities – a trend amongst many well-to-do Palestinian families who were ambitious for their children's education. 'Why not Britain?' I asked.

'No,' said Maher's wife firmly, 'it's better in America.'

That was a view shared all over the Arab world, but how ironic to find it here, I thought. It seemed incomprehensible that the very country which perpetuated Palestinian misery by giving Israel the arms it used against the Palestinians, by funding its excesses in the lands it occupied, and by shielding it from all censure, should have become the destination of choice to give their children better futures. One of the UNDP workers, a young man called Ayman, came over from the other side of the room and introduced himself again. He was dark and well-built with a friendly, warm manner. We discovered that his family had been known to mine in Tulkarm years before. Though their place of origin was Qalqilya, which lay to the north of our town, the two families had often visited each other.

Such connections were common amongst Palestinians, where families were rarely anonymous. A link by marriage or a trade in common was soon discovered when people met. It did not mean that everyone was equal. Families were classified according to their reputation or wealth or status, and they were usually associated with particular towns or villages, for example, the Tibis from Tayybeh, the Touqans from Nablus, or the Husseinis from Jerusalem. After the Nakba, the hunt for family origin and connection became vastly more important as a way of keeping contact with the old Palestine and maintaining its traditions. Nevertheless, people from the old established families complained about the social mix that occurred in exile after 1948. No one knew who anyone was any more, they said. All sorts of upstarts and people of low origins and insignificant families could pop up in positions they would never have attained in Palestine. Some of those who disagreed with the policies of the PLO attributed its failings, as they saw them, to the indiscriminate appointment of such people to high office.

For me, discovering someone who had known my family was immensely pleasurable and comforting; it made me feel connected to a past and gave me a context in which I belonged and could claim as truly mine. When later in Amman I mentioned Ayman to my father, he instantly recognised the surname, and recalled times when he had met some of his relatives. 'Mind you,' he said, 'they were always thought to be a bit shady, rather dishonest in their business dealings. And I think one of them had to leave the country because he was found out. It left a question mark over the rest of them, and you should bear that in mind with this chap, however nice he seems.'

Ayman invited me to come to the UNDP office and meet his colleagues. 'It sounds like a good place,' I said. 'Are you happy in your job?' He nodded vigorously, but then lowered his voice and said that we should talk further when I visited him. 'You might get a better idea about life here,' he said a little ominously. 'Many of us are thinking of leaving.' I was taken aback, but before I could question him further, our hostess asked us to move to the sitting room, where coffee was served. One of the consuls I had been introduced to when I first arrived was now sitting next to me. He smiled and asked what I was doing in Ramallah. I told him, and he nodded politely. He probably had similar conversations with new people all the time, and I thought he was a little bored, but observing the courtesies

'How are you finding it so far?' he asked dutifully, looking round the room.

'Well, I'm still shocked after having seen the wall at Abu Dis just before we came here,' I said.

'Oh, the wall!' His wife rolled her eyes. 'It's awful, isn't it? I couldn't get used to it for ages.'

'And now you've got used to it?' I inquired.

Her husband said nothing. 'What do you think of the wall?' I asked him.

He shrugged. 'You heard what my wife said.'

'And is that also your opinion?'

He was starting to look faintly irritated. 'It doesn't matter what I think. The Israeli government feels that its security is best served by building the fence as a way of deterring terror- ists. And that's the position one has to deal with.' He clearly wanted the conversation to end there. But I could not leave it alone. His diplomatic manner, so reminiscent of scores of fruitless meetings with impassive Foreign Office officials in London over the years, when they maintained a studious silence over their opinions and just stuck to the official line, made me belligerent. It was one thing to be non-committal in London, far away from the scene of conflict, but quite another in this place, literally surrounded by it. I knew that I would transgress the social code of that pleasant evening if I per- sisted. But the memory of the monstrosity I had just seen at Abu Dis was acutely fresh in my mind, while we sat here, but a few miles away from it, behaving as if all were right with the world.

'You can't say it doesn't matter what you and all the other foreign representatives like you think.' I looked at the second consul, sitting further away. 'For a start, this wall is illegal in international law, which I'm sure you believe in, and then it causes immense suffering for anyone unlucky enough to live near it. I've just seen what it's done to one family, split up by it, meeting only if the husband gets a permit.'

He raised his eyebrows and looked me straight in the eye, unsmiling now.

'Look,' I said in a conciliatory way, 'I do understand that Israel feels it has to protect its people against suicide bombers, and of course it's a terrifying thing if that happens. But I don't think building this wall is the answer, do you?'

He said nothing, while his wife continued to look at me with a distressed expression.

'All right,' he countered after a moment, 'let me ask you something in return. Supposing I agree with you, what do you imagine I can do about it?'

I stared at him. 'A lot. You can start by asking your government to make its disapproval of Israel's actions known. And if that doesn't work, there's a lot more. I don't have to tell you that European states are very powerful if they want to be. The EU could use all sorts of weapons against Israel, like refusing to trade with it, or cutting subsidies to its science programmes, and many other things. Even the threat of doing some of this would be effective.' I had slipped into my activist mode as if I was at a political meeting.

'We love Palestinians,' his wife said earnestly. She had clearly not been expecting any of this. 'We know you've been very unfairly treated. Believe me, we're on your side.'

The consul put up a restraining hand. 'I can see you feel strongly,' he said to me. 'You all do, and of course, I understand that. But in the real world, the world of politics where real things happen, we must deal with what is possible and has a chance of succeeding. I am always telling my Palestinian friends, you are too emotional, and it solves nothing.'

I was momentarily nonplussed by this reply and knew it was futile to go on, but was impelled to respond. 'What you mean is, in your real world, as you put it, no one's going to put themselves out and do anything about Israel, isn't that it?'

Maher came over and took my arm. 'Doctora, you don't know Marius' – the consul – 'he's a good friend of the Palestinians, and he defends our cause whenever he can. But he's a diplomat and he's not free to do as he likes.' He smiled warmly at the consul. The rest of the guests were chatting gaily to each other, and some had left the room. Few of them were aware of the heated conversation that had just taken place.

'Dear friends,' said Maher, turning to the others. 'What about another cup of coffee?'

But everyone declined, and began to take their leave. Annetta, who had been out of the room, came in and indicated that we should leave too. I was aware of Ayman looking at me. We thanked our hosts, and the gynaecologist and his wife, who also lived in Beit Hanina, invited me to visit them. As we stood by the front door the UNDP chief whispered to me, 'Cool down. We all need clear heads around here. The consul's a good man, but his hands are tied. Come over to the office soon and let's have a chat.'

CHAPTER 4

Dr Farid

As the days succeeded each other, it seemed to me that I was beginning to get the hang of life in Ramallah. This was no ordinary place. Living there was like being at an international conference, where one had to be constantly alert not to miss anything important. In ordinary life, conferences are anomalous things; they impose an artificial suspension of normal routine, as if one had gone to a desert island where a selected group of individuals with similar interests were assembled to do nothing other than listen and talk to each other. Such events are also by their nature short-lived, a few days at most, and, when at their best, so intense and engrossing that by the end I would often find myself welcoming the return to humdrum reality. In Ramallah we lived in a perpetual international conference. Each day was full of incident – a meeting, a visiting foreign delegation, a press conference, a new government announcement, a violent army eruption, an angry demonstration – and each day brought a new dimension to my understanding of life there, all memorable, all seemingly momentous at the time. Being in such a place was at once exhausting and exhilarating, and unlike anything I had experienced before.

Life at the ministry did not improve. Hanan, who had proposed to visit and explain matters to me, was back at her post the day after the trip to Abu Dis, but I saw nothing of Esperance. The heat made one disinclined to do much work, as the growing number of office staff congregated around the coffee room, idly chatting, testified. Bilal the coffee-maker was much in demand, and offered me coffee without my asking. He came into my office with a cup on a tray, smiling cheerily. Close behind him followed a tall, thin, middle-aged woman in a headscarf and a floor-length overcoat with long sleeves in a dreary beige colour, the so-called *libas shar'i* (dress code approved by shari'a). This was Um Ali (mother of Ali), the ministry cleaner, whom I had seen once or twice hanging around the other offices gossiping. 'Um Ali's here to clean your office,' explained Bilal, eager to please. He seemed afraid of her. 'Sorry, Doctora. She had all the others to do first, or she would have finished yours before.'

Um Ali was not sorry. She eyed me suspiciously, looking pointedly at my uncovered head and bare legs, and I instantly identified her as a member of the Esperance camp. She had brought a bedraggled broom and dustpan and brush with her, and proceeded to sweep the floor around my desk, and then my feet, in a desultory manner. All it did was to shuffle the dirt around. A much-used duster which she produced next and which she passed over my computer had the same effect, and some of the dust settled on my skirt. Bilal had meanwhile brought in a bucket and floor cloth, which she told him to set down in the doorway. The water inside it was murky and I assumed it had already done the rounds of the other offices before reaching mine. I declined this last part of Um Ali's cleaning ritual. She nodded at me grimly, as if it was only to be expected from someone so evidently godless, since cleanliness is a central tenet of Islam, and refusing to be clean is a sort of heresy.

Alone once more, I decided to continue working on my media strategy plan for presentation to Dr Sabah. I divided it into sections by topic and tasks appropriate to each, in the way I was accustomed from working in the NHS. For years I had drawn up strategy documents for what was called 'health service provision' with 'bullet points' and 'targets', dreary exercises far duller than this, and I had no difficulty in writing the report. I laid out a critique of the current media strategy and proposed ways of correcting faulty practices, and then added a long section on foreign and especially Israeli media outlets and the importance of getting the Palestinian message across to the enemy camp. It was an almost total departure from the ministry's existing media strategy, and I anticipated strong criticism. It might have been more restful, I reflected, to simply tinker at the edges of the document to show that I had done some work on it, and not put myself to the trouble of overhauling it. But in a strange way I felt quite committed to the task and taken up by it.

Suddenly the telephone on my desk rang. Surprised that it was even working and wondering who could be contacting me, I answered.

'Hello, Doctora Ghada! *Marhaba!*' I vaguely recognised the genial voice at the other end. 'How are you? What's happening with you? It's Dr Farid here.'

I had so thoroughly lost hope of ever seeing Dr Farid that I did not immediately respond. 'Oh, hello, Dr Farid,' I said. 'How very nice to hear from you.'

'I should have been there to welcome you, please forgive me. But I was travelling, you know how it is. Yes, yes, leave that for later' – clearly addressing someone beside him – 'I'm back now and I will be over to see you shortly. Are they looking after you? Yes? Good. I'll see you soon.' As he rang off, Hanan appeared at my door.

'Hello, Doctora. Just to tell you, Dr Farid is coming over and Miss Esperance wants you to go to the meeting room with the others.'

'What happened to you, Hanan?' I asked. 'I tried to phone you several times yesterday, but there was no answer. I wanted to postpone our meeting because I went out.'

She looked flustered. 'I know, I do apologise. I should have phoned you myself first to say that my daughter was sick and I had to stay with her. I promise I will come – even this evening if you like.' I shook my head. 'No, come when you are less busy. Maybe tomorrow.' She nodded. Through the open door I saw movement and a flurry of people leaving their offices.

What did I remember about Dr Farid? I had met him on and off over many years, at conferences or when he had been in London speaking to the Palestinian community. He was an affable, soft-spoken man with an engaging personality and a warm smile. Though his figure was somewhat rotund, he was always well turned out and charming, face-to-face or in small company. His English was proficient and he had often appeared on TV in the English-speaking world. From his student days in Cairo he had been a loyal member of Fateh and a faithful lieutenant to Yasser Arafat until the latter's death in 2004.

An event that occurred not long after the signing of the Oslo Accords, when optimism about a peaceful outcome to the Israeli–Palestinian conflict was high, came back to me. Arafat and the PLO leadership were based in Gaza in those days. It was not long after they had left Tunis and been allowed by Israel to re-establish themselves there. I had been invited to a lunch at the Palestinian leadership's newly built compound in the centre of Gaza city, and I remembered being greeted warmly by Arafat, whom I had met several times in the past, with a kiss on my forehead when I arrived. With him was Dr Farid, cheerfully organising people and directing the guests to their places. It was there that I first saw Shulamit Aloni, a Jewish member of the Knesset, the Israeli parliament. A youngish Israeli man was with her and another older man, who I was told was the head of Israel TV at the time. Several Palestinian members of Arafat's inner circle were also present.

What I recalled of the occasion above all was Dr Farid's easy camaraderie with the Israelis. He made a special fuss of Shulamit Aloni, paying her extravagant compliments and teasing her playfully. She belonged to the Meretz political party, which she had led at one time and which was more liberal than the other Israeli Zionist parties, and supportive of the Palestinian right to statehood. She met Palestinians regularly and counted many amongst her friends. On the strength of this record, she was regarded by Palestinians as one of the few 'good Israelis' who bothered with them, and it seemed that the lunch was in her honour.

Arafat presented her afterwards with a beautiful Palestinian hand-embroidered shawl as a token of his appreciation for her work. Throughout the meal, however, he was markedly quiet, wary almost, in striking contrast to his ebullient lieutenant, Dr Farid, who, oblivious of Arafat's mood, ploughed on laughing and joking with the Israelis. They in turn reciprocated good-humouredly enough but by no means with enthusiasm. I thought they were bemused by the whole situation and assessing how to make best use of it – even more so when Dr Farid, with an air of celebration as if the conflict had just been declared at an end, left his seat next to Arafat and went round the table to Aloni's chair. Taking her hand in his, he declared fervently, 'It is a very happy day for us that you are here. We will welcome you many, many more times, and long may your work continue!'

The meeting room at the ministry was no more than half full of office workers, some of whom I had not seen before. Esperance was strikingly absent, as was Dr Sabah, who had not come in that day at all. As I went to find a seat around the table, Dr Farid and his entourage, far bigger than Dr Sabah's had been, entered. He had a large presence and seemed to fill the room. Everyone stood up as he came in. His appearance had hardly changed, except for a more rounded belly and a fuller double chin. His smile was as broad as I remembered, as if at some private joke, and he came towards me effusively and kissed me on both cheeks. Linking his arm through mine, he made for adjacent seats at the head of the table. His assistant, Adel, a thin, prematurely balding, nervous young man whom

I later came to know well, sat on Dr Farid's other side and laid a file of papers before him. Three or four other men who had accompanied Dr Farid into the room, all visibly armed, hung around at the back.

'Hello, everybody,' beamed Dr Farid. 'How are you all? Are you looking after Doctora Ghada here?' He turned his smile on me. 'Naturally, you know who she is?' Blank faces met this, but one or two murmured something inaudible. 'You don't? How can that be? She's the best commentator on Palestine in Britain! Always arguing our case and fighting for us abroad. You have to cherish her!' People looked at me curiously, some smiled, but no one said anything. Though I did not know it then, Dr Farid's enthusiastic endorsement of me was not destined to last, and I regretted the loss of his esteem for a long time afterwards.

'Well,' he continued briskly, 'where have you got to in the media work since I was last here?' Two of the men responded by telling him about their own areas of work, and then Hanan said I had been drawing up a new strategy. The others said they had not been directly involved and, as Esperance was not there to give him an overview, I stepped in to explain about the new media strategy and contributed a new idea I had been thinking about. I said I wanted to suggest that we set up a media committee to oversee the aims and general direction of the work. In the NHS this had been a time-honoured way of doing nothing and not feeling badly about it. Committees usually had the effect of delaying all decision-making, for extended periods if necessary, and took up so much time and effort that people involved with them had the illusion they were contributing something useful simply by being on the committee.

That was not my intention here; given the isolated situation I was in, I felt a genuine need for other people's ideas and support.

'Excellent idea!' responded Dr Farid instantly, and I wondered if he, like the NHS managers I had worked with, was also glad that my committee proposal would let him off the hook of having to do anything more. 'Let's think about it now. What's your opinion, Adel? Who should we invite on to it?'

The latter, busy making notes, looked up anxiously. 'I'm not sure,' he said hesitantly. 'You know best, Doctor. You decide.'

Dr Farid turned to the others. 'Are you all happy about the suggestion that we set up a media committee of experts?' Everyone nodded, though I doubted they cared much. To them it must have seemed yet another foible thought up by the boss, and they could carry on with life as usual at the ministry.

'Right!' said Dr Farid, slapping his hand on the table heartily. 'We're all agreed then. Go ahead, Doctora, and arrange for the first meeting of the new committee.' He gave me several names of potential members I did not know but which sounded appropriate; and I later added Muhammad, the Hebrew translator from the ministry, and Aref, a media coordinator from Bir Zeit University whom I had met a few days before. He had worked for the BBC in London for a while and knew my family.

When Dr Farid finally left I went back to my office and tried to digest what had happened. Though I had found his attitude to me gratifyingly positive, almost too much so, in marked contrast to Dr Sabah's, I was not sure if he was genuine. Behind the affability there was a glint of steel in his eye. Before he left, he ordered Adel to sort out a local mobile phone for me, which I had asked for from Esperance when I first arrived and which request she had studiously ignored. I was grateful for Dr Farid's initiative and felt that with his return, things might be looking up.

The next day I came to the ministry with more enthusiasm than I had felt for days, and set about making contact with the names on Dr Farid's list of proposed committee members. The ministry switchboard, which one always had to go through to make a call, was mercifully free that morning. Among the proposed members was a man called Amin Shalabi, who worked

with Dr Farid and who phoned to tell me he would be repre-
senting him on the committee. I then spoke to Muhammad, the
Hebrew translator, and invited him to join us. He looked inordinately pleased to be approached and said he would be ready
any time he was needed. Other people on the list I spoke to also
seemed pleasantly surprised, and agreed to join with alacrity.

The committee was beginning to take shape, and I called
Hanan in to find a room and date for our first meeting. It took
a long time for her to appear, and when she did, she stood
hovering in the doorway, unwilling to come in any further and
looking anxiously behind her.

'Sorry, Doctora,' she said in a hurried whisper. 'I can't help
at the moment. But are you free this evening? Can I come to
see you?'

Oh no, I thought, what now? 'Of course, Hanan. How
about six o'clock?' She nodded and disappeared. I got up and
found Bilal, who was carrying a large coffee tray on his way
to the offices upstairs. He had not offered me any, unlike his
usual custom.

'Bilal, please make me a coffee when you get back.' He
nodded reluctantly. I looked about me at the open office area
where the girls who worked for Dr Sabah were sitting. I said,
'Good morning,' but no one answered. Puzzled, I returned to
my room to find a man I did not know sitting in one of the
chairs. He got up and held out his hand.

'I'm sorry if I startled you, but they pointed me straight in
here without warning you, I think, and you weren't there. I'm
Amin, Amin Shalabi.' He was shorter than I was, probably no
more than five feet in height, with thick dark hair growing low
on his forehead and plump, baby cheeks. 'I thought it would
be good for us to meet face-to-face and plan for the new committee. I tried to phone to tell you I was coming, but your
switchboard was busy.'

'Please don't worry. It's a very good idea indeed for us to
meet.' I might have found a friend, I thought. When Bilal

appeared, I asked for a coffee for the guest, whom the boy seemed to know. 'Hello, Doctor,' he said warmly but respectfully. 'Nice to see you here.' Amin smiled back at him. Many people I met in Ramallah, and indeed in Amman, had the title of 'Dr'. In most cases this referred, not to a medical degree but to a PhD, which a remarkable number of individuals seemed to have acquired. I did not know if it was an indication of their unusual proficiency in higher education, a feature for which the Palestinian people as a whole was renowned, or a reflection of the fact that, through no fault of their own, most had only managed to get accepted by lesser universities in minor states in the US where academic standards were more relaxed. I had no idea where Dr Sabah had acquired his doctorate, or, for that matter, Dr Farid. Suffice it to say, it was a highly prized title that people sought earnestly to attach to their names; it lent them prestige and set them a cut above the rest.

Amin, as he told me at some length, was a 'Canadian Palestinian', just as I was a 'British Palestinian'. He had spent many years in Toronto, and, while telling me about his past life, kept lapsing into Arabic-accented Canadian English as if to establish a common bond between us. He had decided to return to the West Bank from where his family originated and join the PA, mainly after he had met Dr Farid when the latter was on a lecture tour of several Canadian cities. So, on an impulse he packed up, left the business he had set up in Toronto, and returned home.

'I sometimes regret it,' he said. 'Life is hard here, but the wife and kids have settled in. How about you?' I told him a little about myself, but I could see he was less interested by that than by his own life story. And he would have gone on talking about it had I not interrupted to suggest we start work on the committee and plan the next step. He thought we should invite Dr Sabah on to it as a courtesy, although it was unlikely he would join. 'Shall we go and ask him? Now?'

I had no desire to see Dr Sabah, but I assented and we walked over to his office. One of the girls at the desk outside stood up on seeing us, and, ignoring me, asked Amin if she could be of assistance. She was a slender, pretty girl and he looked at her appreciatively. 'Hello. We'd like to see Dr Sabah. Is he here?'

'Sorry, Doctor.' The girl seemed embarrassed. 'He's in a meeting and asked not to be disturbed.'

'Not even for a minute?'

She shook her head vigorously. 'No, no. Not at all.'

Back in my office, Amin, looking annoyed, said, 'We'll have to go ahead without him. I'll try to phone him later. We don't want problems at the start, do we? Or better still,' he mused, 'maybe I should ask Dr Farid to do it.'

'I wonder why Dr Farid didn't think of doing that himself.'

Amin looked at me strangely as if about to say something, but then thought better of it. 'I tell you what. Let's just go ahead and set up the first meeting and see what happens. Have we got an agreement from all the members?'

I went through the list with him and said all the members I had approached had accepted the invitation to join. He looked pleased. 'What a good idea of ours it was to do this! I think I'll phone round and talk to them myself just to make sure.'

'Why would that be necessary? I've already talked to them.'

'No, no,' he said firmly. 'Thank you for what you've done so far, but I will now take this on. You just find us a room to meet and let me know.' Lapsing back into English, he continued, 'And let's get on with it and not mess about any longer!'

That afternoon a rocket was fired from Gaza and hit a target in the Israeli border town of Sderot, killing an Israeli woman. As soon as I heard the news I started to dread the next stage, which usually entailed some form of Israeli revenge against the people of Gaza. I found Ahmad at the gate of the Gemzo Suites, chatting to Atallah. When they greeted me, I said,

RETURN

'Have you heard about Gaza?'

They looked at each other and shook their heads. 'They fired a rocket which killed an Israeli woman,' I said.

'Oh, that,' said Atallah without surprise. 'Don't be scared, Doctora. The Jews won't do anything to us here.' Ahmad agreed. 'They'll go there, to Gaza. Not here. So nothing to worry about.' Palestinians generally referred to Israelis as 'Jews', *yahood*, a leftover from the time before 1948 when there was no such thing as Israeli nationality and the new immigrants who came into Palestine called themselves Jews.

'What about those poor people in Gaza?'

Both men looked up to heaven, turning the palms of their hands in supplication. 'What can they do? They have no one but God to help them.'

Their apparent indifference to Gaza's plight, which had taken me aback, was not callousness, as I was to understand later. It was the effect of their closed lives spent inside the parcels of land into which Israel had confined them. Inevitably, they learned to think solely of their own affairs inside their parcel, and feared only for its safety. To them a village a few miles off was far away, let alone Gaza, which could have been on another continent.

Within a short time of the rocket attack, Israel sealed the borders and stopped all movement of people and goods in and out of Gaza. That evening Israeli troops killed six Gazans. Not long after, skirmishes also broke out between Hamas and Fateh in Gaza City, and two more people were killed. 'Oh God,' exclaimed Annetta when she and I watched the news on TV. 'As if poor Gaza hasn't had enough death and destruction from Israel.'

There had been a long-standing enmity between Fateh and Hamas, whose ideologies diverged widely on Israel and on the solution to the conflict. For Hamas, Islam was central, and its ultimate goal was an Islamic state in all of Palestine. Fateh, the far older and more secular party, had started life on a purely

66

nationalist platform, aiming for total liberation of the usurped homeland. But with time and increasing setbacks it adapted to the reality of Israel's superior power, and after years of ineffectual struggle downgraded its ambitions to a claim for just one fifth of the original Palestine. By the time I was in Ramallah, it had made many more compromises with 'the enemy', drawing criticism and dismay from many Palestinian quarters at what was seen as a gradual surrender.

Hamas's main power base was in Gaza, which had always traditionally been conservative, while Fateh was strongest on the West Bank. When I was working for the PA it was dominated by Fateh members, and many in Hamas openly despised the leadership for what they called its subservience to Israel and the corruption of its members. Conversely, Fateh people disapproved of Hamas's tactics, and especially the rocket attacks against Israeli targets which rained Israeli vengeance down on the hapless Gazans. Such passionate disagreement and friction between the two parties ineluctably led to spurts of open and increasingly deadly violence.

Hanan was as true as her word. She arrived at the Suites where I was waiting for her soon after six o'clock. We sat in the lobby which was quite empty, and I ordered coffee. But she declined, saying we should go to her house afterwards for dinner. She was a nice-looking girl with an open, smiling face and a warm manner, and I had taken to her from the start.

'You said there was something you wanted to tell me. Can you talk now?'

She hesitated a little, looking around her. And then she spoke. There were bad problems at the ministry, the worst of which was that the minister and his deputy detested each other and each did his own work without reference to the other. Because Dr Farid's office was in another building, also designated the Ministry of Media and Communications, his deputy had taken over the building where we worked and regarded it as his fiefdom. Strictly speaking this was not permissible and Dr Farid was supposed to be able to override him, but in practice Dr Sabah had been left to his own devices. As a result, no policy was coordinated, and differing, sometimes conflicting, messages emanated from each ministry. Both men resented each other's plans and countermanded orders given to staff.

'I had no idea,' I said. 'I could see that something was wrong, and that Dr Sabah didn't care for me, but I did not realise it went so far.'

'You are another problem – sorry to say, Doctora. Dr Sabah didn't want you as soon as he found out that it was Dr Farid who appointed you.' I remembered the lack of an office when I first arrived, the grudging efforts of Esperance to find me one and the fact that no one was expecting me.

'And Esperance?' A look of pure hatred passed over Hanan's features. 'Dr Sabah spoils her. She's a spy for him, her job is to spy on us and report back. And she spies on you too, Doctora.' I frowned. 'You've done nothing wrong. Actually we think you're a breath of fresh air, you listen to people and you try to get us to work together. But they want you out.'

I pondered this. If it was true, what would happen to me? Would Dr Farid intervene on my behalf? I was alarmed at how powerless I felt, as if I were dependent on Dr Sabah's favour or what support I could look to from Dr Farid. I had forgotten how I came to be in Ramallah in the first place, that my contract was with the UNDP, not with the ministry or anyone else at the PA, and that my presence there was in the nature of a free benefit to them, not the other way around. If I felt like that after only a few weeks at the PA, how did the more junior office workers feel, I wondered? My self-confidence seemed to have seeped away.

'I don't suppose you know,' continued Hanan, 'that Dr Sabah's given orders to all of us not to talk to you or assist you or deal with you in any way.' I remembered Bilal's reluctance with my morning coffee.

'For how long?' I asked.

'I don't know, but I suppose until you find it so impossible you'll leave.'

I said nothing for a moment. And then I asked, 'you don't seem to like Esperance very much, do you?'

'Ah, if you only knew, Doctora, how I've been treated, and it's all due to her,' Hanan said bitterly. It turned out that a few months back the ministry had stopped paying her salary, on the grounds that she was registered to work at another ministry and could not draw a salary from both bodies. 'But I wasn't at the other ministry any more. I'd finished with them. Maybe they hadn't taken my name off their books. I told Esperance, but she wouldn't believe me. I went back to the other ministry and asked about their register. No one knew anything, and I didn't know what to do.'

'How did this ministry know about you having been registered for work at the other place?'

Her eyes glittered with anger. 'That's just it. I started digging and found out that Esperance had asked Abdullah' – this was an office worker who Hanan said worked closely with Esperance – 'she asked him to check up on me, and he kept nosing around until he came out with this business of the other job I was supposed to have.'

'But why? Why did she ask him to do that?'

'She hates me. I saw Dr Sabah when I applied for this job, and he appointed me without telling her. She's hated me ever since.'

Hanan's salary was not reinstated until Dr Sabah intervened. He found that she was indeed not an employee of the other ministry and she was exonerated. However, she never received the back pay that had been denied her for months while the matter was being investigated. 'They won't give it to me and say that I was paid when I wasn't.' She suddenly burst into tears.

'I'm so sorry,' I said. 'Can no one help, not Dr Sabah?' She shook her head. 'He's not around much and he doesn't want to be bothered with me again.'

'I'm very sorry,' I said again.

'Thank you, Doctora.' She dried her eyes and smiled. 'I shouldn't trouble you with these stories. Let's go and have dinner. My daughters are so looking forward to meeting you.'

My spirits suddenly rallied. 'Tell me, Hanan, will *you* be talking to me in the office tomorrow?'

She nodded. 'Of course I will, so long as Esperance doesn't see me.'

'Fine. Then I'm going to ask you when you get into the office tomorrow morning to book a room for the first meeting of the new media committee.'

'I will,' she said. 'When should I book it for?'

'The day after tomorrow. The sooner the committee meets and we start our work, the better.'

'What about Esperance and Dr Sabah?' she asked nervously. 'They don't want you to do another thing at the ministry.'

I looked at her and smiled. 'We'll just have to see, won't we?' I said.

CHAPTER 5

A Concert in Nablus

On 7 July 2005, London was rocked by a series of terrorist explosions. Several bombs hit the London Underground at major central locations, King's Cross and Edgware Road stations, and inside a double-decker bus which was driving through Tavistock Square. Fifty-two people lost their lives and over 700 were injured. The emergency services worked indefatigably to evacuate the dead and wounded, and hospitals in the vicinity were overwhelmed. The perpetrators, as it turned out, were Islamists apparently engaged in a war against the West, and the outrage caused a wave of violent anti-Islamic feeling. Muslim communities in major British cities, such as Birmingham and Bradford, became objects of hate and fear.

Hearing about all this in faraway Ramallah, I was immediately anxious to make contact with my daughter and those I cared about in London. But having done so and been reassured that no one I knew had been in the centre of London that day, I returned to the minutiae of life around me, as if they were more important than the death and destruction in the city which had been my home for more than five decades. It was not that I did not care, or was not horrified by the death toll and the grief it must have caused; but it was that London now seemed so distant, as if it belonged to another planet and another life. Nor of course had I forgotten a whole lifetime in England in the space of a few weeks, but that the Ramallah 'international conference' effect I was living through was so immediate, so compelling in its detail, that its every twist and turn kept me riveted.

The battle with the ministry over setting up the new media group and organising its first meeting dominated my thoughts. It was at the forefront of my mind throughout the evening at Hanan's house, although she and her little family made me welcome and entertained me with touching hospitality. Her eldest child, a shy girl of eight, who had turned her head away when I was first introduced, came up close after a short while and put her hand in mine. The younger one, who had also hung back, soon followed suit, and the three of us ended up all sitting cramped together on the small sofa. They chattered away excitedly throughout the meal, and when I left, Hanan's husband, a warm and welcoming young man, walked me back to the Gemzo Suites. On the way he begged me to help his wife in her fight to get the salary owed to her. I could not tell him that I felt as powerless as she did, so I nodded and said that I would do my best.

The next morning I awoke still thinking about the media group, and found myself dreading the idea of going into the office and facing another day with no one speaking to me. So I decided to avoid the place altogether and went instead to the Cultural Palace, where I had been told that a meeting about Israel's separation wall was to be held that morning. It had been called to discuss the wall's impact on Palestinian lands and livelihoods. A number of local dignitaries, researchers from the PLO Negotiations Support Unit (NSU),[1] a few foreign diplomats and Western journalists were assembled in one of the meeting rooms when I arrived. I knew no one personally there and took a seat unobtrusively at the back.

The meeting was addressed by a senior PA official at the foreign ministry, a small, dapper man with a slightly

---

1 The NSU was a British-funded organisation whose purpose was to provide well-researched factual studies for the use of Palestinian negotiators in the peace process with Israel. It was staffed by bright young professionals who came from all over the world and whose reports and briefings were widely regarded as accurate and authoritative.

self-important air. He had served for many years as a diplomat at the Palestinian Mission to the UN, where he was
well regarded and, it was said, had been reluctant to return
to Ramallah. But his position in an important ministry of the
Palestinian government had somewhat made up for the loss of
freedom he had enjoyed in New York. He did not see himself
staying long at the relatively lowly rank to which he had
been assigned, and it was rumoured that he had ambitions to
become the PA's foreign minister in due course.

Pictures of the wall, taken at various locations and from a
number of angles to show its most egregious features, were
projected on to a large screen. The official, who I thought
looked either bored or perhaps weary, expounded on the
wall's origins and history. It had been the brainchild of Israel's
prime minister Ariel Sharon, who claimed that a barrier wall
was needed to provide protection against Palestinian terrorist
attacks on Israel. Accordingly, in 2002 Israel started building the huge, insurmountable shield of high concrete wall and
electrified fencing, parts of which I had seen at Abu Dis and on
the route to Jerusalem. Despite the wall's concrete reality, the
Israelis called it a 'security fence', and the Palestinians, who
saw how it imprisoned them within their towns and villages,
called it the 'Apartheid Wall'.

At this point, pictures of the wall were replaced by a large
multicoloured map of the West Bank. This had been drawn
up by the young researchers at the NSU and depicted with
impressive clarity the circuitous route of the wall through the
West Bank. We saw how it dipped into Palestinian territory
here and there to surround Jewish settlements and shield them
from the Arab areas around them, and how it also enclosed
the Palestinian cities to prevent their inhabitants from
leaving except through one or two exit gates under Israeli
guard. More detailed maps of towns and land affected by
the wall followed, all similarly expertly drawn. Photographs
of farms severed by the wall and angry villagers confronting

Israeli soldiers showed the effects of the wall on Palestinian communities.

Throughout this presentation the PA official related the hardships that the wall inflicted on the population in a flat, monotonous voice, and reminded his audience that what Israel was doing was illegal under international law. At no point was his speech enlivened by a personal story, an anecdote, or a living example of individual experiences; just a toneless delivery of a list of misfortunes. He ended his monotone with another reminder that in 2004, the International Court of Justice had issued a majority judgment about the illegality of the wall and called on Israel to dismantle those parts of it that crossed over into West Bank territory. He then asked his dwindling audience (several of the Western diplomats and journalists had left quietly while the lights were lowered during the slide show) for comments and questions.

'Thank you for that excellent exposition on the wall.' The speaker was a young American journalist who had stood up. Everyone looked round at him curiously. The official nodded without changing his expression. 'What I would like to ask is what you intend to do about it. I mean, does the PA have a policy with regard to the situation? Are there any plans to address the problem?' He sat down.

The PA man smiled faintly in his direction. 'What paper did you say you worked for?' When the journalist gave his credentials again, the diplomat nodded, cleared his throat and continued, 'Let me turn the question around. What would you do if you were us?' He spoke English with an American intonation, no doubt picked up from his years at the UN in New York. There was no immediate reply. 'Hmm?' He now smiled more broadly at the young man. 'You see? Not so easy, is it?'

Why not tell the truth? I thought. Why not say that there is nothing, absolutely nothing, you or the PA can do to stop one inch of this wall being built? It would at least be honest. Instead, the official began a long-winded account of how the

PA would pursue the international route, make new representations to the International Court of Justice, publish more information about the wall and publicise the plight of those affected by it. I slipped out quietly in my turn as he was speaking, and was accosted by a young woman outside. She gave me a glossy, expensively produced booklet about the wall from a pile on a table outside the meeting room. It showed the same maps and photographs we had just seen, with the same commentary on the wall's illegality we had heard. The two or three young people manning the table were chatting to each other and exchanging animated accounts of what they had been doing the evening before.

On my way out of the building I saw an elderly man with a *hatta* and *'igal* on his head, such as villagers wear.[2] His face was lined and weather-beaten, especially around the eyes, and as we looked at each other he smiled at me. I smiled back. I concluded that he was probably from one of the villages affected by the wall, and must have been at the meeting. I wanted to ask him how he had found it. But he knew nothing about any meeting. It turned out that his daughter worked at the Cultural Palace and his only reason for being there was to visit her.

That afternoon Zeina got in touch. She wondered if I would like to go to a roundtable discussion on 'solutions to the Israeli–Palestinian conflict' being held at the Grand Park Hotel. This was Ramallah's most expensive hotel, and host to many top-level meetings and conferences. Zeina, whom I had got to know not long before, was an attractive, intelligent young woman who had taken me under her wing, an

---

2   This is a traditional Palestinian male headdress, usually worn by rural people, in which a rectangular white cloth is folded to form a triangle and placed over the head. It is then encircled by a black rounded cord, leaving the sides of the triangle hanging on either side of the face.

odd thing to happen given the difference in our ages; but I rather thought she felt sorry for me. She worked for one of the Palestinian ministries and knew her way around. She kept an invaluable calendar of Ramallah's events and had a wide circle of interesting, mostly political, contacts. Her views of life under occupation and the future prospects for young Palestinians like herself were refreshingly forthright and honest. 'In a word, grim,' she said.

The roundtable discussion she took me to that afternoon had been organised by a non-governmental organisation (NGO) based in East Jerusalem.

'What, another NGO?' I said. 'There are so many here.'

She shrugged her shoulders eloquently. 'Yes,' she said, 'but what else do we have? When my job at the ministry ends, I'll have to apply to an NGO, and I might get accepted if I'm lucky.'

NGOs were important sources of livelihood in the Occupied Territories, where farming land and natural resources were in short supply and the restrictions on travel and freedom of movement between places made most kinds of ordinary work impossible. They attracted the best educated and most talented Palestinians, like Zeina, to the extent that many people thought NGOs had been deliberately introduced into the Palestinian territories by pro-Israeli Western agencies to siphon off the pool of available Palestinian talent and prevent it from being used to mount any resistance to Israel. It was certainly the case that the people who worked for NGOs were kept inordinately busy, as one of their main tasks was raising funds to continue in work (and have their salaries paid). They spent the last three months at least of each year working on proposals for the next year's projects, thereby hoping to ensure a renewal of their contracts.

Ramallah was full of NGOs at the time, perhaps as many as eighty, working on myriad aspects of Palestinian life from health and education to sanitation and the environment, as well as less tangible matters like psychosocial issues and what was known as 'capacity building'. You could hardly go from one street to the next without coming across yet another NGO. They were all funded by foreign, usually Western, agencies, charities, societies or associations. USAID, the largest American aid organisation, was a major provider of funds for NGOs in the Occupied Palestinian Territories, as were various European charities, in addition to the European Union and the UN. All projects in the Palestinian areas were funded by one or more of these bodies.

This extraordinary profusion had come about after the Oslo Accords, when everyone thought that Palestinian statehood was within reach. As a result, Palestinians were encouraged to prepare for it through engaging in 'state-building' initiatives, many in collaboration with Israeli organisations. To help them do this, NGOs sprang up all over the West Bank and Gaza, including a small number in East Jerusalem. I noticed how they used a particular jargon to describe their activities. Expressions like 'capacity building', 'sustainability', 'democratisation', 'empowerment', all previously unfamiliar to Palestinian society, became commonplace. People were not slow to pick up on the potential of this new vocabulary in attracting funds from outside; all they had to do was pepper their applications with enough of these buzzwords to enable them to raise the funds they needed.

Filling in a 'proposal' was the key to setting the whole process in motion, and knowing how to do that effectively was often the best qualification for getting the job. The news soon spread, and in one local story a *mukhtar* (village headsman) from a poor village close to al-Bireh and desperate for funds once turned up at the municipality offices and asked an official there, 'Tell me, my son, where can I get hold of one of these "proposals" everyone's talking about? God knows we need the money.'

The NGO which had organised the meeting in Ramallah had a slightly more daring range of activities than was the norm for these organisations. It was well known that the work of NGOs had to conform to guidelines set by the financial backer, and as a result, political or other potentially controversial topics were generally best avoided if one wanted to secure the funding. Some donors even imposed specific types of censorship on NGOs before funds could be released. But in this case, no such restrictions seemed to apply, and the topic to be discussed was part of a political series this NGO apparently specialised in.

The workshop had already begun when we arrived. Dr Wajdi Sallam, the chairman and head of the NGO, an urbane globetrotter who attended many international conferences where he was famous for his outspoken criticisms of Israel, was introducing the discussion. People wondered how he got away with it, for he seemed to travel in and out of the country without difficulty. But then, they said, it was probably because Israelis did not care how much Palestinians like him screamed their heads off, as long as they did not do anything else. Israelis were thought to be extremely clever; they deliberately allowed the odd Palestinian like Dr Wajdi to let off steam in public, because it was good for their image as 'the only democracy in the Middle East'. I remembered how the Arabs I had known in London were similarly impressed by Israelis, and also imputed Machiavellian powers to them.

Dr Wajdi and I knew each other from various international meetings we had attended in the past, and he made much of greeting me as I came in and inviting me to sit next to him at the head of the table. He was an amiable-looking, fatherly man in his sixties with a smooth face and a broad smile. About fifteen people were present, among them young, mostly foreign, assistants he had brought with him from Jerusalem. The rest of the participants consisted of an assortment of researchers and journalists, some members of Fateh though none in government, one or two men who were Hamas sympathisers but not members, and several others who seemed knowledgeable about the subject in hand. People spoke in both English and Arabic.

'We're talking about the future,' Dr Wajdi explained, turning to me as I sat down. 'What solutions we can see for the problem, what strategies we need to employ. As I see it,' he was now addressing the room, 'we have limited options – things either stay the same, which no one wants, or we try for the two-state solution. You all know that this is the solution the Palestinian leadership has chosen. But we've been waiting for our state to materialise, and it seems that it's further away than ever.' He swept the table with his eyes. 'My friends, you see how the settlements are being built all over our land. What have we got left to put our state on? And as for Jerusalem,' he rolled his eyes up to heaven – 'our capital, our city, I know many of you can't even go there – I'm saying this for the sake of our foreign visitors who may not know that most Palestinians can't go to Jerusalem except with a permit from the Israelis, which they don't often get. But Jerusalem is already gone, lost, I assure you. So what is left of the Palestinian state we've been hoping for?'

He paused to let that sink in, and then resumed, 'Or, we go for the last option: a binational state, a "one state". No partition, no division, just one land shared between us and them.' He paused. 'That's how I see it. What do you think, Dr Ghada?' I was not expecting this and found it embarrassing. I smiled and shook my head at him.

'Never mind,' he said, 'let's hear from the others. Nawwaf, tell us what you think.'

Nawwaf, a middle-aged Fateh man, cleared his throat and put his cigarette down. He nodded his head in greeting at everyone around the table and answered in Arabic. 'Thank you, Dr Wajdi. You have given us a good summary of the situation. But you said that no one wants it to stay the same. I disagree. Israel wants it to stay the same. And Israel will make sure it doesn't change. They're building their settlements, they've got

Jerusalem as you said, no one stops them. So it couldn't be better for them.' He coughed and looked at his colleagues. 'It's only us who don't want it. So, it's us who've got to change it.' The other Fateh men, also smoking, did not comment.

Looking pleased, Dr Wajdi translated what had been said for the benefit of the non-Arabic speakers. 'Yes, very good, brother Nawwaf, very good. Please continue. We want to hear what you have in mind.' He looked round and gestured at everyone, encouraging them to join in. His smiling, pleasant manner never changed throughout the discussion, despite its gravity. He looked ever happier as people became engaged. The Hamas sympathisers, who had at first said little, eventually spoke up to assert that it was not a matter of which option, but of a failed PA strategy.

'You know, brother Wajdi,' one of them said, also speaking in Arabic, 'that the president has turned his back on any policy which could threaten Israel, that's the truth, isn't it?' At this time, Mahmoud Abbas was the PA president, having replaced Yasser Arafat after the latter's death. Not everyone agreed with his total renunciation of the armed struggle, and many accused him of surrendering too readily to Israeli and American demands. Hamas, the Islamist Palestinian party and Fateh's chief rival for power, was the spearhead for these views: it regarded all forms of resistance to Israeli occupation as equally legitimate and disapproved of the change in Fateh from a previous revolutionary force to a party only wanting to stay in power, even at the cost of abandoning its past honourable record in fighting for Palestine's liberation.

The discussion went on, getting more heated as people relaxed and spoke their minds. But after two hours of this the workshop ended inconclusively. No new strategies emerged, and the options that Dr Wajdi had outlined at the beginning were scarcely developed further. However, the atmosphere was amicable enough as the meeting broke up, people exchanging cards and continuing the discussion in smaller groups.

Dr Wajdi urged me to visit his offices in Jerusalem and left with his assistants, and Zeina and I left as well.

'That was very interesting,' I said to her, 'but not very satisfactory. Surely Dr Wajdi wanted something more out of it?'

'Oh, not at all,' she said. 'That's how all his meetings go. He brings together lots of really worthwhile people, and the topics are usually good. But if nothing much comes out of any of them, he's happy enough as long as he can get a report written about it. That's why he tries to provoke people to engage, so he can make something exciting happen which will be worth writing about.' The workshops he organised led to published reports which his team put together, and then added to his NGO's annual output. This was then submitted to the NGO's backers in anticipation of a renewal – usually granted, Zeina said. I could see that she did not care for Dr Wajdi.

'Aside from wanting funds for his NGO, do you think he has any genuine interest in the topics he deals with? Like today's, for example?' I asked her.

'I honestly don't know if he has. But it wouldn't surprise me if he didn't. I'm glad you never said anything, by the way. He would not have taken it in, just used it as another thing to put in his report. I don't think he listens to anyone other than himself.'

It was early evening by the time she drove me from the hotel back to the Gemzo Suites. I invited her to join a group of us going to Nablus later that evening, but she said her parents were expecting her back for dinner. Like all unmarried people in Ramallah, Zeina lived at home with her family, and would only leave when she got married. Telling Annetta about the workshop when I saw her, I found that she knew Dr Wajdi well and thought him an impressive 'operator', as she put it. His NGO was always in funds, and she admired his ability to survive the hostile and demeaning environment of Jerusalem.

'It's not easy for any Arab living there,' she said. 'Israelis think it's theirs by divine right, you know.'

We were in Annetta's car driving towards Nablus to attend a recital given by two women from Ramallah, one a soprano singer and the other a pianist, and the event had been prominently advertised in 'This Week in Palestine'. The sheer normality of such an occurrence was striking, as if we were in some ordinary country with the leisure to enjoy concerts and listen to music. Samir came with us and also Reema, Annetta's activist friend who had been at the Abu Dis demonstration against the wall. It was a balmy night with a star-studded sky and a full moon whose light you could almost read by, so wondrously beautiful it was almost worth living through the scorching summer's day that had preceded it.

All through the eastern Mediterranean people stayed up into the early hours on such nights, enjoying the cool gentle air. It brought back to me an early memory of childhood in Tulkarm, not far from where we were now, when we used to sleep the night on the flat roof of my grandfather's house looking up at the moon and the stars. In the place we were in on this night, however, such pleasures were curtailed by the vigilant presence of Israeli army units never far away. The Palestinian territories were subject to tight Israeli military control over the whole area which was rigorously policed. I turned towards the open car window and let the fresh breeze blow over my face. If I closed my eyes I could imagine myself somewhere else entirely, on holiday perhaps in some Mediterranean resort. But as soon as I opened them I could see the yellow lights of Israeli settlements high above on all the hilltops we passed. In the valleys below it was pitch black, with just the dark outline of vegetation against the horizon. The road, empty but for the occasional car, was bathed in pale moonlight.

This was the old main route from Nazareth in the north down to Bethlehem in the south, a central artery that followed the foothills of the West Bank mountain ridge. After Israel's occupation in 1967 the road became obstructed by checkpoints and ran past numerous settlements with guarded entrances, and was no longer the convenient link it had been. Not long after leaving Ramallah we passed on our left the huge settlement of Yitzhar, a religious colony known for its fundamentalist Jewish zealots and their violent anti-Arab hostility. It was said that men and boys from the settlement would go out with their guns on most days to harass the people of the nearby Arab villages, as if enjoying a kind of gruesome sport.

But nothing was stirring there that evening as we drove by. After another twenty minutes we reached the village of Huwwara just outside Nablus. Here there was a large checkpoint, notorious for the long hold-ups and massive car queues that built up on either side trying to cross it. It had a reputation for being manned by aggressive soldiers who treated the local people with particular roughness and brutality. Palestinians said that was because Nablus was a city with a proud and solid Muslim Arab identity which refused to succumb or compromise with the enemy. The town was traditionally a source of resistance fighters against Israel. The huge Ballata refugee camp just inside the town's perimeter was the main centre of resistance and the target of many Israeli raids, when soldiers would seize young men on Israel's 'wanted list' and take them away for interrogation and usually imprisonment.

When we arrived at the checkpoint there were no queues in our way and we passed through without difficulty, no doubt thanks to Annetta's Israeli-number plate and the fact that, as three women with only one man amongst us, we were seen as less of a threat.

Annetta drove to Nablus's main university, An-Najah, and parked just outside. The recital was being held in the main auditorium, and when we arrived, it was already quite full. The university rector, a handsome middle-aged man, recognised

Annetta as we entered and came over to greet us.[3] He showed us to a row of seats near the front with a good view of the raised platform on which stood a piano where the two ladies would perform. I looked round at the hall, the young women in *libas shar'i*, their heads covered and their bodies hidden by long, plain-coloured coats. Many men were there too, the ones seated next to the women presumably their husbands or relatives. All age groups seemed to be represented, and from their large numbers I supposed this was a grand event for Nablus.

But I could not help wondering who had thought to organise such a European-style recital in a place like this. Nablus had always been one of Palestine's most conservative and traditional cities and religiosity was conspicuous everywhere, probably the town's own way of withstanding Israel's repeated onslaughts. I could not see how it would fit with the music we were likely to hear that night. However, when the recital started there was a hush in the audience and a rapt attention to the music. The pianist and the singer, who had come up to Nablus for the event, were impressive, given the acoustics in the hall. The songs had been composed by the pianist, and the singer performed them in a strong soprano voice that filled the auditorium. Even though she sang in Arabic, the style was unmistakably European, and I waited to see how that would go down with an audience reared on a very different musical tradition.

But to my surprise they were enthusiastic and clapped appreciatively after each song. There was long and loud applause at the end.

'Aren't they great?' said Samir excitedly afterwards.

'Yes, those two ladies are wonderful,' said Annetta. 'I've heard them before.'

'No, not the musicians, I meant the people, the great people of Nablus!' We were back in Annetta's car on the start of our

---

3 This man, Rami Hamdallah, was appointed Palestinian prime minister in 2014.

return journey. 'Look at them!' His eyes were shining. 'Their spirit! Their guts! You'd never think that just down the road there was an army camp or that hideous checkpoint we went through. They were goddamn well going to enjoy that concert, what the hell, no matter who was playing what kind of music!' He moved his head from side to side in admiration. 'Goddamn it, they're just great!'

I had always found Palestinians like him, brought up in the US and speaking like typical Americans, rather disconcerting. They did not come across as Arabs but as part of the 'enemy camp', the country that had nurtured Israel for decades and was its most loyal friend. I felt guilty even having such a thought, for Samir's patriotism and utter commitment to the cause were not in doubt. And yet his reactions to what went on around him, however passionate, were still somehow those of an interested tourist or an outsider looking in. It was a fear I had about myself. How much, I wondered, did my English accent and manner place me in that much older 'enemy camp', the one which was the source of the problem, which had created Israel and was so infinitely more culpable? Perhaps I was also something of a tourist, an observer of a scene I was not part of.

We came up to the Huwwara checkpoint still discussing the concert. The soldiers this time were different to those who had earlier let us through without difficulty. The young soldier who gestured to us to drive up to the checkpoint was weighed down by his large helmet and the heavy gun slung over his shoulder. When we stopped, he bent down and peered at us through the car window. Annetta greeted him with a friendly smile, but it had no effect. He straightened up and turned towards a colleague, a taller, older man. They conferred in rapid Hebrew and then the soldier told us to get out of the car.

'Something wrong?' I asked. He ignored me and just repeated the order, speaking in poor and heavily accented English. We filed out of the car and handed him our passports as was usual at all Israeli checkpoints. The sky was even starrier and the moon shone down brightly. The soldiers examined the passports and lingered over Samir's.

'*Haviyya*?' the older man demanded. This was a Hebrew rendering of the Arabic *hawiyya*, or identity card. West Bank Palestinians all carried these cards, and although Samir, whose family originally came from Ramallah, had a US passport, the West Bank ID was the only thing that counted under Israeli law. The soldiers examined his ID closely, and then looked at the rest of us as they checked our passports. They asked where we had been.

'We were at a concert in Nablus,' replied Annetta.

'You know many people there?'

'Well, yes. I have friends in Nablus.'

This seemed to irritate them. 'And you?' They were looking at me.

'No, I don't know anyone there. But what is all this about? Why have you stopped us?'

I could see Annetta trying to dissuade me from saying more with a faint shake of her head. Reema said nothing.

'Yeah, come on, give us the reason,' Samir said pugnaciously, seemingly ready for a fight.

The soldiers just stared at him. 'But of course you don't need reasons, do you?' Samir was now in a rage. 'You think you're God almighty here, don't you. And we've got to do what you say no matter what. Well, buddy, you picked the wrong people!'

In this unwise diatribe, which I doubted the soldiers' English was good enough to understand, I recognised his outrage, that of a man used to living in a free country with rights and a rule of law. He had been an activist in America and knew about the harassment of Palestinians at Israeli hands. It had angered him long before he left San Francisco for Ramallah, only a few months before, and I could see he was all fired up now.

I started to feel nervous. The soldiers had turned on their walkie-talkies, and the older soldier began speaking into his. Samir was not deterred.

'So you don't have a reason. Good, so let us go.' He turned towards us. 'Come on, guys, let's go!' He took my arm and that of Reema's and motioned to Annetta to get back into the car. Meanwhile, a queue of vehicles had built up behind us.

Samir's last interjection was like a red rag to a bull. The soldiers sprang into action and shoved him roughly to one side. 'You go there. You wait,' they shouted at him. 'You!' they said to us. 'Get back in the car and go!' None of us moved. 'Go!' they shouted again, and the younger soldier pushed Annetta towards the car. At that moment an army jeep, driving fast, came into view and with a screech of brakes stopped abruptly next to us. Two more soldiers, also heavily armed, got out and started talking to the ones who had detained us.

'Please return to your car.' This new soldier was more courteous, and seemed senior to the rest. He was fair-haired and European-looking and spoke good English. 'It is better for you.'

'We can't leave our friend here,' said Annetta. 'Perhaps you could explain what the problem is.'

His manner was still courteous. 'We have a few questions for your friend.'

'And then you will let him go?'

'Depends,' he said without elaborating.

Meanwhile, Samir's temper had not improved. 'You have no right to keep me!' he yelled at the new soldiers. They ignored him and, moving nearer, edged us towards the car.

'We'll wait for you, Samir,' Annetta called out. 'We'll park just the other side.'

The new soldiers checked our passports again, and the fair-haired soldier looked at me.

'You live in London?'

I nodded. 'Where in London? I love London!' he said. 'I often go there to see friends.'

'I live in a part called Golders Green, but you probably wouldn't know it.' If indeed he knew London, I thought, he could not fail to know Golders Green. We had moved there in 1949, when we took refuge in England following the loss of Palestine. It was an enormous irony that of all places my father had chosen Golders Green, one of London's foremost Jewish areas and full of German Jewish refugees at the time. Our next-door neighbour was a German Jewish doctor whose services we used for a while, and more than half the girls in my class at school were of similar origin. My father always explained afterwards that he had not known his way around London and had little idea where he was taking us. What an incongruous sight we must have been, the only Palestinian family in the middle of a Jewish neighbourhood, and it was a subject of hilarity for everyone who heard about it.

The soldier's eyes lit up. 'Golders Green?' he said smilingly. 'Of course I know Golders Green. My girlfriend lives there. I went many times. I love it.'

We exchanged experiences and stories about Golders Green, which I spun out, and he seemed to be enjoying himself. The other soldiers stood in the background.

'When are you coming to London next?' I asked. 'How about you visit me in Golders Green?'

'Sure, why not? I will be there maybe in October.'

'Excellent. That's a date!' I exclaimed. 'So now, won't you please let our friend go? He really hasn't done anything. We were all on our way back to Ramallah.'

He paused and then turned to the other soldiers and said something to them. And then, to me,

'Listen. For the sake of Golders Green I will think about it! Go in the car and wait.'

We did as he said and drove through to the other side of the checkpoint and parked. Not long afterwards we saw Samir walking slowly through the checkpoint towards the car. He still looked angry, but he came quietly enough.

What part Golders Green had played in his release we never found out. But it made a good story for a long time afterwards.

CHAPTER 6

A Tale of Two Ministers

'Are we all set to go?' asked Amin. It was the day of the new media group meeting at the ministry, and he had come to my office early that morning, ahead of the other members. I thought he looked especially dapper in a light suit and striped shirt with matching colour tie. Hanan had been as good as her word, reserving the main meeting room for us and printing copies of the agenda to be given to the group members. These would be five in all, since Muhammad, the Hebrew translator, had been forbidden by Dr Sabah to attend. All staff were instructed not to cooperate with us, including Bilal, who was not to make us coffee either.

On hearing of Dr Sabah's instructions, Amin instantly picked up the phone and asked to be put through to him. After several insincere pleasantries he asked if Muhammad could be allowed to join the group.

'No? I don't understand. What are you saying, Dr Sabah? We can have no help from the ministry, no facilities, nothing? Is that what you're saying?' The loud voice at the other end made Amin hold the receiver away from his ear. He looked really angry. 'All right, all right, I understand that's what you want, Dr Sabah. Fine. We'll see.' He put the phone down and looked at me. 'It's as you said. He's not giving us anything from here, no facilities, nothing.' He picked up the phone again. 'We'll have to speak to Dr Farid about this straight away.'

But Dr Farid was unobtainable, despite three attempts to contact him. 'Come on, let's not waste more time. We should go down to the meeting room and wait for the others.' On our way out of my office, he caught Bilal walking towards the coffee room. 'Bilal!' he called out authoritatively. 'We'll want coffee for all of us at the meeting when I tell you. All right?' Bilal nodded unhappily and mumbled something.

I had not seen Esperance that morning as she was closeted with Dr Sabah in his office. Outside, the secretaries were all bent over their work with unusual diligence. I asked Hanan in a half whisper if she would take the minutes of the meeting, but she looked frightened and shook her head. We found the meeting room set up with paper and pencil at each seat and a jug of water with glasses. Not long afterwards the other members arrived.

Despite that unpromising start, the meeting was a success. Everyone was enthusiastic and genuinely interested and full of ideas. I took the minutes, and we resolved to meet regularly and draw up a multimedia plan for promoting Palestine which would extend and complement the one I had already drawn up. They asked for copies of this, but I explained it would have to wait until Dr Sabah had approved it, as was formally required of me, though if he bothered to read it or not was another matter. As the meeting broke up we set a date for the next one, also to take place at the ministry, and heedless of the consequences.

Upstairs in my office once more, Amin tried to phone Dr Farid again and this time he succeeded. There was a tense exchange between them as Dr Farid, I presumed, was taking in the information from our end. 'Yes, yes,' Amin nodded vigorously into the phone. 'I'm leaving now. I'll come to see you as soon as I return.' He turned towards me. 'There will be trouble now,' he said portentously, 'big trouble. I think you'll see some changes.' He put his papers together and buttoned up his jacket purposefully. I walked out with him towards the front door just in time to see Dr Sabah on his way out too. He smiled genially at the two of us, as if we had been the best of friends.

'Dr Sabah,' I said, 'I wanted to let you have the media strategy I've written for the ministry.'

'Excellent!' He was wreathed in smiles. 'Thank you. I'm on my way to Amman just now I'm afraid, but back tomorrow. Please give it to Esperance and remember to ask her for whatever you need here. All the facilities we have are at your disposal.'

It was impossible to know what had occasioned this sudden geniality, but the next day the changes that Amin had warned me about became apparent sooner than I had expected in the shape of a heated row between the minister and his deputy. Amin told me that Dr Farid had made an angry phone call to Dr Sabah and demanded to know why an official from his office and I, a consultant to the ministry, had been denied the facilities of that ministry. This had impeded our valuable work, he said, and we had also been deprived of the services of a Hebrew translator on Dr Sabah's orders. To which, as Dr Farid reported, his deputy had retorted rudely that it was I who had set up the meeting without asking his permission first and I should take the consequences. But was that not part of my proper work at the ministry? asked Dr Farid. That did it. Dr Sabah began to shout that he had never wanted me at the ministry in the first place. No one had consulted him. If truth be told, he said, not even he, Dr Farid, really wanted me. I had been imposed on them both by the head of UNDP, and if Dr Farid cared that much, he should move me out and put me in his own building.

The same day Amin was in touch to propose that I should indeed join them at the main ministry building. He explained that he would be on leave for two weeks, and I could use his desk while space was found for me. Until then, he suggested, I could move between ministries so as to reduce the time spent in Dr Sabah's vicinity while also continuing the work we had begun there. This arrangement, though presumably well meant, filled me with apprehension. I saw that I would

RETURN

have to speak to Dr Farid myself, but was told he had just left for Gaza. I wondered if these travels were connected with US Secretary of State Condoleeza Rice's visit to the region, and the talks taking place between her and the Palestinian president. When I inquired about this, no one at the ministry knew or was even interested. I asked Esperance for permission to have Hanan's help in my office.

'Why do you need her, Doctora?' she asked expressionlessly.

'To type out the minutes of the media meeting.' I resented having to justify myself to her, but knew that those were her orders. She seemed to consider for a moment, and then said grudgingly, 'All right, as long as it's not for too long.'

That evening Zeina took me to a fund-raising dinner at the Grand Park Hotel, where I had gone for the workshop a few days before. The event was in aid of Jerusalem and had attracted many guests. The money raised was to go to needy Palestinians there and to publicise the plight of the holy city to the world outside. Ever since Israel took over the Arab half of the city in 1967 and seized control of its Muslim and Christian holy places, Jerusalem had become a unifying cause for all Palestinians. Israel's increasing grip on the city and its determination to turn it into an exclusively Jewish place had rallied not just Palestinians but the whole Arab and Islamic worlds to the cause of saving it from such a fate. Campaigns to denounce the judaisation of Jerusalem and preserve its multi-religious character sprang up in different countries, and events such as that night's became commonplace throughout the 1990s. Even in Britain's mosques, most of them run by Muslims from the Indian subcontinent, congregations were passionately concerned about this issue and many Friday collections were held to raise funds in aid of Jerusalem's holy places and its Arab inhabitants.

The hotel's large terrace had been set up for the occasion with round tables covered in starched white tablecloths and

92

facing a raised platform fitted with an assortment of micro-
phones and loudspeakers. Bouquets of flowers on tall stands
adorned the front of the platform. A band was playing as we
arrived, and Zeina and I sat at one of the middle tables. The
air was cooler but still warm as the evening set in. Several
people greeted Zeina, especially the men who clearly found
her attractive, but I did not recognise anyone. Many of the
women wore expensive jewellery, even the ones in hijab. The
people who joined our table were all middle-aged couples,
pleasant enough, but their conversation was mostly about
how expensive things were and how unreliable workmen had
become; dishonest shopkeepers who overpriced their goods
were another scourge.

The star speaker of the evening was the young grandson
of the legendary Abd al-Qadir al-Husseini, after whom he
was named. He seemed nervous and looked straight ahead
of him, and I thought how little he could have known about
his grandfather's significance to my own history. Husseini was
a Palestinian patriot and hero who fought valiantly against
the Zionists at the time of the British Mandate when I was a
child. He was killed in April 1948 at the battle of al-Qastal,
a hilltop village five miles west of Jerusalem, and so named
after the twelfth-century crusader castle which stood there.
Strategically situated on the Jaffa–Jerusalem road, the village
had been conquered by the Jewish army, the Haganah, in the
battle to control the road it overlooked. On 8 April Husseini
retook it in a desperate battle during which he was killed. His
followers, shattered and demoralised by his death, were said
to have left their positions to attend his funeral the next day,
thus allowing Jewish troops to recapture it.

I remember seeing al-Qastal on my first visit to Israel in
1991, the Israeli flag flying over the hilltop on which it stood
and a plaque in Hebrew and English commemorating the 1948
Jewish victory over the Arabs. Husseini's death had been followed the next day, 9 April, by the massacre at Deir Yassin, a

village to the west of Jerusalem. This was a notorious incident in which Jewish paramilitaries killed some 120 inhabitants of a village previously at peace with the Jewish militias. The massacre had a devastating impact on the Palestinians, especially those in nearby Jerusalem, who, terrified they might be the next victims as the Jews had threatened, began to flee their homes. Menachem Begin, the leader of the gang that had perpetrated the killings and later one of Israel's prime ministers, boasted that Deir Yassin had been worth a thousand military tanks in the war against the Arabs. When I visited Deir Yassin in the 1990s, I found it had been turned, perhaps fittingly, into a mental hospital, its old Arab houses a reminder of a previous age.

It was Husseini's defeat together with the Deir Yassin massacre so soon afterwards that finally pushed my family into leaving Jerusalem, my place of birth. My mother had sworn that nothing would make her abandon her home 'to the Jews', as she put it. But in the end she was persuaded that we could no longer stay in such a dangerous place. It was in April 1948, before the State of Israel was declared, an aberration we thought would never materialise. So my parents saw our departure as a temporary measure until the situation had 'calmed down'. It never did, for us at least, and fifty-seven years later, there I was sitting in Ramallah, no nearer to returning than on that April day in 1948, and marking the loss of what had been my native city.

Abd al-Qadir's grandson, a slight, delicate-looking young man with a fine, wispy beard, spoke passionately about the danger facing Jerusalem from Israel's project to turn it into a Jewish city. He listed the Israeli encroachments on the city's archaeology and architecture, and how Jewish extremists were trying to turn the Aqsa mosque, sacred to millions of Muslims throughout the world, into a synagogue. Everyone there knew these facts but listened politely and then clapped enthusiastically at the end, more for who he was than what he said. I thought there was something brave and touching about him standing there alone, as if through the passion of his words he could reincarnate his grandfather in himself.

The dinner succeeded in raising a substantial sum of money for Jerusalem, but I wondered how many of the people who made donations to its cause believed that any of it would make the slightest difference to Jerusalem's fate. Years of campaigning of my own in London, holding similar functions, organising major lectures and what was called awareness-raising about Jerusalem never succeeded in halting Israel's advance on the holy city by one inch.

Nonetheless, the event made a pleasant night out and gave people a warm feeling of doing something good. No member of the PA was there as far as I could see, and certainly not the minister for Jerusalem Affairs, a nice woman I met soon after and felt rather sorry for. Her position was more a lofty title than an actual job, since all her activities on behalf of the city were strictly limited and subject to Israeli permission.

The next day I moved to Dr Farid's office inside the presidential headquarters. These were a compound of imposing new white buildings on a wide, tree-lined avenue with sentries standing outside and the Palestinian flag flying from the roof. Armed guards stopped me as I approached the entrance to ascertain who I was, and then let me through. They were friendly and polite, and as soon as they cleared me, resumed the chat they had been enjoying with one another when I arrived. Dr Farid's ministry was to the left of the compound, on the ground floor next to the head of cabinet's office. Facing me was the president's headquarters with another sentry in a box outside.

I entered the building and went through into a cool spacious interior that was a big improvement on the dark, gloomy ministry I had just left. The coffee room on the right of the corridor, however, was as poky as the other one had been, and had an equally overworked young man running to answer people's calls for coffee. Dr Farid's main office, which I passed first, was an ambassadorial-style room on the left. Further along was a large sunny office overlooking the back of the building. There were three desks here, one of which was Amin's and temporarily to be mine. The rest of the space was taken up by a leather suite of sofa and two armchairs in a brilliant mustard-yellow colour. It cluttered up the room and seemed totally out of place.

When Adel, Dr Farid's secretary whom I had first met when he accompanied Dr Farid to the other ministry, came in to welcome me and to inquire if I was comfortable, I could not help asking him about the yellow suite. 'It's a very nice suite,' I said as tactfully as I could, 'but isn't it too large for this room?'

Adel and the two men who sat at the other desks looked at one another and smiled. 'It's a bit of a story, Doctora. Do you really want to hear it?' I nodded, now even more curious. 'Well, you're right, the suite doesn't belong to us. It was originally ordered for the head of cabinet's office next door, but when it turned up it was apparently the wrong colour. The minister came out to see it for himself, and asked for it to be taken back and the correct one delivered. But the delivery men refused. There was quite a row.' Adel turned to the two men, listening avidly. 'You were here, closer to it than I was.' They nodded and chimed in to say that the row had got very noisy and heated and people came out of their offices to see what was wrong.

Neither side would back down, and the delivery men, who were tired and bad-tempered from dragging the furniture around, made to leave. This enraged the cabinet office staff, who began to push the sofa and armchairs out into the hall. The minister, called on by his subordinates to solve the problem, came out again and ordered the delivery men to remove the suite. The men announced they had no orders from their company to take anything back, and the furniture would have to stay.

'In the end,' continued Adel, 'Dr Farid intervened and told us to take the sofa and chairs into our own office. So we did, and the whole thing died down.'

'I see, but now you're lumbered with things you didn't want.'

'Oh, not really, you'd be surprised,' he answered. 'They come in quite handy when we've got visitors waiting to see Dr Farid. Or you yourself, Doctora, might want to sit in them and relax. The sofa's really comfortable.'

When I told the story to Zeina later, she was not amused. 'Oh, really?' she scoffed. 'The wrong sofa and chairs? Did they also tell you about the drama of the desks? When a two-drawer desk was ordered for that same minister it should have been at least a three-drawer desk, according to the protocol. The greater the number of drawers the higher the office rank of the person, you see. So there was a terrible row about that too.'

I smiled and shook my head in wonderment at what she was telling me. 'If only that was all we had to worry about with this minister,' she continued more seriously. 'You don't know what goes on yet, Doctora.' There was a strong rumour that the head of cabinet owned a cement company which had made him wealthy through supplying Israel with cement for the building of Jewish settlements in the Occupied Palestinian Territories. I found this allegation too disturbing to believe. It had been shocking enough to observe Palestinian labourers building these places, erecting settler houses on the very lands that Israel had taken from their villages; whatever their feelings, which I imagined to be ones of bitter resignation, they were forced into such work by poverty and the lack of other sources of employment. But it was another matter for a PA official in comfortable circumstances to support the same enterprise for personal profit. I never managed in the end to find out if there was any truth in the rumour, which stuck to the minister like a bad odour. But when I met him I found him a mild-mannered man with a sweet smile and gentlemanly ways. It was hard to see him as the traitorous villain people described.

Dr Farid finally arrived with a noisy flourish, flanked by his entourage of armed young men, and was welcomed at the door by Adel and Firyal, the office secretary. Soon afterwards, Adel, wearing his usual worried look, came to fetch me. When I entered Dr Farid's sumptuous office, expecting to see him alone for us to talk about my transfer from the other ministry to this one, I found him being interviewed by Swedish TV. I had heard that his media appearances were quite frequent, as were the interviews he gave to various international newspapers. He spoke eloquently and in fluent English about the peace negotiations with Israel. At this time there had been another of those frequent hold-ups in the 'peace process' that was launched in 1993 and had since then proceeded by fits and starts, mostly in line with Israel's whim. He spoke candidly about this Israeli intransigence and the Palestinians' readiness to cooperate, and made the PA sound for all the world like the established government of a state on a par with Israel. Had I not known better, I might have believed it.

There was no hint in anything he said of an underlying reality that he must have known would belie all his criticisms. Israel's lack of cooperation in the peace talks was not replicated in its close coordination with the PA on security matters. This arrangement, whereby the two sides worked closely together to police Area A, supposedly under sole Palestinian control,[1] had existed since 1994. Its main aim – as Yitzhak Rabin, Israel's prime minister at the time, put it – was to 'safeguard Israel's security' in the Palestinian territories it occupied. To this end, Palestinian security forces were trained by CIA personnel to collaborate with Israel in the surveillance and

---

1   The Oslo Accords led to a division of the West Bank into Areas A, B and C, the first controlled by the PA, the second under joint Palestinian-Israeli control, and the last and largest under sole Israeli control.

detention of any Palestinian caught planning or perpetrating hostile acts against Israeli targets. These security arrangements were augmented by the creation in 2005, a few months after my arrival in Ramallah, of a special 8,000-strong Palestinian 'counter-terrorism' force under the direction of a retired US army officer, General Keith Dayton.

In the event, these Palestinian forces did their job rather too well. In 2008, while pursuing Hamas, the PA's sworn enemy and a terrorist organisation according to Israel, they killed eight of its members and tortured others, including anyone they defined as a suspect – a state of affairs much to Israel's satisfaction. By way of reward for the Palestinian security forces doing Israel's job for it, as it were, the Israeli army reduced the number of West Bank checkpoints and eased other restrictions on Palestinian movement.

I sat listening to Dr Farid on the comfortable sofa they had shown me to and thought how wrong it was of him to project an image of equivalence, however unintended, between an occupying power and the people it occupied, and to pretend that his 'government' had any option but to submit to Israel's diktat, no matter how damaging that might be to Palestinian interests. I wondered also why so many other Palestinian spokesmen did the same thing. Did they think they could fool the world into believing they were representatives of a Palestinian state that existed in all but name? The amazing thing was how many people did believe it, and especially Palestinians, who longed for it to be true.

When the interview was over and the TV crew had withdrawn, Dr Farid got up and greeted me warmly, then clapped his hands. 'Come on, where is everyone? It's lunchtime. The Doctora here would like to have some lunch and so would I. What do you say to kebab?' he asked me. 'Adel, get the boys in.'

Two of the armed men appeared as summoned, and he told them to go and bring an assortment of grilled meats, hummus, *mutabbal* (grilled aubergine with tahini) and salad. He took out several shekel notes from his wallet and gave the guards the money. 'Don't take too long. We're all famished!' His laugh was hearty and infectious. 'Forgive me, Doctora. Just one minute.' Adel hovered over him, setting letters and documents before him which he signed without reading.

'Have you settled in yet?' he asked me absentmindedly, not expecting a reply. I wondered how it was going to be possible to have a private conversation with him about my position, or Dr Sabah, or the other ministry and the work I was to do. He gave Adel several instructions in a low voice, and made some phone calls. Then he welcomed into the office two visitors who had put their heads round the door, with a jovial 'Come in, come in, this is Doctora Ghada Karmi – you know her, no? She's from London and is here to work with us.'

The conversation carried on in this cheery vein until the guards arrived with the food in large carrier bags. Firyal took charge and laid a makeshift cloth over the polished wooden table in front of the sofa I was sitting on. She set out the take-away boxes covered in silver foil, a dozen cans of Coca-Cola and Seven-Up, napkins and paper plates. It was all rather cosy, as if we were eating in our own homes in front of the television. Dr Farid came out from behind his desk and joined us. He called out to all his armed guards to come in and enjoined us all, visitors included, to 'tuck in'.

As everyone was busy munching, he told me that the two visitors were in the process of composing a new Palestinian national anthem. 'What's wrong with the present one?' asked one of the guards, a cheeky lad with a black-and-white check kuffiyya wound loosely round his neck. The same question was in my mind too, but Dr Farid, not put out by the young guard's interjection, explained that the current anthem was not specific enough and needed updating. At the time two national anthems were in use by Palestinians. The first was 'Mawtini' (My Homeland), an unofficial version written during British

Mandate days by the prominent Palestinian national poet, Ibrahim Tuqan, and very popular. The second, and official, anthem was 'Biladi, Biladi' (My Land, My Land), adopted by the Palestinian National Movement in 1972 with the alternative title 'Fida'i, Fida'i' (Freedom Fighter, Freedom Fighter), to reflect the Palestinian national struggle against Israel.

The visitors, it turned out, had brought cassettes of various alternative compositions of the new anthem for Dr Farid's approval. After lunch, he said we would all listen and give our verdicts. I could see any hope of speaking to him alone evaporating rapidly, and began to feel slightly desperate. As the food was cleared away and the visitors went to wash their hands, I seized the opportunity.

'Dr Farid, could we have a moment to speak alone?'

His smile did not waver. 'Of course,' he responded, 'any time.'

'Would it be possible this afternoon?' To my surprise I felt diffident, even nervous, about asking him as if I had been a student facing my professor.

'Not this afternoon, Doctora. We'll be working on the national anthem as I said. I hope you'll stay and give us your valuable opinion.'

'Tomorrow then?'

'I'm sorry, I'll be on my way to Cairo. But not for long. I'll be back soon and we can certainly talk whenever you want. Or,' he turned his head in Adel's direction, 'there's Adel here. He knows all about me, don't you, Adel? He can tell you anything you want.'

The visitors had come back into the room, and Dr Farid called out to them. 'Come in, brothers. We're all waiting anxiously to hear what you've recorded for us.'

I stood up and excused myself. 'Not staying?' asked Dr Farid distractedly. I could see his attention had moved on elsewhere. I slipped out and walked back to my assigned office.

* * *

The next day I made my way reluctantly to the old ministry, in conformity with the new arrangement suggested by Amin of dividing my time between the two buildings. It was unusually hot that day and I found my office, which Um Ali had obviously not cleaned, stifling. It seemed that people knew about my transfer to Dr Farid's ministry and regarded me as having left for good. Hanan seemed pleased to see me, without the fear she had shown before. When I queried this, she told me that Esperance had been unconcerned about her movements ever since she understood that I had gone.

'But I haven't gone,' I protested. 'I'm going to work at both ministries, which is why I'm here today.'

Hanan looked surprised. 'Oh, Dr Sabah told us you'd left.' She frowned. 'It might be difficult for you to be here if that's not the case.'

'Well, that's too bad,' I retorted. 'I'll be coming in according to my schedule.'

In fact I deeply regretted having returned to the place, which I had only done out of a misplaced sense of professional duty. I wondered why I was trying to be so correct in my dealings, when no one else was. There was no reason to have taken my commitments so seriously, because these were pretend places like the rest of the PA's 'ministries', indeed like the 'Palestinian state' they were supposed to be part of. Everyone who worked in them was also pretending, playing a part in a charade created by the international donors who encouraged the Palestinians to believe that they needed to have all the appurtenances of statehood ahead of attaining their state. The reality, however, was that the moment the money stopped the whole thing would collapse, like the proverbial house of cards. But while it lasted it was a convincing show that everyone was irresistibly drawn into and ended up believing in. Even I could feel myself succumbing to the same illusion.

When Hanan left, to my surprise I had a second visitor, Muhammad, the translator, who had been barred from joining my media group. He greeted me nervously and asked diffidently if he could come in.

'Of course,' I said, 'come and sit down.' He closed the door after him and took a seat opposite me.

'I was so sorry, Doctora, that I couldn't join your group the other day,' he said, 'but Dr Sabah was insistent. I wanted to see you to explain but couldn't find you.' He paused. 'You know how hard it is for us here. I've got three children, and my mother depends on me, and I have an unmarried older sister.' As the eldest son that I presumed him to be, he was responsible for the womenfolk in the family. 'I can't go against Dr Sabah's orders and it's not the first time he's done things like that. But what else can I do? What choice have I got but to obey?' He looked miserable. For the first time I noticed his down-at-heel appearance, his dusty old shoes and the frayed cuffs of his cheap shirt.

'I understand, really I do. Don't worry. We may well be able to find a way for you to join our group.'

He shook his head. '*Inshallah*, but I don't hold out much hope.' He obviously had something more on his mind. 'It's not just that, Doctora, I have other problems. Dr Sabah has not treated me fairly in another matter. The ministry owes me money, they should have paid me a year ago, but they're refusing to pay it. I've begged Dr Sabah to look into my case, but he says it's nothing to do with him and I should go to the finance department.'

'And have you?'

He shook his head. 'It's hopeless with them. They said they couldn't do anything unless Dr Sabah authorises it, and he won't. They owe me hundreds of shekels which I can't afford to forgo. I've got no reserves.'

'I'm very sorry to hear that. It reminds me of a similar case also at this ministry, but the details are different.'

He suddenly frowned. 'If you mean Hanan, it's not the same as my case and it's not true. I know about her story, she's told many people how she's been unfairly treated, but none of it is true. She's a terrible liar, Doctora, and you mustn't believe a word she says.'

I stared at him. 'I find that difficult to believe. I've found her very nice and very helpful. She's told me about some financial troubles she has and I feel very sorry for her.'

'Yes, I know, the old story about the salary the other ministry owes her. She's trying to get money out of them with this fake story about not having been paid. Be very careful of her, Doctora, there's not a word of truth in anything she says.'

'Why are you telling me all this?'

'I just wanted to warn you against her. She's pretty convincing unless you know her, and I was afraid you might try to give her money or something. I'm sure you're a good person, Doctora, and you'd want to help someone in need. But please be on your guard against Hanan.'

I recalled Hanan's tears that had seemed genuine enough when she spoke of her predicament, her little family, her nice, kind husband. Could they have all been part of some villainy? Or was it Muhammad who was lying to me, and if so, why?

I ended our meeting with some soothing remarks and was relieved when he went. There was nothing more for me to do there and I left for the Gemzo Suites. I sought out Annetta and told her the latest of my adventures, especially my last encounter with Muhammad.

'Don't give it another thought,' she advised briskly. 'You'll never get to the bottom of it, believe me. Each of them will accuse the other of lying and drag you into it. You don't want that, so I suggest you never mention it to either of them again. All these workers are poor, you know. They've got low salaries and can barely manage. If there's an administrative mess-up, they're usually the first to lose out, and there are many mistakes and blunders in these places, losing papers and not making proper staff registers. So there's often some problem, and both your people are probably telling the truth.'

'But then, why the smear against Hanan? She really struck me as genuine.'

'She may well be. But, you know, too little money and too many claims. If your man can knock her out of the competition, there's a better chance for him, isn't there?'

I sighed. 'It's difficult being here,' I said. 'I remember what you told me about working with the PA when I first came.'

'Yes, but that was with me. With you it should be different. You're one of them. It should not be like that.'

'Ah, but maybe I'm not one of them,' I said lightly, not wishing to enter with her into a discussion of identity and belonging, issues which had plagued me for most of my life, wondering who I was exactly, English or Arab, or a hybrid? 'Maybe they see me as some odd figure, neither Arab nor foreign. And that is why they treat me so strangely.'

She laughed. 'I'm sure you're wrong. You're one of them all right, anyone can see that: an Arab and a Palestinian. No, no, there must be some other reason.' She thought for a bit. 'I tell you what. Why not go to see Mounir in Jerusalem at the UNDP office? He's no good if you ask him things on the phone. But face-to-face, he's much better.' She saw me hesitate, doubtful that her suggestion would make any difference. 'Go on!' she said, slapping me on the back.

CHAPTER 7

A Trip to Jerusalem

The next morning I went to Jerusalem. I expected the way there to be difficult and I was not wrong. Since I had no car to take me this time, I had to go by taxi from the Gemzo Suites to the Qalandia checkpoint, disembark and go through the crossing on foot to pick up the Jerusalem bus on the other side, as it was not permitted to cross to the Ramallah side. The checkpoint marked the boundary between 'Palestine', that is, Area A, and 'Israel', Area C. The road that led to the checkpoint was uneven and full of holes, and cars had learned to manoeuvre around the potholes with considerable adroitness. Because it was in Area A and under Palestinian jurisdiction, the PA should have repaired it but had not done so. Around the checkpoint on both sides were fruit sellers and young boys selling cold drinks and snacks, an informal trade that had grown up to serve the traffic around the checkpoint. The separation wall rose incongruously to the right, its surface covered with paintings and graffiti expressing freedom and struggle. A huge slate-grey watchtower at the end of the wall oversaw the proceedings, a disembodied voice booming orders through a loudspeaker from it at the Palestinians below.

The whole area was a mess: rubble, bits of unfinished separation wall, kiosks, taxi drivers calling out to prospective passengers, heavy traffic, and Israeli soldiers shouting at people trying to cross the checkpoint. After waiting in a long queue to enter the turnstiles that led to the other side, I found the Jerusalem bus. It was nearly full and ready to move off. A few more passengers joined us and we started on our way. We had not gone far before the bus was flagged down by an army jeep. Two soldiers jumped out and climbed on board, one standing by the entrance while the other went round demanding that passengers show their identity cards. The UNDP office had previously informed all its employees like me that we were not required to show our passports in such situations; the UN employment card we had been given was sufficient, and that this had been agreed with the Israeli interior ministry. If we were challenged about it, we were to report the officer or soldier concerned.

I had not tested this out yet, but suddenly decided to do so now, affronted by the arrogance with which these soldiers could impede a whole busload of passengers from getting to their jobs or other appointments with a mundane request for IDs that had already been checked at Qalandia a few minutes before. When the soldier reached my seat I gave him my UN card. I doubted he had ever seen one of these before, but he barely glanced at it and demanded again, 'Passport'.

'This is instead of my passport. It's my ID here.' He clearly did not understand English and looked confused. 'Passport. Passport,' he reiterated. 'No,' I said firmly, determined to hold my ground, 'I've just told you, not necessary. See this?' I showed him my card again.

He walked back to his friend at the entrance and they conferred. He then turned and ordered me off the bus behind him. As I walked through the aisle, the passengers on either side looked at me with annoyance. I could hear them grumbling behind me, the men getting angry, and one woman shouted out, 'Give them your passport for God's sake. We're all in a hurry.' As I got off, the bus drove to the side of the road and parked, to wait there until I was released. Outside, the sun was hot. The soldier who had asked for the IDs stayed with me and his companion went back to the jeep.

'You have no right to do this,' I said angrily, 'I'm going to report you. Give me your name and number.'

I must have sounded more confident than I felt, for he meekly eased his shoulder out of the rifle slung over it and took the pen and paper I offered him. He put the paper against the cover of a small notebook he had and wrote his name and number as I had asked. His hand was shaking and I looked at him more closely. He was very young, with curly red hair, a wide face and high cheekbones. I could see he was nervous, and when I took the paper from him I read his name, 'Dimitri Ovanov'. A Russian immigrant, I thought, and probably not even Jewish. It was estimated that about 40 per cent of the Russian citizens who had emigrated to Israel, supposedly as Jews coming to the Promised Land, were in fact Christians. He repositioned his rifle and stood there uncertainly; it was in my mind to speak kindly to him, even to say: why would a nice boy like you want to join this army and serve such people?

Hardly had these thoughts taken shape than I saw a new army jeep driving up to join the other. At this the young soldier straightened and motioned me to follow him towards the second jeep, where he left me. Inside and lolling on the front seat with his foot on the dashboard was a thickset, dark-skinned soldier sucking on a straw and looking at me with faint amusement. He remained inside while I stood in the heat outside.

'Come here,' he said in Arabic. 'I understand you have a problem with showing us your passport, is that so?'

This man was obviously in a different category to the youth I had just been able to browbeat. 'No,' I answered in Arabic, 'there's no problem, but my passport isn't necessary. I have a UNDP employee's card which is all you need.'

He laughed loudly. 'Listen, we decide what we need, not you. Now give me your passport.'

His arrogance and total air of command made me nervous. I could see he was a Druze, from a minority Arab Islamic sect which had thrown in its lot with Israel back in 1948, soon after the new state was created. Its members went on to make loyal Israeli citizens, proud of being nationalist and patriotic, and many were members of the Druze Zionist movement. They spoke about a 'blood pact' between them and Israeli Jews, and early in Israel's history had been categorised as an 'ethnic community', unlike other Arabs. Nevertheless, they remained non-Jews in a Jewish state and their community was still subject to discrimination, although to a lesser degree than other Arabs. And, unlike the latter, they were recruited into Israel's army, many of them to serve as border police. This force was employed to control the Palestinians of the occupied territories and was widely feared by them for its harshness and brutality.

What an anomaly, I thought, looking at this Druze soldier. Here we were, both Arabs, but on opposite sides, he a servant of a state that had oppressed Arabs since its inception, and I one of its victims. By all that was just, we should have been comrades, not enemies. Nevertheless, I knew I could expect little mercy from him if things went wrong.

'I told you,' I said, determined to hold out a little longer, 'I have a United Nations ID which is all you require. You can check with your people, or with the UN office in Jerusalem, and you will find it is sufficient. Here it is. Look at it.' I put my card up to show him. He did not even bother to turn his head to see it, but he did sit up from his recumbent position inside the jeep and fixed his eyes on me.

'I want you to understand that here in Israel your card and your UN and whoever else you like to mention is worth not so much as an onion peel! We don't give this much for any of them!' He clicked his thumb and middle finger against each other. 'Only our law counts. Only what we say and do counts. Get it? Now give me your passport.'

I saw it was no use and handed it over. He took his time leafing through it, as if he were studying every page, and then made a phone call. After a conversation in which he seemed to be joking and finding whoever it was at the other end hilariously funny he went back to lolling on the seat and putting his foot up against the windscreen. Not looking at me now, he held out the passport through the window and motioned me to move.

I saw the Russian soldier watching all this, and walked back to the bus feeling shaken and humiliated. I stepped on silently, avoiding the passengers' eyes, and went back to my seat. I remember little of the ensuing journey, thinking of what had happened, furious and embarrassed by my little show of defiance which had come to nothing. No wonder the other passengers had submitted their IDs with so little resistance.

We all got off at the central bus station near the Damascus Gate of the Old City. I had only a vague idea of where the UNDP office was, but so-called Arab Jerusalem – what was left of the eastern part of the city still relatively free of Israeli settlements – was so small that it was unlikely I would get lost. Each time I came to this part of Jerusalem it seemed to me that the Arab city had shrunk further, with yet another street infiltrated by Jewish settlers, or some Israeli-owned hotel or other Israeli building, as if to stamp it with a seal of Israeli ownership. With each change of this kind East Jerusalem lost more of its distinctive character, and I could see that in time and perhaps before too long the pluralistic, mosaic city of my birth would become something unrecognisable.

Such a transformation had already taken place in the western half of Jerusalem, occupied by Israel in 1948 and the early focus of attempts to convert it from an Arab city to a modern, quasi-Western 'Jewish' metropolis. Lacking a 'Jewish' architecture to replicate, the city planners ended up with a hybrid of building styles derived from what they had seen in Europe or America. As the transformation progressed, West Jerusalem became an ever more strange and unfamiliar place. Were it not for the old Arab houses, like the one we had lived in, still standing here and there to give it a distinctive charm, that half of the city could be mistaken for somewhere in Canada or Europe. A large beautifully landscaped public park was created in the centre, and modern streets, wide highways that led to and from the city, flyovers and tunnels; rush hours and traffic jams completed the picture of a new metropolis in the Western mould.

I imagined that West Jerusalem's Jewish inhabitants and its Jewish visitors, especially ones from Western countries, admired its modern urban look and felt at home. I even recall one Palestinian woman with such views, a native of Jerusalem before her family's expulsion from it in 1948, admitting she was impressed on seeing the city for the first time in the 1970s. 'You've got to hand it to them,' she had said with admiration. 'I know they took it over and it's not theirs, but my God, how beautiful they've made it!'

I walked down from the bus station towards the Damascus Gate, still trying to shake off the memory of the altercation with the Druze soldier. The Old City wall to my right, I reached the bottom of Salah al-Din Street opposite to Herod's Gate. On the corner and across from me was the post office, a large building with the Israeli flag flying from it and Hebrew lettering over the door. Apart from this intrusion Salah al-Din Street was still overwhelmingly Arab, and as I walked through it I felt a surge of nostalgia pass through me, faint echoes of childhood perhaps, since al-Ma'mouniyya, the primary school I attended all those years ago, was in the vicinity. The crowded pavements, the noise, the village women in their colourful embroidered caftans sitting on the pavement with baskets of fresh fruit and vegetables around them, all brought back indefinable, half-conscious memories and with them an ineffable sadness.

As I was ushered into Mounir's office at the UNDP office which I had finally found, he rose to welcome me with a great show of enthusiasm and friendliness. I had a sudden urge to open my heart and tell him about the incident with the bus. The memory still burned in my mind, but I did not know what he would make of it and thought it would somehow be to my disadvantage. Annetta had warned me against complaining too much or burdening him with my questions and anxieties. 'Just tell him the facts,' she had advised.

Taking a breath to steady myself, I reminded him of the situation with the two ministries and the battle between the two ministers, and explained how I had been moved from one to the other, although not completely, and that the position was unsatisfactory. I wanted to add that he must have known about all this long before I came, but nevertheless had thrown me into the middle of the fray without warning.

'So, in view of the situation,' I continued, still careful to keep my tone light and casual, 'I wondered if it was possible for me to be moved altogether, to another ministry or institution.' To my surprise he seemed unruffled by my report, his smooth manner and smile unchanged and as friendly as ever. 'What you're asking is not easy, you know. We've had no requests for consultants' services recently from any of our institutions, and, may I add, no complaints from any of the other consultants either. So, even if you could move, I have nowhere to send you.'

I found this hard to believe, but no matter what suggestions I made, he remained adamant. 'You're here under the UNDP programme for expatriates. We agreed you would be placed as a consultant, and that's what you're doing.' I knew he had been a key figure in devising this programme and was proud of it. My objections could only spoil what he saw as a considerable achievement: to reconnect a people split apart by expulsions and occupations, bringing expatriates home to what remained of Palestine. I admired the project and could not begrudge him his success. But at the same time, I also realised I was being sacrificed to this noble effort, condemned to serve out my time at the Ministry of Strategic Planning at whichever site and with whichever absurd minister it would happen to be.

'Don't take such details to heart,' said the UNDP chief, Tim Rothermell, when I unburdened myself to him afterwards. 'Look at the bigger picture!'

He had invited me to the American Colony Hotel, a short walk away from the office, and we sat drinking coffee at a shady table in its beautiful tiled courtyard surrounded by leafy trees and elegant potted plants. Famous for its charm and cosmopolitan atmosphere, the hotel was regarded as politically neutral ground in this divided city and was a meeting place for people from all communities: international residents, journalists, casual visitors, Palestinians, and also many Israelis who found it a congenial oasis in a hostile Arab Jerusalem. Two years later it would serve as the part-time residence of Britain's former prime minister, Tony Blair, on his mission as Middle East peace envoy to the Quartet.[1]

'I've been studying the situation here for years, you know,' Rothermell continued. An American with a long experience of international work, he was calm, relaxed and easy to talk to. 'You might think it looks bad, and on the surface it does. But I want to tell you that I don't envy Israel. I wouldn't give much for its chances against these Palestinians.' I raised my eyebrows. 'Oh, yes,' he said firmly. 'Every time I look at the young people, like Ayman' – this was the young man I had met at Maher's house, who had intrigued me by his enigmatic remarks about life at the UNDP office – 'or, better still, look at that group over there, I see how vibrant, clever, and resourceful they are. Real survivors. Whatever Israel throws at them, they bounce right back.'

In another corner of the café and at a larger table than ours sat a striking, dark-skinned man with an air of command,

---

1 This consisted of the UN, EU, Russia and the US and was set up in 2003 to oversee the resolution of the Israeli–Palestinian conflict, without success at the time of writing.

surrounded by a small group of young men all talking loudly and gesticulating enthusiastically.

'That,' said my companion, dropping his voice, 'is Muhammad Dahlan. He's an important figure worth watching in my estimation. He might even become the next Palestinian leader after Mahmoud Abbas.' I knew of Muhammad Dahlan long before I came to Ramallah. He was a prominent member of Fateh and a strongman whom many found charismatic and who inspired either love or hate. Born in a Gaza refugee camp, he had risen to prominence as a young Fateh activist, for which Israel imprisoned him some dozen times. While in jail he had learned Hebrew and emerged, as was often the case with Palestinian political detainees, even more politically active than before. He rose swiftly in the ranks and was appointed by Yasser Arafat head of a 20,000-strong security force in Gaza. This inevitably involved him in dealings with the CIA and with Israeli intelligence.

He established himself in Gaza which he virtually ruled as security chief with his own private army, and made himself into an independent force within Palestinian politics. For that reason he was considered a threat to the Palestinian president who, although he had appointed Dahlan minister of the interior in 2003, saw in him a rival and was wary of him. On the surface Dahlan's patriotic credentials were irreproachable, but his high-handed ways and public criticism of the PA for having no coherent policy earned him enemies. It was widely rumoured that he was too close to the Israelis, and some even suspected him of being their man amongst the Palestinians. It was also said that he had diverted nearly half of PA tax collections into his own account, amassing a considerable private fortune.

'Dahlan is a controversial figure, I know,' continued my boss, 'but with all his faults, it's an indication of how irrepressible the Palestinian people are. I really wouldn't want to be Israel facing this generation, I can tell you!' Remembering the grinding daily queues at checkpoints, the bitter loss of land and water to Israeli settlers, the imposed divisions of village from village and town from town eroding Palestinian society, I wondered if he could possibly be right.

That evening I had an encounter of a totally different kind in West Jerusalem. Crossing from the (Arab) east to the (Israeli) west of the city was a short car drive, but it might as well have been a journey to another country. The old dividing line that had separated the two parts of Jerusalem until 1967 had physically vanished, yet for most people it was still there, especially for Israelis, who did not like to cross it towards the Arab side even though it no longer existed on the map. But for me, Jerusalem was an undivided city where our old house still stood as testimony to Jerusalem's Arab past – no matter what artifice Israel had later imposed on it.

It was at that house that my evening encounter was to take place. A week earlier I had received a surprising invitation to visit the *New York Times* bureau chief, Steven Erlanger, in his apartment in West Jerusalem. I had not met him before, nor would I have expected to. The newspaper he worked for was not known for its sympathy with the Palestinians or their cause, and I did not imagine its Israel correspondent would have felt otherwise. Erlanger had written to me out of the blue, having somehow obtained my contact details, to tell me that he believed he was living in the flat above what had been my old home. He had identified it, he said, from reading my memoir, *In Search of Fatima*, which had described my early years in that house.

I was intrigued, not least by an approach from such a source, and agreed to his invitation to visit and see for myself. Rami, a young Palestinian lawyer and the son of the doctor and his wife who had been fellow guests at Maher's house in Beit Hanina, drove over from Ramallah to Jerusalem to take me to see him.

Before 1948 we had lived in a newly built area called Qatamon, north of the old German Colony, and at the time one of the more desirable suburbs of West Jerusalem. In those days it had been predominantly Christian, but many Muslim families such as ours lived there too, as well as a scattering of Jewish immigrants and other foreigners. Its detached stone villas, frequently surrounded by gardens, were much admired for their architecture and setting. After we and our neighbours were forced to leave in 1948, the Israeli government moved poor Jewish immigrant families into the vacated houses and the area underwent something of a decline. Some years later, however, it revived and became increasingly sought after by a well-to-do Israeli middle class which thought it was chic to live in old Arab houses because they had 'character' and 'features'. Whether any of the new incumbents wondered about the Arab owners who had once lived in those houses was not talked about, but they reminded me of a similar aspiring class in English society, which also sought to live in Victorian or earlier historic houses with 'period features'.

I did not know if our street had had a name when we were there, but it was now called Mishmar Ha'am, Hebrew for 'Guard of the Nation', a rather grandiose name for what had been a modest, homely place. To get there we drove up the Qatamon hill, a gentle, tree-lined slope with our turning off on the right near the top. After several manoeuvres around the baffling one-way system – another Israeli innovation introduced since our time – we reached it and drove towards the house. Strange, I thought, how even now Qatamon still retained its old tranquil atmosphere, as if time had stood still since the days of my childhood. My memories of that time were hazy, but I could still recall those peaceful, quiet siesta afternoons spent playing with Randa Issa, my friend from across the road, while our parents were asleep.

The streets and villas we passed had different inhabitants now, people from faraway places we had never heard of in those innocent days of 1940s Palestine: Kiev, Minsk, Pinsk, Byelostok, Riga, Vilna, Lodz – all towns and cities in Lithuania, Ukraine or Poland that could have been from Mars for all the connection they had with us Palestinians. Rami parked across the road from what had been our house. I got out and stood looking at it, the iron garden gate, the trees on either side, the steps leading up to the veranda with its mosaic floor, all still there. It was not the first time I had been back to see it after 1948. My first visit was in 1998, coinciding with Israel's fiftieth anniversary, when the American Jewish tenants who lived there then allowed me inside, although with much trepidation; and again in 2000 when the Israeli tenants who succeeded them did not. My daughter, who was a teenager then, had been with me on that visit, and it was she who went up to the closed gate and asked the man standing behind it, staring at her pugnaciously, if I could look around as I had lived there many years before. He was a stocky Orthodox Jew with sideboards and skullcap. 'No!' he had shouted in a fury. 'Go away or I'll get someone on to you!'

To the side of the house was a flight of steps leading up to the second storey, presumably the flat where Erlanger awaited us. When he opened the door he turned out to be a civilised, pleasant-looking middle-aged man with brown hair and glasses. He welcomed us in and invited us to his veranda overlooking the garden. It was still light although swiftly darkening into dusk, as is the way in the Middle East once the sun has set. I asked him if he knew when the upper storey had been built, since the house we had left was a typical Palestinian villa with no second floor. He could only say that the *New York Times* had acquired the flat and started to place its bureau chiefs there sometime during the 1980s, and so it must already have been in existence at that time.

'You were right,' I said. 'The villa below was indeed our house.'

The atmosphere was slightly awkward and he looked ill at ease. I wondered if he had regretted inviting me to come.

'I thought so,' he responded. 'The description fitted so well. And by the way, your book was marvellous. I enjoyed it. It's good to meet you. And thank you, Rami, for bringing her.' Rami smiled and nodded.

'Well, thank you for reading it,' I said. 'But I'm curious to know why you decided to get in touch. Was it just to confirm your suspicion about the house?'

'No, not just that,' he said earnestly. 'I found parts of the book fascinating, particularly the description of life here in the 1940s. Great stuff, and I wanted to meet and maybe show you your old house. You see, I know the people downstairs, they're really nice and we talked about you coming to visit. They'd be delighted to meet you. I want to take photos of you in the house that you can keep. Here,' and he pointed to a large professional-looking camera on a table in the sitting room.

'Were you thinking of writing a piece about it for your paper?' I asked.

He looked taken aback. 'No, no, the photos are for you, I thought you would want to have a memento of your old house.'

'That's very kind, but have you thought of doing an article on this story?' I persisted. 'It would be a bold step, I grant you, for your paper to agree. But it would make a refreshing change to present this story from the Palestinian side, don't you think?'

He cleared his throat. 'That's not the idea at all. I simply wanted to have you get inside your old home, because I know that's not so easy for many Palestinians to do. I know how they get turned away when they try.' The memory of the aggressive Orthodox Jew who had lived here before flashed through my mind. 'So, there's a friendly family living in the house who're happy to let you in. You can look around for as long as you like.' He made it sound like largesse from the current owners. 'And we should go while it's still light.'

'Thank you. It's an offer I won't refuse. But can I ask you another question?' He looked faintly alarmed. 'You've read my book and identified this place as being my family home. You also know that we're no longer in it because of what happened in 1948. The fact that you're here, your newspaper's here, and your friends downstairs are here is because we're not here, if you see what I mean. I know you didn't need my book to tell you that. But it gave you the story again from a personal, human angle, how it felt to have to leave this house and the details of what happened here.' He nodded, waiting for me to continue.

'So, knowing what you know, seeing me right here in front of you, and Rami too whose parents were dislocated from their homes in 1948 just as we were, I wanted to ask how that makes you feel about Israel now.'

Clearly he had not anticipated any of this. After a pause, he said he was aware of how difficult matters must have been in 1948, but that was in the past and things had moved on since then. He had not answered my question and I felt it was important for him to do so, even though it must have seemed ungracious to respond in that way to the kindness he was perhaps doing me by inviting me to see my old house. But there was an underlying smugness about him which I found irritating.

'What I'm really asking you is if you feel comfortable being in a country which came into being like that? Which had to get rid of people like me and take their place to build its state? Which keeps me from returning, from getting my house back? I mean, you can see the result: you're physically occupying a house which belonged to other people. And you feel nothing about that?'

'Look, these things are difficult. They're not black and white. You have to remember history's important here. Some things aren't either right or wrong.'

I pressed him further to answer my question and not to evade it, to examine the contradictions in his position. But no matter how hard I tried, he remained evasive, sticking to his line that it wasn't that simple, historical reality could not be ignored, and the like. Should I have expected anything else from him, a man employed by the *New York Times*, whose line on the Middle East was consistently pro-Israel? Yet Erlanger struck me as one of a type I was familiar with and usually liked, cultivated New York Jews with refined tastes and good minds, descendants of Eastern European immigrants who came to America in the early years of the twentieth century; they were frequently liberal, left-leaning or radical about many political issues, and so should have been capable of understanding the Palestinian situation.

Yet I also knew that for many such people the liberal positions they held on human rights abuses in countries from Africa to Latin America ceased to apply where Israel was concerned. The logic of this contradictory position was that the Jewish state could not be judged by the same yardstick as any other, for it had been created in answer to a moral need, that of rescuing the Jewish victims of persecution, most especially Nazism, an imperative that overrode all other considerations at the time, including the displacement of people like me. Who but an anti-Semite could possibly argue with that, they would have said? So compelling was this logic for many people that it invalidated any factual evidence to the contrary, let alone any counter-argument.

However, not everyone was comfortable with such a position. There was a Jewish minority which, confronted with the actual situation on the ground, began to perceive a different reality from the one they had previously cherished, and were troubled by it. I used to call this condition 'Zionist angst', the turmoil of decent people trying to reconcile a devoted commitment they had always held towards Israel with the plain evidence before them that challenged not only this idealised image, but also their liberal and egalitarian notions about how things should be.

I remember once being on a delegation to the Palestinian areas with a group of British writers, one of whom was a Jewish publisher, a refined, interesting woman who had joined us because, as she said, she wanted to understand more about the Palestinians. In that sense she was what might be called a 'liberal Zionist', someone who was sympathetic to the Palestinian cause but was also a staunch believer in the Jewish state and its right to exist as such. Hence she supported dialogue between the two sides so as 'to understand each other better' and work towards peace.

But by the last days of our journey she had changed. It was evident she was deeply troubled, said she was not sleeping well, and told me she was haunted by the things she had seen. She said she could not comprehend why Israel was behaving the way it did, and it weighed on her conscience. I could see she was wrestling with an internal dilemma she could not resolve.

Her distress affected me and I often wondered after we parted if she ever went any further with her questioning, ever let the angst she had felt lead her towards its logical conclusion, the abandonment of her ideas about Israel's moral rectitude. I never found out, and the only time I saw her again was a chance encounter at Heathrow Airport. She acknowledged me, but without warmth. We exchanged a few pleasantries before she hurried away. I could only assume the whole business had been too uncomfortable and she wanted to put it and me behind her.

Meeting Erlanger, who had taken the unusual step of reading my book, an account unmistakably written from the Palestinian point of view, and a person I found to be congenial and civilised, led me to imagine that he might have been one of that minority of Jews whose first-hand experiences had made them question the whole Zionist enterprise. But nothing in his responses to my probing suggested anything like that had happened, although he remained courteous and pleasant. There was no more to be said, and we went down to the ground floor, where his friends came out to greet us.

They were agreeable, liberal Israelis, whose origins, like Erlanger's, most likely lay in Eastern Europe. They welcomed me into the house solicitously, as if I had some disability which made me especially fragile. Retiring tactfully, they left me to see the rooms inside on my own. I felt like a cross between a tourist and a prospective house buyer, and I wished I had not come. Nevertheless, I forced myself to look around, but all I could think of were the many alien people who had lived in these rooms after us, and how each one erased more and more of our presence there.

Outside once more, I let Erlanger take photographs as he had proposed. He took a great many of these and did so with such enthusiasm that I was tempted to think it might have been a form of recompense for his earlier prevarications. But nevertheless it had been a kind act, and, I think, well meant.

I never saw him again for the rest of my stay in Palestine. We didn't move in the same circles, and he made no further contact beyond that occasion. If my visit had meant anything to him it didn't show in his subsequent pieces for the *New York Times*. I doubted that I had set him on a course of the kind that had so tormented the Jewish publisher of my earlier trip, and for all I knew may have succeeded only in reinforcing the views he had held before we ever met.

CHAPTER 8

Hebron

In June 2004 Israel's prime minister, Ariel Sharon, convinced his government to agree to what he called a 'Disengagement Plan' for Gaza. Israel would evacuate its forces and settlements from the Strip which it had occupied for thirty-seven years, and would do so on 15 August 2005. The plan was much-trumpeted as a generous, unilateral step towards peace, and a painful sacrifice on Israel's part. In reality it was nothing of the sort. By a shrewd calculation, Sharon had decided to ditch Gaza with its troublesome, hostile population in favour of concentrating all efforts on colonising the West Bank more thoroughly. As he presented it, the Gaza disengagement would secure the West Bank for generations of Israelis to come. His ultimate vision was of a territory dominated by large Jewish settlement blocs connected to each other and to the Jordan Valley, in which the Palestinian inhabitants were locked away behind the separation wall that his government was actively building.

Israel's decision was taken without even a cursory nod at the Palestinian Authority supposedly in charge of Gaza, and the plan omitted to mention that after the coming 'disengagement' the Israeli army would retain control over Gaza's every border, land, sea and airspace, exactly as before, and reserved the right to enter Gaza at any time to protect what it called its 'security'. By the time of the disengagement in 2005 there were twenty-one Israeli settlements dotted along Gaza's coastline and its interior, to the north near the border with Israel, in the centre of Gaza and to the south, cutting the Strip into non-contiguous areas and entirely blocking the towns of Khan Younis and Rafah from access to the sea. The settlements sat on top of Gaza's best agricultural land and controlled its aquifers; all together they took up a third of Gaza's land area, although only 8,000 settlers lived in this third, leaving Gaza's 1.3 million Palestinian inhabitants to be crammed into the remaining two-thirds.

A vigorous Israeli publicity campaign accompanied the Disengagement Plan, mounted well in advance of the evacuation to show the world the extent of Israel's 'sacrifice'. Gaza's Israeli settlers were seen weeping hysterically and clinging to the land they regarded as theirs as they faced the prospect of being driven out of it. With the date of evacuation drawing near, ever more dramatic scenes of settlers clashing with the Israeli army and defying its orders to leave, even though many of the soldiers were openly sympathetic to their cause, filled the airwaves and television screens in America and other Western countries.

I was struck by the fortuitous coincidence of my presence in the area at a time when I would have the chance of seeing this unique event first-hand, and had come to Dr Farid's ministry that day deliberating that I would tell him of my intention to go to Gaza. As I reached my office, Firyal, who seemed to be standing in for Adel, followed me in. 'Could you join Dr Farid in his office as soon as possible, Doctora?' I had noticed that there was an air of excitement in the building, and more people than usual hanging around in the corridor. The coffee boy told me that a meeting was in progress in Dr Farid's office to discuss what he had heard was a new and important project. At that time my working arrangements had not changed: I was still only supposed to attend part-time at this ministry, my desk on loan from Amin until his return, and as before to alternate my attendance between one ministry and the other. Otherwise, life at the two places carried on as before, and the antipathy between the two ministers was as keen as ever. Neither man met the other, and both still issued contradictory directives to their subordinates.

'Ah! Doctora Ghada! Come and join us.' Dr Farid smiled expansively and beckoned me in. A group of people, several of whom I recognised from the media group I had set up at the other ministry building, were seated around the low table where we had had our kebab lunch not long before. An extra chair was brought over and space made for me to sit with the group. Dr Farid passed me a document which set out the object of the meeting. This turned out to be a proposal for an international conference to define a media strategy for how best to communicate the Palestinian point of view to the outside world. It was handwritten and contained a list of proposed topics and another list of possible participants, but no date or programme. It was clear someone had been working hard on it, and it appeared that it was Dr Farid himself.

'I think you'll agree, Doctora,' he said, 'that this is an important task for us, one which all too often we've failed to accomplish. It's the main reason why I welcome you among us. You'll know better than most how to guide us in these matters.'

'I'm not clear what you mean, Dr Farid,' I said. 'Has the decision about this conference already been taken? Are we not going to discuss it first?'

'Oh but we already have, before you came.' The others nodded in agreement. 'But of course if you have something you want to ask, Doctora, please go ahead.' He turned to the others. 'I think we've come to some decisions, haven't we, friends?' They seemed to be listening raptly. 'As you see, we aim to bring together some of the best brains in the media world to bear on this question. You know, brothers, I am very aware that we've never been able to communicate our side of the case adequately or convincingly. The Doctora knows how many of us have tried, and yet there are these incidents all the time when Israel has so clearly been in the wrong but we still didn't manage to get our message across.' He frowned. 'And now, there's an Israeli disengagement from Gaza about to happen. You can see the hype they've been giving it already. We surely don't want to let them put out their version on that business without challenging it, do we?'

He was looking at me, but I was at a loss to say anything and examined the proposal again. 'Well,' I said, weighing my words carefully, 'can I ask what you think a conference like this will achieve? I mean, I've been working on a media and communications plan for the Palestine case since I came to the ministry. I gave Dr Sabah a copy and sent one to you. Amin and I then set up a media group with these gentlemen here to discuss the strategy, and it's already met once. So, I'm sorry, I don't fully understand the point of a conference on the same topic.'

Dr Farid looked a little pained at this. Aref, the media expert from Bir Zeit University, a friendly middle-aged man who had been in my media group, answered for him. 'You see, Dr Farid – and I understand his point – thinks the matter so important that it needs a higher profile. And a major event like an international conference, with eminent speakers, is necessary to give it that profile. Am I right?' He looked at Dr Farid.

I thought back on the major conferences I had organised in London, back-breaking work needing professional help that was seldom available for our modestly funded group, the long preparation time and advance notice necessary for prominent speakers to find space in their busy diaries. If this conference went ahead, who would do that work here? Adel, already weighed down by Dr Farid's workload? The young and inexperienced Firyal? Or did Dr Farid intend for that person to be me?

As if reading my thoughts, he continued, 'Don't worry, Doctora, there are many helpers on hand to do the work. Our friends from Bir Zeit University, the Palestinian Media Centre, and all the others here. You just direct them and I'm sure they'll be willing.' From their expressions I doubted whether any of them, having suddenly grasped the enormity of the project Dr Farid had in mind, would be willing at all. 'And, as soon as Amin comes back he'll be working with you on this as well.' It was evident he assumed that both of us would be as delighted at the prospect as he was. 'But seriously, the conference must go ahead, and the sooner the better. So we mustn't delay. If you look at the names I've jotted down, there are important people there, and we need to send out invitations as soon as possible.'

'Is there a budget to cover the costs?' It was common knowledge that the Ministry of Media and Communications, like all the others, was strapped for cash and lived from day to day on the promise of funding from international donors and the tax revenues generated by the PA's external trade. Relying on the latter was always precarious, partly because of Israeli restrictions on the free movement of goods and people, but also because Israel, which collected the tax revenues and was supposed to pass them on to the PA, did so irregularly depending on its state of displeasure or otherwise with the Palestinians. The economic uncertainty and dependence that resulted from this unsatisfactory situation left ministries with chronic cash shortages and an inability to draw up a proper budget.

'Don't you worry about that, Doctora,' beamed Dr Farid confidently. 'We'll find the money. You just start working on the conference – you know, statement of aims, draft programme, list of speakers, that sort of thing. As you see, I've already drawn up something. Just build on it.' There was an air of finality about his manner, indicating that this particular subject had been adequately covered and he would like to move on. 'But as I say, anything you need or want to know, Doctora, please get hold of me, or if you can't, Adel always knows where I am.'

Well, well, I thought, I've just been demoted from 'Media Consultant to the Ministry of Media and Communications' to the lowly state of 'conference organiser'. It made me quite angry, but with the Gaza visit on my mind, I decided I would think about the conference later. 'Dr Farid,' I said, as the others filed out of the office leaving him momentarily alone. 'I would like to talk to you about another matter. I have been thinking I would like to go to Gaza, especially now with the disengagement coming up. Would you mind if I went there for a few days?'

But Dr Farid had other ideas. 'I don't think that would be a good idea, Doctora. I will be there myself and we can't both go. I would want you to stay behind and take care of interviews and any media work that comes up here.' What media work, I thought? Most of the world's media would be in Gaza, covering the events there, not here, and he must have known it. It was obvious that Dr Farid, despite his avowed admiration for my media skills, wanted the field clear for himself.

When I phoned Mounir later to tell him what had happened and ask how I could get around it, he advised me not to try. 'Look, I'm the first to agree someone like you should be there. We need all the spokespeople we can get, but it'll be difficult for you to go to Gaza when he's specifically said no. He has contacts everywhere and you don't want to antagonise him. Just go along with what he says. But if you want to go to Gaza now, before the disengagement, I can arrange that. You could join one of our UNDP trips and I don't think he'll object.'

As soon as Amin returned to the ministry and learned about the new project he had been assigned by Dr Farid, he flatly refused to take it on. It was not his area of expertise, he asserted. I was clearly the best person to do it, he said. Had I not organised conferences and workshops in England before? He would be able to help with getting invitations printed and sent out, or he might make a few phone calls, but he was in no position to compose conference statements, draw up programmes or find appropriate participants. None of the members of the group who had been at the meeting with Dr Farid was any more forthcoming, although Aref from Bir Zeit agreed to look at anything I wrote. I saw that I was alone and could expect no assistance from anyone there.

'I will not do it!' I fumed at Annetta afterwards. 'I don't believe in it. It's a stupid waste of time and money, and I want no part of it. I'll have to get out of it somehow.'

She sighed. 'You know that's what happens around here these days. Such projects make people feel they're doing something important when the truth is, nothing they do is important. They're all trapped here with nowhere to go. You've seen how it is: got to get permission for this, permission for that, can't travel anywhere without a permit, can't connect with the outside world, can't do anything that matters. So what can they get up to, except this sort of silliness?'

Trapped indeed, but in a trap of their own making, I would have added. When Yasser Arafat and his men, veterans of the old PLO and now working for the PA, returned to Palestinian soil in 1994 on the basis of the Oslo Accords – an ambiguous agreement with the enemy who had driven them out of Palestine in the first place – they became hostage to the vagaries of whatever Israel threw at them. That was inevitable in a place under military rule. And Israel had thrown much in the way of restrictions, controls and loss of independence.

The men who had returned with Arafat were generally disliked by the Palestinians they joined, accused of being hangers-on and opportunists. But that was unfair, for amongst them were those who had been genuine revolutionary activists and had fought at one time for the total liberation of the homeland, only to find themselves now grounded and powerless in a remnant of the old Palestine, still unliberated. The ideals of the Palestinian revolution – expressed in the famous Fateh slogan, 'Revolution until Victory!' – had long faded; no one was aspiring for total liberation any more, but just for one small part of the homeland to call a Palestinian state. And even that was out of reach. Outwardly, many of these men had made the transition from the revolutionary vision that had once inspired them to the narrower quest for a modest political solution. But inside themselves there must have been memories and regrets they now sublimated in the pursuit of the limited and sometimes trivial enterprises that Israel's military rule allowed.

Dr Farid had not been one of these fighters, but he had joined Fateh as a young man, believed in its early revolutionary ideals and remained loyal to Yasser Arafat, the symbol of the Palestinian struggle, until the latter's death. His role had chiefly been as a strategist and spokesman for the cause, which he fulfilled well, with a suave and pleasant manner that impressed the Western media. He had been at the heart of events during the Madrid peace negotiations in 1992,[1] and was involved again in the talks that led to the Oslo Accords a year later. He tried to maintain that political role despite the change in Palestinian fortunes, and retained a determined optimism that all would be well in the end – even as the land of the Palestinian state everyone was now striving for shrank around him, and the settler numbers swelled. I suppose it was a sort of steadfastness in the face of relentless adversity, and in its way a part of the old nationalist struggle, however slim the chances of its success. In such circumstances a shift of focus from the larger to the smaller issues was the inevitable result.

The next day, in an effort to set aside the dispiriting affairs of the ministry by a total change of scene, I took up an offer to visit Hebron. I would join a British journalist, Chris Horton, who had worked for the BBC but was now a freelancer, and Pietro and Filippo, a couple of Italian activists working for a human rights NGO, who were driving down there. I had

---

1 The Madrid peace conference was held under the auspices of the US and Russia, and sought to find a solution to the Arab–Israeli conflict.

first visited Hebron in 1996 and been deeply affected by what I saw there at the time. Since then, more of Hebron's land had been seized for new settlement building and the number of extreme religious Jewish settlers, who had first implanted themselves there soon after the 1967 Israeli conquest of the city, had increased and were even more entrenched inside it. Hebron was a tormented place, notorious for the violence of these settlers and their army backers. I anticipated that there would be little to enjoy when we reached our destination and wondered for a moment why I was going at all.

Although we set off early in the morning it was already quite hot, and would get hotter by the time we reached Hebron. We drove to Jerusalem and from there due south. Because we were all foreigners in an Israeli-registered car, it did not take us long to get there. Had we been locals, it would have been a prolonged and hazardous journey over rough roads and tracks with the constant risk of being stopped at flying checkpoints en route, and Israeli soldiers ready to turn the car back to Ramallah. We approached Hebron from the south, driving along well-paved roads, all under Israeli control and full of settlements. Apart from army jeeps, most of the cars that passed us were driven by settlers and their wives. The scenery here was richly beautiful, lush farming land, fertile red soil for which the Hebron countryside was famous, and acres of vineyards and leafy plum and fig trees.

Our first stop was at a farm off the main highway, one of the few still owned by Palestinians. The car turned off the road and entered a narrow driveway leading up to the farmhouse. The land here too was filled with vineyards, but a closer look showed them to be in poor shape, yellowing and parched. By contrast, the vineyard in the adjoining farm, which had been taken over by settlers, was richly green and healthy. A tall, grey-haired man stood waiting for us outside the farmhouse. He was thin and had a dusty, unshaven look. Pietro and Filippo, evidently well known to him, went forward to shake his hand. A young woman in a headscarf, either his daughter or granddaughter, was hovering shyly in the doorway of the house behind him. He welcomed us into a modest front room with plastic chairs and plain stone flooring. As soon as we sat down the doorway was crowded with children, teenagers or younger, all staring at us. The farmer, who I presumed was their grandfather, shooed them away.

'How have you been, Abu Ibrahim?' asked Pietro in a concerned voice.

Abu Ibrahim looked away and shook his head. 'Not good. Not good.' He spoke passable English and I could see he was used to talking to foreigners such as these about his story. Pietro gave us the background. It appeared that until recently the farm and the wide expanse of lands next door, now fenced off and in the possession of the settlers, had all belonged to his family. Its main produce was grapes, and at that time of year its vines should have been flourishing and swollen with fruit, to be sold in the markets of Hebron and other West Bank cities. However, a couple of years before, the family was served with a military order that the lands were to be confiscated for 'army use'. A battle in Israel's courts contesting the order ensued, but, as was the way with the majority of such cases, it failed. The land was duly expropriated and soon afterwards turned over to the settlers who now farmed it.

It had been painful enough for Abu Ibrahim and his family of some eighteen people to watch the Israeli newcomers farming the land that had been theirs. But it did not stop there. The settlers, intent on driving the family off what remained of their farm, had started to harass them. Abu Ibrahim and his children were subjected every day to a variety of assaults: the settlers often barged aggressively into his farm with large, fierce dogs, played loud pop music sometimes all night, held raucous gatherings with other settlers, and encouraged their children to taunt Abu Ibrahim's grandchildren with insults and curses.

But despite it all, he remained implacable. 'Whatever they do,' he vowed, 'they will never, ever, drive me off this land! It was my father's and my grandfather's and his father's before him. Praise be to God, I have strong sons who will fight after I am gone.'

It was almost unbearable to listen to him. How many stories like his had I heard over the years? The same defiance against injustice, the same brave spirit, and the same powerlessness to affect the doomed and inevitable outcome. Chris, the journalist, was making notes, and asked several questions which Abu Ibrahim answered with alacrity.

'Did you complain to the Palestinian Authority?' I asked. The activists, who knew the story, nodded at me. 'Did anyone help?'

'The Authority? What Authority?' Abu Ibrahim asked bitterly. 'They did nothing for a long time after we contacted them. And then finally they sent two men round a few months ago who came and sat here and talked. I don't know if they were trying to help, but they talked a lot and in the end they offered me a few hundred dollars in what they called compensation.' He made a snorting, angry sound, and after a pause he looked directly at me. 'You and your friend, on the other hand –' he indicated the journalist. 'You can help. Tell everyone outside, tell the whole world what's happening here. These good people,' he pointed at the activists, 'they care. They come to see me regularly, God bless them.' He lit another cigarette. His fingers were nicotine-stained and there was cigarette ash down the front of his shirt.

But that was not the end of the story. Recently matters had got worse for Abu Ibrahim. The Israeli authorities which came to connect the settlements around his farm to Israel's national water carrier had at the same time disconnected his supply. They were deaf to all entreaty, and as a result he was forced to use an old well that had been on the farm since as far back as he could remember. But after a while the Israelis came again and blocked the well. This was a common practice, usually employed against Palestinian farmers in areas close to settlements with the aim of forcing them off their land. Starved of water, Abu Ibrahim's vines began to wither.

'Come and see for yourselves!' he exclaimed and jumped up. We followed him out towards the vineyards. He pointed at them with a shaky hand and urged us to come closer, although the deplorable state they were in was obvious. 'Look at this one!' he cried. 'Or that one! Look how yellow and shrivelled they are. See my grapes, so small, they never had a chance to ripen before they died.' He strode agitatedly from vine to vine, holding up their desiccated branches for us to see. He was shaking with anger, and I wondered how many times a day he looked at them in just this way and felt the same rage each time. I thought he looked ill, his eyes hollow and unnaturally bright, and I doubted his body could withstand all that anger and shattering loss for much longer.

And yet withal he had a dignity that commanded respect. Chris told him how sorry he was and promised to publicise the story, and I murmured something too. But I felt ashamed of my impotence in the face of his tragedy. No matter what I said, it would only have been to try and comfort him, for what could I or any of us do that would make the slightest difference to the reality he was living through? Matters would take their course, the settlers and their army protectors would win and Abu Ibrahim and his family would lose. We said nothing about that and bade him goodbye, leaving him standing on the path, touching in his defiance and looking after us as we got back into the car and drove off.

It was a short distance from the farm to the outer perimeter of Hebron. Approaching it from this direction brought us to the neighbourhood of the Old City and the Ibrahimi mosque. The road was quiet as we drew up to park near to a couple of lone Arab shops standing in view of the mosque and the army checkpoint opposite. They sold grimy, old Hebron souvenirs and soft drinks. No customers were to be seen, not surprisingly since hardly any Palestinians were allowed past the checkpoint. I thought the shops looked rather pathetic standing there, like two small islands stranded in a sea of Orthodox Jewish settlers and Israeli soldiers. Yet the shopkeepers were cheerful and friendly. They called out to us in broken English and offered us coffee. For some reason we declined, and when I looked back on that incident later, I deeply regretted the churlishness of not accepting their small kindness, a gesture of acknowledgement of their presence that would have cost us nothing.

The mosque, an imposing medieval Islamic edifice enclosed by tall stone walls, stood high up on an incline to our right, the Israeli flag flying from it. A number of cars with yellow number plates were parked in the area beneath its entrance, and groups of black-coated, religious Jews were walking up towards it. The Mamluks, an Islamic dynasty that ruled Palestine from Egypt at the time, had built it in the fourteenth century. They renovated it from an older mosque built at the time of Saladin on top of what had previously been a Byzantine church.

For centuries the Ibrahimi mosque served as one of Palestine's major shrines, until Israel's occupation of Hebron in 1967 turned it into a battleground between Palestinians and Israelis. Jews held it in especial regard as the site where, according to ancient tradition, the biblical patriarchs Abraham, Isaac and Jacob and their wives were allegedly buried. The biblical story went that here beneath the ground was a cave, called in the Bible the Cave of Machpelah, which Abraham was said to have purchased for the burial of his wife, Sarah. The religious structures built in later times were supposedly constructed on top of the Cave.

Feelings amongst religious Israelis were strong that the mosque they believed to be standing on top of the biblical Cave should belong exclusively to Jews, and in 1994 a

fanatical American Jewish settler, Baruch Goldstein, who
shared this view, shot dead twenty-nine Muslim Hebronites
praying inside the mosque. Thereafter Israel partitioned the
building into Jewish and Muslim sections, neither of which
was accessible to the other. When I first saw the place in 1996,
the Jewish part, which contained the major holy shrines and
was the mosque's main entrance, had been made to house
a synagogue and a cafeteria. Visiting it this time there were
more changes, which I was only able to see because the
Israeli woman soldier at the sentry post outside was too
busy chatting to my companions to be aware that I was a
Muslim; had she realised, I would certainly have been barred
from entry.

The mosque's central quadrangle open to the sky, a classic
feature of mosque architecture, had been transformed into a
Jewish religious space. The attempt to convert it from what it
had been looked to me clumsy and contrived. New cupboards
and bookcases, filled with what I presumed were Hebrew religious writings, had been placed in various corners; there were
benches and seating areas for Jewish worshippers at which
several men and women sat reading or talking. We were the
only non-Jews there, but attracted no one's attention. The
worshippers were too intent on their devotions by the shrines
of the patriarchs to notice.

The sacred tombs could be discerned through the ornate
grills that protected them inside the enclosures sculpted
from the mosque walls when it was originally built. Massive,
octagonal-shaped sepulchres, they were draped in rich coverings bearing Quranic verses. Abraham's tomb was the most
impressive, covered in emerald-green cloth ornamented with
gold Arabic calligraphy. This tomb was the main focus of
worship; several men sat before it intoning prayers or touching its grill repeatedly with their foreheads. A woman with a
huge Hebrew tome on her lap sat quietly mouthing the words
she was reading.

I marvelled at the incongruity of the scene before me: how could the people so devoutly praying in this place persuade themselves that it was a Jewish site? Had they ever bothered to look at it properly, to see its Islamic architecture, its classic medieval arches and pillars, its typical mosque layout and design? Or the tombs they so venerated, archetypically Islamic shrines in shape and structure, draped according to Muslim tradition in coverings inscribed with Quranic verses? How could they claim this place, so manifestly the creation of another people and another religion, as exclusively theirs? Or did they dream they were in some other universe where the tombs of their prophets and the Cave of the Patriarchs shone through all that Islamic camouflage?

When afterwards I voiced my astonishment at this, Chris Horton disagreed. 'I don't find it a bit surprising,' he said phlegmatically. 'You know how it is with religious people the world over. They believe in things quite blindly, whether they can see them or not. In this place it seems that devout Jews believe for whatever reason that their patriarchs are buried here. And so it doesn't matter to them what's covering the tombs of their prophets or who made the coverings. They see what they want to see – with the eye of faith, if you know what I mean.'

We had walked away from the mosque towards the checkpoint at the bottom of the Old City. Pietro and Filippo said nothing about the mosque, which they must have seen many times before, and seemed keen to move on. At the checkpoint that marked the bottom of Hebron's covered souk, the traditional Arab marketplace, a couple of soldiers examined our passports without much interest and waved us on. We found ourselves in one of the long, narrow streets of the souk which had in the past been a hub of economic activity. The busiest part of all had been al-Shuhada Street, the main thoroughfare linking the west of Hebron to the east, and previously its most important commercial centre. But ever since three of Hebron's four Old City settlements were built over it the street had been closed by the Israeli army, and Palestinians, whether in cars or on foot, were barred from going there.

Hebron was an important place, the West Bank's second-largest city, and accounted for a third of its economy. The disruption to its commercial life caused by these closures had been massive. We found al-Shuhada Street deserted, a dead, ghost place, its Arab shops long since closed down and Hebrew graffiti all over their shutters, some of them in English, telling Arabs to get out, and the Star of David painted on the shop fronts. As we walked along, a group of armed Orthodox settlers stopped to stare at us with undisguised hostility. The women settlers with them were, if anything, even more overtly hostile than the men. Several Israeli soldiers standing near the settlers came over and unsmilingly ordered us to leave. I could see they thought the place belonged exclusively to them, to the Jews, and no non-Jews were tolerated there.

I was more than glad to get out of that sad, shabby street and return to the rest of the souk, far more familiar to me with its typical small shops set close together, its neighbourly shopkeepers sitting in front chatting to each other, and people wandering along its narrow winding streets and stopping every now and then to buy something or just to look. But all was not well here either. The typical bustle of such Arab souks, the noise, the crowds and the jostling were all missing, and the further down one went towards the checkpoint at the end the quieter it became. Despite the gaily coloured displays of Hebronite goods, hand-painted ceramic plates, embroidery, pottery and glass, all locally made, there were scarcely any customers. Only falafel and other food stalls attracted the few shoppers. As soon as they saw us, the souvenir sellers pounced eagerly. We later found out that they lived off the monthly stipend the PA paid them to keep their shops open and fend off the settlers' attempts to have them shut down.

The 500 or so settlers who lived within the Old City under

army protection had one aim in life: to force the Arabs out of the area altogether, and to this end had devised all sorts of tactics to bring it about. Those living in the high-rise settlement buildings above the souk ejected all manner of offensive detritus, soiled nappies, sanitary towels, rotten food, dirty water and even heavy rocks on to the souk below. The shopkeepers had roofed over the street with steel mesh netting to catch the rubbish that was incessantly hurled down on them, and it made an unpleasant sight if one looked up.

We stopped to talk to one shopkeeper who spoke English well and asked who we were. As soon as he heard that one of us was a journalist, he focused all his attention on him. 'Please,' he said. 'Please look around you, sir. You see how terrible this place is, how terrible our lives are. Please tell Britain when you are back, tell the world, what is happening to us.' A torrent of similar pleas poured out of him. I thought he was about to pull on Chris's shirt in his agitation. 'Everyone here will tell you the same. We have no hope, no future, no end to this situation. It is like living in hell. Can you see, sir, can you see?' For all his efforts to speak calmly, his distress was evident. He grabbed a map he had in his shop and opened it up. 'Look at the settlements choking us. See, here is Kiryat Arba.' This was the oldest and largest of the settlements in the vicinity of Hebron, lying a short distance to the west of the city and home to about 6,000 hard-line religious settlers who believed in the absolute Jewish right to possess this land; they had imposed themselves on Hebron soon after the 1967 war, forced the Israeli authorities to recognise them and remained there ever since.

The shopkeeper jabbed at his map. 'See, here we have the settlements in the Old City, four of them. They're right in the midst of us and the army protects them. There's nothing we can do against them.' There was more in the same vein. I tried to speak to him in Arabic to say we understood the difficulties, but he was focused on the Englishman. In the end we all bought a few souvenirs from him, and Pietro and Filippo, who obviously knew him, calmed him down. As we walked away, a group of Israeli soldiers passed us pursuing a couple of Palestinian youths who they stopped roughly and harangued in broken Arabic. The two boys looked terrified.

At the top end of the souk, where it opened into the main part of the city, it was a different scene. Here there were more people, noisy traffic and crowded shops, almost a different city. Hebron was one of Palestine's most conservative places, more so than Nablus, and all the women here wore hijab. 'They must get hot in that, surely,' said Chris looking at them. Outside the Old City the rest of Hebron, which constituted about 80 per cent of the total area, was Palestinian-ruled and densely populated. Having had to compensate for the loss of the important Old City market, it was vibrant and quite successful. We would have gone further, but there was no point. From here on it was an ordinary Arab town like the others and of little interest to my companions.

'The Hebron deal was in my view one of the worst mistakes Yasser Arafat ever made,' said my host. 'How on earth could he have sacrificed the most important part of it to the Israelis?' I had returned to Ramallah in the late afternoon, feeling physically and emotionally drained by the trip. What a day of unrelieved gloom and foreboding it had been. I was reluctant to go out again, but did not feel I could back out of Ilan Halevi's invitation at such short notice. Halevi, a Jewish Israeli living in the heart of a Palestinian city, and more with the Arabs than the Israelis, was an interesting anomaly in a country of anomalies. I had met him many years before in London, but never saw him again until I came across him at the PA foreign ministry in Ramallah. He was a short man with a goatee beard and warm dark eyes, attractive and lively. His background was curious; born into a Jewish family in France where he was brought up and educated, he had gone to Israel as a young man to learn about the conflict with the Palestinians.

What he saw and learnt there changed him forever. He threw his lot in with the Palestinian resistance movement thereafter and formally joined the PLO in the late 1960s, becoming a member of Fateh. Yasser Arafat took him on as an adviser and appointed him PLO representative in Europe and delegate to the Socialist International. When Arafat moved to Gaza, Halevi returned as well, to become a senior figure in the PA's foreign ministry and a member of Fateh's Revolutionary Council. Not surprisingly, for Israel he was a traitor and an abettor of 'terrorism'. But this did not deter him from pursuing the course he had chosen for himself.[2]

It seemed he held these dinner gatherings from time to time at his home, a beautiful old Ramallah house with many original features and a shady garden of olive and fruit trees. I knew none of the group he had invited. They were sitting out on the patio when I arrived. It was a balmy, still evening, a welcome relief from the day's fierce heat. Among the guests was a veteran PLO activist, two women working for NGOs concerned with education and women's rights, an academic from Bir Zeit's law department, the Palestinian Authority's delegate in Paris, who looked to be in his early fifties and was on a brief visit to Ramallah, and a tall, youngish German woman working for a German-funded institute who I gathered was Halevi's partner. A little later we were joined by a Palestinian journalist and his Italian wife.

I told them about my trip to Hebron that day and how it had affected me. Apart from Mamdouh Nofal, the PLO man, who had belonged to the PFLP (Popular Front for the

---

2   Mahmoud Abbas later conferred a Medal of Distinction on Halevi for his support of the Palestinian struggle. Tributes from the Fateh leadership poured in when he died in 2013. But an Israel official commented, 'Halevi crossed the lines, and this is unacceptable for the Israelis.'

Liberation of Palestine), a rival faction to Arafat's Fateh and frequently at odds with it, none of the others seemed especially interested; probably, I thought, because they had heard it all before.

'Just *one* of Arafat's mistakes?' asked Mamdouh with scorn. 'When did he ever do anything right?'

'Now, now, my dear friend, no need for that,' responded Halevi. 'We will never agree about Arafat. Let's just say he should never have gone along with the division of Hebron, which was bound to lead to the misery our friend Ghada saw there today.' He was referring to an agreement drawn up with Israel which Arafat signed in 1997, ceding control of Hebron's Old City to Israel in return for Palestinian rule over the rest. At a stroke it left some 30,000 Palestinians stranded in the Old City, living in close proximity to the settlers and at their mercy, as I had witnessed that day.

'Come on,' said the PA delegate from Paris. 'It's not that bad. The PA's put a lot of money into developing Hebron's historic sites. I've seen it for myself and it's really quite impressive.'

He turned to the Bir Zeit academic. 'Legally,' said the latter, 'the Hebron Agreement is watertight. I don't know how it can be broken.'

'By a mass uprising, that's how!' exclaimed Mamdouh vigorously. 'The PA would be better employed organising that before renovating a few old buildings. Or are you going to tell me that buildings are more important than people?'

Khalil, the journalist, and his wife, who had lived in Ramallah for many years, were looking at me as if I were some curious specimen. 'Didn't you know all that about Hebron before, Doctora?' he asked with an edge of disbelief. 'I thought you people outside kept up with everything that happens here.'

'Well, yes,' I said. 'But seeing it close-up like that is different.' Why did I have to justify what seemed to me obvious? He smiled faintly and shrugged his shoulders, and it made me wonder when was the last time any of them had visited the places I had seen that day. The women from the NGOs said nothing during this exchange, but one of them eventually suggested we change the subject. She was smartly dressed and self-assured, and spoke fluent English. The other woman, who was younger, was talking on her mobile phone much of the time. They represented a class of educated Palestinians I was growing familiar with in Ramallah, people at home in the world of NGOs and international solidarity work and not given to nostalgia over past campaigns for the liberation and return of the lost homeland. I could not fathom what it was they cared about exactly; they were a new breed of Palestinian reared in the era of occupation and, knowing no other, had learnt to find roles for themselves within its reality. Yet our host, Israeli though he was, did not feel the same way. He, no less than Mamdouh, belonged firmly to a past of revolutionary struggle and the idealism of another era.

It was a pleasant enough dinner party: good food, plentiful wine, an affable host and intelligent conversation, but nothing I could identify with. Halevi was clearly cultivated; his library of books, some of them his own writings, which I had seen on coming into the house, attested to that, and he was one of a type of anti-Zionist Jew I had often worked with in the past. But he was not forthcoming about that aspect of his life here, and seemed more anxious to fit himself into the Palestinian society he had adopted than to discuss anti-Zionist politics. None of the Palestinians he had invited that evening showed much interest in who I was or what I thought, beyond knowing that I had come from London to work for the PA. No one asked for my views about what might be done with Hebron, or, coming from the outside, how I found the Palestinian situation overall.

I had introduced myself as a '1948 Palestinian', shorthand for a story they all knew well, but, with the exception of Mamdouh, clearly felt remote from. I found that strange.

For me, it was we, the 1948 generation, who were the proper custodians of our national history, the vital witnesses to the dispossession and loss of the homeland which lay at the the root of the bitter conflict that had blighted all our lives. Without that knowledge, the conflict today was incomprehensible. And what would we be without a national narrative of our past, still alive in memory and on record?

My life's work had centred on the fundamental facts of 1948 from which all else was derivative. It never occurred to me that any Palestinian alive would think otherwise. But here I was, a 1948 Palestinian and one of those custodians of history I believed so precious, beginning to realise that people like me were irrelevant in this place, far removed from the reality of daily life with the Israelis, their army and their settlements. Whatever had happened in the past made no difference to the immediacy and harshness of the occupation people now endured. To them, my memories of what had caused the initial problem were all very well, but in the scale of things, much less important. And in the here-and-now, I was as irrelevant to the current situation and this generation of Palestinians as Halevi or Mamdouh.

CHAPTER 9

Interlude in Amman

My father telephoned from Amman yet again to ask when I was coming to visit. The desperate loneliness in his voice made it impossible for me to turn him down. I promised to go over at the weekend, which in Ramallah, as in Amman, meant Friday and Saturday. The media conference hung over me like an incubus. It dogged my waking moments, because I still had not found a way of confronting Dr Farid with my refusal to comply with his request that I should work on it. And the longer I put off doing so, the harder it became. He had been in touch several times after the meeting in his office, asking how I was getting along with the preparations and if I could send him the conference statement I was supposed to be drawing up. Each time he telephoned I gave a vague reply to fob him off, aware of my cowardice in not telling him the truth. Nor was I sure why I so feared confronting him. I kept reminding myself that he was not my employer, I owed him nothing, but on the contrary: he was in my debt, as a consultant who had come all the way from England to offer my expertise to his ministry.

In the end my hesitancy and lack of resolve led me to take a middle course between doing as he had asked and doing nothing. So it was that before leaving for Amman I found myself trying to write something down to send him, like throwing a bone to a growling dog. I had gone to my office in Dr Sabah's building for the purpose, not wanting to meet Amin or anyone else at the other ministry. It had been some time since I had gone there, and to my amazement Esperance greeted me with great warmth and said how much they had all missed me. Had I been ill, she inquired solicitously, joined by Bilal the coffee boy and then Hanan, who came over from her office to see me. I could make nothing of this sudden change and wondered whether it was genuine. Baffled, I went to my office and sat trying to collect my thoughts. Like a schoolchild forced to do some hateful piece of homework, I sat staring at the computer screen, devoid of ideas. In the end I made myself compose a brief statement of conference objectives full of meaningless clichés, and added a skeleton programme of sessions and workshops with appropriate-looking titles. I thought very little of what I had produced but hoped it would be enough to satisfy Dr Farid, at least temporarily, until I summoned up the courage to tell him how I felt.

The next morning I set off early for the crossing to Jordan. From Ramallah the road went due south towards Jericho, and then to the Allenby Bridge. Going across the Bridge from the Israeli side was no less unpleasant than doing it the other way. Long queues of cars waited in the heat at the checkpoint before the bridge, allowed in one by one after lengthy inspections of the passenger documents and the vehicle, including the boot, by bored-looking Israeli soldiers in no hurry to do their work. They chatted to each other as if they were on holiday, kept the cars waiting for no apparent reason, and then languidly examined each one, still chatting to their colleagues. The taxi drivers, who knew the drill, meekly complied, careful not to react or antagonise the soldiers in any way and prolong the journey even more.

This part of the crossing finished, there was the departure building to negotiate, with more delays and a hefty exit tax on top. All of this took an hour or more, and by the time I'd finally crossed the bridge to the Jordanian side, found a taxi to Amman and arrived there, it was already early afternoon. My father lived in Shmeisani, one of the older residential areas of West Amman, the more prosperous side of the city. Shmeisani

used to be considered a 'good' address, but increasing commer-
cialisation had lowered its status. Its pavements were broken
up and the large metal municipal bins along its streets were
often overflowing with rubbish and open plastic bags, spilling
their rotting contents on to the road for the legion mangy,
skinny cats of the neighbourhood to rummage in. Even so, the
older streets were still genteel and attractively tree-lined.

My father's flat was not in one of these but in an apartment
block on a busy road, directly opposite a large supermarket. The drive to Amman took about forty-five minutes, and
as we entered the city we joined long queues of traffic and
a muddle of roundabouts, bridges and underpasses that all
looked alike to me without a distinguishing mark to help one
recognise them afterwards. I saw a heavily built-up conglom-
eration of apartment and office blocks of differing elevations
and designs, some ultra-modern, all glass and steel, and others
built in old-fashioned white stone. There was no pattern to this
assortment of buildings, which looked to have been erected
without the benefit of any discernible municipal planning.
In the midst of all that concrete there were no public spaces,
parks or children's playgrounds in sight. But the recently built,
wealthier residential areas were attractively laid out, although
in some cases the trees that adorned them had been planted
in the middle of narrow pavements which forced one to walk
round them. The needs of pedestrians seemed to be the last
thing on anyone's mind, and a walk in Amman meant dicing
with death to avoid the traffic along the roads.

Here and there were sandy, rubbly open areas of ground
strewn with litter, awaiting development into more buildings.
Construction sites for flats and offices were everywhere, and
we passed a large number of hotels, many of them branches
of international chains like the Marriot, the Sheraton, or the
Four Seasons. Although I had visited Amman many times in
the past, I still found it hard to find my way among its streets,
which all looked alike and whose names were forgettable

because hardly ever used. To the casual visitor, it was a place without charm or character. Although it stood on an ancient site with a long history, there was little of that to be seen today beyond the downtown area, where the remains of the Roman citadel, forum and amphitheatre were located. The rundown older houses below the citadel and the souk downtown had a more authentic Arab character with its bustle and crowds. Though not to be compared with the historic souks of other Arab capitals, it had an attractive, friendly atmosphere.

Palestinians tended to regard Amman and Jordan as a whole as late, artificial constructs created by British imperialism. Amman in particular, and for all its buildings, restaurants and hotels, was seen as more of a haphazard encampment in the desert than a proper city. Historically it had been a small village for most of its life, with a few thousand inhabitants at most. Only with the arrival of the British in the region at the end of the First World War did its fortunes revive. My father was a young man of seventeen when the British conquerors divided Palestine and created out of its eastern bank what was then called Transjordan; they set the Emir Abdullah, the Sharif Hussein of Mecca's second son, at the head of this new principality in 1923. Abdullah, totally dependent on the British who were the real rulers of the land on both banks of the Jordan river, assumed the title of king in 1946 when Transjordan gained independence, and made Amman the capital of this new kingdom. But it remained insignificant until 1948, when fleeing Palestinian refugees arrived in their hundreds of thousands to swell its small population. This seminal event set it on the road to becoming a large city.

My father had never intended to live out his last days there, but when he and my mother grew older they decided to move from London, where they had lived for forty years by then, and go to Amman. There was no history to connect them to the place, least of all my mother, who was a Syrian by origin. But it was the closest point to the Palestine they had left behind in 1948, and in the old days, before the 1967 war and the checkpoints and barriers that Israel set up, it took no more than forty minutes or so to reach Jerusalem from Amman. By going there my father joined much of the Karmi extended family which had also ended up in Amman, more than 150 of them. But in truth he had never been much interested in his relatives, and did not seek them out. His life, like theirs, had started in Tulkarm, among its farms and village folk of whom our family was a part, but he had abandoned it as soon as he could and never lived there again. The later course of his life took him on a widely divergent path to most of the family, and he became estranged from his origins in mentality and outlook.

He did not like being in Amman. 'Don't any of you come to this country,' he would warn us. 'It's not a good place. Don't ever think about it.' Many people would have disagreed with him, especially other Palestinians who had settled there. For historical and geographical reasons, Jordan was the only country outside Palestine where the Palestinian presence was so concentrated and pervasive. Though no official statistics for the number of Palestinians in Jordan existed – and were in any case, it was said, unofficially played down – it was estimated that they made up at least 60 per cent of the total population, and over 70 per cent in Amman. This was not surprising, in view of the events after the first large refugee exodus of 1948. The Arab–Israeli war in 1967 and the first Gulf war of 1991 led to further inflows of hundreds of thousands more Palestinians. In Jordan's refugee camps, set up in 1948, there were two million people by the time of my parents' arrival.

Thus Palestinians felt at home in Amman. They talked the same kind of Arabic, shared the same jokes, had suffered alike some misfortune or other because of being Palestinian, and cherished the same attachment to the homeland. I remember feeling at home too the first time I went to Amman, where the

Arabic spoken around me was the one I had grown up with and it was a pleasure to hear my first name (for years variously mangled by the English as 'Gharda', 'Rada', 'Khada', or simply 'Dr Karmi' when they had given up trying) pronounced correctly at last. It was also the one place where I could line up at the airport immigration desk labelled 'Jordanians', feeling myself an authentic citizen of the country, while the other desks were for 'Foreigners'. Jordan conferred its nationality on all Palestinian refugees who came into the country in 1948, and especially those from the West Bank. Although we had lived in Jerusalem and gone to Damascus as our first place of refuge in 1948, our family's origins in the West Bank town of Tulkarm qualified us for Jordanian citizenship.

Becoming Jordanian felt natural, since Jordan was contiguous to Palestine, indeed had been carved out from it, and made us at least equal with the natives, who at that time were mostly made up of large family clans and villagers, Bedouin tribes originally from Arabia, and an added minority of Circassians, Chechens and Armenians. The cynical view of Jordan's ostensible generosity towards the Palestinians in 1948 was that King Abdullah needed the numbers to people his new state, and what better than well-educated Palestinians who could help build the country? Amman was subsequently expanded and developed at the expense of Jerusalem, which Jordan had annexed along with the West Bank in 1950. The Holy City was relegated to secondary status, to serve as a religious centre but little more. In years to come, that earlier Jordanian willingness to integrate Palestinians into its society gave way to increasing hostility and discrimination against them. They were rarely appointed to government or other official positions, which were filled by native Jordanians ('meaning, Bedouins', Palestinians would say scornfully), and were downgraded to secondary or lower-ranking jobs. Jordanian nationality became ever harder to obtain, and eventually was no longer freely offered to Palestinians.

Yet, undeterred by these unfavourable circumstances, Palestinians still flocked to Jordan from all over the world, as if following some homing instinct. They bought houses, set up businesses, and sought spouses for their children. I knew many Palestinians in London who owned second homes in Amman and went in and out of the country regularly. How ironic that such a thing should happen. For years Israel's dearest wish had been that Jordan should become the Palestinian state everyone sought to create in the Occupied Territories. Many an Israeli leader would argue that since Jordan's population was mainly Palestinian already, what more natural than for the two communities, currently divided by the Jordan River, to come together in Jordan, leaving their previous lands to Israel? No one else accepted this idea, least of all Jordan, which rejected it vociferously. But like it or not, there it was being realised before our very eyes, and without Israel having to fire a single shot.

It was siesta time when I arrived at my father's flat. I paid the taxi driver, who responded with a 'Thank you and welcome home, Auntie.' However many times I came to the Arab world, I never got used to being addressed in this way. It was always the same: as soon as I arrived in Amman I became an instant old lady, someone's aunt or, worse still, a *hajjeh*. The latter, strictly speaking, was the designation for a woman who had undertaken the annual pilgrimage, the *hajj*, and nothing to do with her age. But in common parlance it was applied to old women, usually from a lower social class, and conjured up an unflattering picture of some poor soul on the edge of her grave. In Arab society women were afforded a short time, usually the years under the age of thirty, in which to be considered desirable and marriageable. By forty and irrespective of her charms, a woman had lost much of her appeal and could mostly look to marrying a man in his sixties. From the age of fifty onwards women ceased to be sexual beings altogether, and were seen predominantly as someone's aunt or mother, devoid of any intrinsic interest as women.

Being over sixty as I was, I had more than attained that unfortunate state, particularly for taxi drivers, shopkeepers and even bank clerks, which should have consigned me to the social rubbish heap along with all the sad widows and disappointed spinsters. But being a doctor and living abroad put me into an indeterminate category, somewhere between a man and a woman, and saved me from that final ignominy.

My father's Sri Lankan maid, Margo, opened the door to let me in. It was a sunny ground-floor flat, well-proportioned and carefully designed to make the most of the available space; it had an open-plan lounge and dining room, a front balcony overlooking the busy road and the supermarket, and a small garden with a veranda to the side. He had planted an olive and a lemon tree in the garden, but the former did not survive. There had been a mature lemon tree in the garden of our house in Jerusalem, just outside my parents' bedroom window. Perhaps he had been thinking of that when he planted the new one.

'Baba is sleeping,' said Margo in her broken Arabic. 'Baba' was what she called him, an Arabised form of Papa. She had been with him since shortly after my mother's death in 1991, and was devoted to him, despite his cantankerousness and irritability towards her. Margo was a sad figure with an unhappy story, like all the other maids from Sri Lanka, the Philippines, Indonesia, or Bangladesh who served as domestics in Jordan. Many of them had previously done stints in Gulf countries, and most well-to-do households employed one or more and often treated them badly. They were overworked, might have no room of their own and so were forced to sleep on the floor either in the corridor of the house or in the sitting room after everyone else had gone to bed. Some maids were 'lent out' to clean the houses of relatives in addition to their employer's, for no extra payment, and could have their salaries withheld for months. There were numerous stories of the cruelties inflicted on these poor women, some of whom were regarded as no better than slaves. From time to time, a maid who could bear it no longer would run away or even try to do away with herself.

Margo by comparison had a much better life with my father. She had her own room and her duties were relatively light, since he lived alone and did not entertain in the way that normal Arab families did. Despite his frequent ill-humour, he was kind to her, gave her extra money when she asked for it, and listened to her incomprehensible chatter when they were alone. Margo had lived in the Arab world for over twenty years, but had still not managed to learn any more than a rudimentary form of Arabic, with words garbled and mispronounced, and only after some familiarity with her could one divine what she was talking about.

When in Sri Lanka, she had been married briefly to a man who abandoned her with their son, and she never heard from him again. Finding no employment in her country, she was forced to leave her child behind and join the legion of domestic workers with similar stories headed for the Middle East. Like all these, the money she made from her work she sent back for the care of her son, leaving her with no savings of her own. My father would often advise her to keep something back for herself, but she never did. She was a kind-hearted woman who always made me and my daughter feel welcome. Her future was irrevocably tied to my father's, and as he had just turned one hundred years old that summer, I wondered what would happen to her when he was gone.

Meeting him, no one would have guessed he was so old. He was still quite handsome, and looked many years younger. His mind and memory were sharp. But his hearing had declined to the point at which, and much against his will, he was fitted with a hearing aid. More seriously, his eyesight had gradually failed and he could no longer recognise faces, or read – a terrible affliction for a man who had spent his life with the written word. He had always read widely, owned an extensive library in Arabic and English, and over many years produced a dozen dictionaries and various other works. His expertise in Arabic literature had won him many fans all over the Arab world, and his weekly programme for the BBC Arabic Service on Arabic poetry and proverbs was widely listened to, from the Levant to North Africa to the Arabian Peninsula.[1]

I admired my father enormously, as did my sister and brother. We adopted some of his ideas and ways of looking at the world, and we quoted his sayings to others. And yet he had not been a good father to any of us in the conventional sense. He took little interest in our personal lives, offered us no parental guidance as we were growing up, and neither my sister nor I saw much affection from him, except when we were very young. Our poor brother fared slightly worse, deprived of fatherly advice on how to conduct himself in the world, or even an interest in his welfare, beyond the most basic kind. Yet our father was not a cruel man, and would have been horrified to hear of our complaints; his behaviour was more a case of benign neglect than deliberate ill-treatment. We all felt that lack of personal concern, and resented him for it in our various ways.

But, such was the power of his status in the family, it over-came all other considerations. Despite lives spent in England, we remained in essence an Arab family where certain tradi-tional norms applied, chief among which was the primacy of the father. He was the source of authority in the family, and it was he who defined its identify. In Arab society, people

---

1 This weekly programme, which ran for nearly thirty years, was called 'A Saying on a Saying', and involved listeners writing in to inquire about the origin of a line of poetry or a proverb they had come across. My father's encyclopaedic capacity to find the answers to these queries, some highly obscure, was celebrated, and he went on recording the programme until he was eighty-three.

were known less for being themselves than for whose sons
or daughters they were. It situated them in society and enabled
others to define them in a way that their own names would
not have done. I always found it disconcerting to be asked
on meeting someone for the first time, 'Is your father Hasan
Karmi?', as if unsure who I was or how to react to me until
they had established this. When they had placed me in that
way their manner would change instantly from indifference to
warm recognition.

The children of an Arab family traditionally *looked up* to
their fathers and wanted to be proud of them. For us, a displaced and isolated Arab family living in the England of the
1950s, where foreigners were an uncommon and unwelcome
phenomenon, this patriarchal structure was even more of an
imperative, and our father became our anchor in the wilderness despite his aloofness. He dominated our lives throughout
that time. And seeing him now, so frail and old, sitting on the
sofa opposite me in his pyjamas and dressing gown, I marvelled at how he could still possess so much of that authority
and power as in the past. We might deprecate or ignore his
more extreme views or joke about some of his irritating
habits, but ultimately, he retained a presence and strength of
character that could not be dismissed.

He asked me about Ramallah and what I had been doing,
but he mainly wanted to tell me about his thoughts on the
world, on Islam, on the Arabs' collective failure, and on
Western duplicity and malice towards the Arabs. Indeed he
eagerly awaited my visits in order to talk about these views.
He had always had such ideas, but as he grew older and more
isolated he brooded on them, and often spoke of little else
to us and to some of his unwary visitors. One of the advantages of life in Arab society for the old was its sociability and
respect for old age. Neighbours, members of the family, and
friends would drop in on my father to ask after his health or
offer help if he needed it. For that reason it had been a relief to

us when he and my mother decided to spend their last years in an Arab country. And as we had expected, all sorts of people came to pay their respects, including many members of the Karmi family who looked up to my father as the respected elder amongst them and visited him regularly.

They usually looked in for a cup of coffee and a little chat about generalities, but might find themselves faced instead with a rehearsal of his often vehement views on Islam and the state of the Arab world. Like many ordinary people who lacked his education and were too preoccupied with the details of their difficult everyday lives to be reflective about such issues, they would listen politely while Margo served them coffee; and then they would leave, no doubt little the wiser about any of the matters he discussed. He would be left frustrated, disgruntled with the society around him and people's lack of intelligence as he saw it.

The grievances that preoccupied him for years were against the imperialist West that had trampled all over the developing world, stolen its lands, ruled its people and ruthlessly prevented them from gaining independence. He veered between pity for the plight of Muslims caught up in these Western colonial snares, and anger at the same Muslims for not being able to stand up for themselves. He revered Islam as a doctrine and a philosophy, wrote and thought about it, but decried its practice by what he called vacuous believers who followed mindless rituals and failed to understand its true essence. Thus he did not agree with women wearing the hijab or men growing beards, and disapproved of the widespread practice amongst these supposedly devout believers of not shaking hands with members of the opposite sex for fear of spoiling their ablutions before prayer.[2] He would say to female relatives

---

2 In Islam, ablutions, or ritual cleansing, are carried out before each prayer. They involve washing the face, arms, legs and private parts. Once performed, the ablutions would be negated by re-soiling of the cleansed parts, which would need to be washed again. However,

of ours wearing the hijab when they came to see him, 'What on earth can you possibly fear from a man of my age, old enough to be your grandfather?'

His diatribes against the West, which became more emphatic as he grew older, were tedious to listen to, and I was often torn between challenging his ideas and patiently letting him rant on. Even so and despite the irritating manner in which he delivered them, his ideas had merit, and I still cited some of them to other people. I could see he was desperate for engagement when he spoke, for his listeners to reciprocate. Yet if one were unwise enough to respond with any comment that disagreed with his views, he would dismiss that person for a fool, incapable of comprehending ideas.

In reality, and no matter how objectively he framed it, I never believed that so much bitter vehemence was really about what it claimed to be. I thought it instead a form of emotional displacement about his own life, about his experience of the particular colonialism that had lost us our homeland. He rarely talked directly about Palestine or his life before 1948, but I did not doubt that there lay the source of his anger and frustration. With what callous disregard for him and his kind did Britain discharge its promise to a foreign political movement, Zionism, and enable it to install itself in our country, against our wishes and, as it proved, to our enormous detriment.

Working as an education inspector for the British Mandate government in Palestine in the 1940s, he had seen first-hand its preferential treatment of Jews, its favouritism towards them, and its scorn for Palestinian natives like him. Without Britain's unstinting collaboration, the Zionist movement and its adherents could never have succeeded so spectacularly; could never have expelled him and us from our home in Jerusalem. When the Mandate came to an end in May 1948, the signal for the

---

shaking hands with the opposite sex is not prohibited at any time; it was a custom introduced by fundamentalists, with no basis in Islamic doctrine.

mass takeover of Palestine by the Jews, he had been on the verge of promotion in his job, his future bright and promising. In a few short weeks that future had been smashed to pieces, and he had to start all over again in another place, with us like a millstone around his neck.

The concept of 'Chosenness' fascinated him, an idea embedded in Judaism and passed on to Protestant Christianity, of a people especially chosen by God, who by inference preferred it above all others. Jews rejected this interpretation: they said that to be 'chosen' in Judaism meant to have been chosen to worship God and do pious deeds in His name. My father did not subscribe to this view and would rail against the Western colonialists who, imbued with the belief in their chosenness, had conquered other people's lands and exploited their riches as if they had a God-given right to them. And what more vivid example of this arrogance than that of one 'chosen' race, the British, conferring Palestine's lands and its riches on another, the Jews? If I reminded him that the seventh-century Arab conquerors of the Near East, Persia, India and Spain had also at one time exploited the lands they ruled, he became incensed and accused me of being a fool along with everyone else. 'It's not the same thing!' he would exclaim. 'The Arabs did not come out of Arabia with an idea that they were chosen. They brought a new religion which they offered to the peoples they conquered, but did not compel them to convert. They did not see those places as belonging to them by divine right. That's a Judaeo-Christian idea, and it's absolutely not the same thing at all!'

This ranting and vehemence worsened after my mother's death. He missed her acutely, although theirs had not been a love match, nor had they shared many interests or ways of thinking. But they had been together for so long that he had come to rely on her constant presence, in his life and to ignore the fact that she had never been the ideal companion for him. They had been married according to Arab tradition, by an agreement between their respective fathers in which they had

had little say. I doubt whether, left to themselves, they would ever have got together. Our father was scholarly and introverted from an early age, and spent his time in reading and contemplation. Our mother was the opposite, she was sociable and gregarious; a lively, vivacious woman who loved other people's company and had a charming penchant for storytelling. But fate threw them together and they had trudged along as best they could.

I did not think that either of them had welcomed our arrival into the world, or at least not so early on in their marriage. My father would have preferred to concentrate on building his career, and my mother probably not to have had children at all. But having children as soon as one was married was what happened in Arab society, and any delay usually resulted in raised eyebrows and suspicions that one or other of the couple – the woman mostly – had a problem with their fertility. None of this mattered much while we lived in Palestine. My parents' marriage was after all no different to many other people's of their time, and the extended family and our neighbours had been there to paper over any cracks in their relationship. We had aunts, uncles and cousins to befriend and turn to. But in faraway London, isolated and in an alien environment, there was no one to call on for help. We found ourselves alone with our two parents, overwhelmed by the change in our circumstances and the new country we were forced to adapt to. We struggled alongside them, trying to cope with the problems of survival in London.

The misery of my first days at school, knowing not a word of English and feeling utterly lost amongst the other children and the teachers, can hardly be described. I hated everything about London, its immense size, its unfamiliar atmosphere and cold weather, and could not find a place for myself in it. The rupture between the warm, close-knit society we had been born into and the denuded nuclear family we had become was never healed. Our parents, struggling with their own lives, were in no position to compensate us children fully for our loss, and unequal to the task of giving us the love and security we needed. I longed ever afterwards for what I thought of as a proper family, whose members loved and supported each other, where the parents were calm and strong and the children felt secure.

We missed the Arab ideal of family united by strong bonds of loyalty and affection, the children helping each other and caring for their parents. Family relations were the bedrock of life that had sustained generations of Arabs in whatever difficult circumstances they found themselves. One only had to think of the Palestinian refugees in their camps, or the people under Israel's occupation who had managed to retain their sanity and humanity in the face of endless abuse, to understand the crucial role the typical Arab family played.

Whenever I was in the Arab world, it seemed to me there were such families all around me. I would see an enviable affection between fathers and daughters, praise such as we had never had from mothers for their children, admiration for any successes they attained, and closeness between siblings. In England, I would come across many young Arabs who had come for work or study, desperately homesick for the loving families they had left behind; they would telephone home every day, and look forward eagerly to spending holiday times with them.

The warmth of these relationships was unmistakeable, and the contrast with the typical English middle-class family was stark: to our eyes these families were cold and fragmented, the children uncaring about their ageing parents and, once grown up, often out of touch with them and their siblings. Arabs were fond of pointing out this contrast, feeling a sense of superiority over these miserable relationships as they saw them, and we felt the same. 'Look at these English,' our Arab friends would say, 'like cats. As soon as their kittens are weaned, they throw them out!'

But in truth many English families did not conform to this stereotype, and when I looked at ours, I could see little to feel superior about. Once past childhood and our shared experience of displacement and struggle, we went our different ways. Our characters and lifestyles diverged, and over time my brother and I drifted apart in 'typical' English fashion. When he and his Danish wife, after living in Copenhagen for more than thirty years, moved back to England and to a small village outside Cambridge, there was a superficial friendliness between us for a while; but it did not last, and we became estranged. My sister, who was the eldest, tried to keep up the connection between us, passing on our brother's news to me and vice versa, and she and I retained a certain closeness. As a child I had been devoted to her, told her my every secret and looked to her for what security I had – until one day she went to live with our uncle in Syria and left us all behind. It felt like a betrayal of all my childish trust and devotion, and things were never the same again between us.

With age, she became ever more religiously devout, faithfully adhering to all the Islamic rituals and reading the Quran every day. In those terms her life's direction and mine could not have been more different. At university I had begun hesitantly to question the Islamic faith I was brought up with, and soon afterwards the whole idea of religion and with it the very existence of God. These questionings hardened with time into a total rejection of all religious faith, as I looked about me at the tragedies and traumas repeatedly visited on innocent individuals and whole nations, without a trace of divine intervention to counter them. No religious explanation for this cruel paradox ever convinced me, nor could I comprehend the even greater paradox of turning to God in reaction to every disaster that a moment's reflection would have shown he either could not or would not avert.

An old friend with terminal cancer, whom I remember once visiting in Amman, told me in response to my concerned inquiry after her health: 'Thanks be to God. We do not question. All that comes from God is good.' While I doubted my sister would have gone that far, still I could see that her faith sustained her in some way and gave her a comfort I would never experience. I imagined she saw her God as a watchful, caring yet incomprehensible presence that held her within its overarching protection, and I would have longed for such security had I only been able to believe.

It grieved me that the three of us were not more close, but I knew it had been our parents' unhappy legacy to us. They never taught us how to love or support one another because no one had taught them either. Censure, rather than kindness, was the currency of our dealings with each other; we criticised each other's decisions and choices, often mercilessly and without sympathy or understanding, reflecting what we had grown up with. It was probably inevitable that we should relate to each other in that way, but I never stopped finding it hurtful and I never ceased to regret that it had to be like that. In many a bitter moment I would think how differently it could have turned out for us had our parents been otherwise, and for that, I think none of us loved them as we should have done. At such times the compassion I should have felt for them, every bit as traumatised as we were by the rupture in their lives and yet trying to give us shelter and care as best they could, deserted me.

So it was that we ended up having neither the advantages of an English family, whose members may have been cold but at least respected each other and had few expectations of the sort we had, nor those of the classic Arab unit with its warmth and closeness. I knew of course that my view of the Arab family I longed for was idealised. Many had their problems: siblings often disliked each other, parents could be neglectful or cruel, fathers were not always strong and dominant, and many a mother had the upper hand to the detriment of everyone else.

My father knew a family of five children whom I also

befriended, and visited whenever I was in Amman. Their material circumstances were good; all had received a decent education and enjoyed comfortable means. But the family was dominated by a strong, inflexible mother who ran their lives, made constant demands on them, and behaved in such a way as to suggest that she looked on them purely as vehicles for her own personal comfort. When I knew them she was quite old and shrunken, yet still wielded considerable power over the family. She never went out, complained that her husband and children had failed her, and yet insisted they should look after her. She refused to have a maid, as someone of her means and class would usually have done, and turned her daughters into servants and made her sons attend to all her other needs. Neither the husband nor any of the children, all of them grown up and with families of their own, could stand up to her. They obeyed her against their will and probably hated her, but were unable to free themselves from the hold she had on them. However, it did not make them stand together in this adversity; she sowed rivalry and competition among them from their early childhoods, and they could not rely on each other for support or sympathy.

One of her daughters, the best-looking and most talented of the girls, was a tragic victim of this set-up. While at university she had fallen for an Australian teacher whom her parents, and especially her mother, could not accept. The teacher returned the girl's feelings and wanted desperately to marry her. But mixed marriage was frowned on in Islamic society and was even illegal if contracted between a Muslim woman and a non-Muslim man. The parents, afraid that her reputation and theirs might suffer 'if people knew', quickly married her off to a doltish cousin who could never have aspired to marry her in the normal course of things; and thereby they felt they had buried her 'shame' in respectability. The girl spent a miserable life with this man, her promising career prospects shattered, and never forgot her first love.

It was this daughter in particular whom the mother picked on to provide for her daily needs, while never ceasing to remind her of the shame she nearly brought on the family. The poor woman meekly accepted her mother's cruelty and lack of maternal feeling, and served her like a skivvy; she was so browbeaten she had long given up any idea of rebellion, as had her siblings, who endured their servitude to the mother in their different ways. It was a sad story, but by no means unique. Here and there were families whose daughters were deliberately prevented from marrying in order to keep them at home as carers for their elderly parents. One of my cousins, all of whose sons had married, made sure of deterring any suitor who came for her only daughter's hand until the girl was considered too old to be marriageable. She ended up living with her widowed mother, a gloomy, embittered woman who would die off at some point, leaving the spinster daughter to a lonely old age.

These terrible stories still did not prevent me from holding to the vision I had clung to for years, of a warm, inclusive family somewhere that offered its love unconditionally and was a haven of security and support. I dreamed of having such a family, in fact spent a lifetime searching for it. The eagerness of that quest used to cloud my judgement of others. I trusted people too easily, mistook their pleasantries for genuine friendship, magnified affection into love, and often felt disappointed and betrayed. By contrast, my siblings, who must have wanted the same thing as I did, seemed to fare better. My sister found it in marriage to a fellow Palestinian with whom she produced four devoted children; and when the husband had gone and she was alone, she found compensation in the greater Islamic community she had joined.

My brother made his own family with his Danish wife and her daughter by a previous marriage, whom he looked on as his own, and later had a son to complete the family unit. Though he ended up living an isolated life in a Cambridgeshire village, he found solace in the company of his wife and the visits of his son and adopted daughter.

But for me it turned out differently. I searched in vain for that sense of inclusion and belonging I longed for and never ceased to regret not finding it, although the ardour of my quest eventually cooled down into resignation. Justifiably or not, I ascribed all the ills that befell me in my life afterwards to the lack of it, to the absence of the love and security that would have insulated me from a pitiless world. And for that I laid the blame squarely on my parents' shoulders. But yet, I should have understood that their part was but a small one in a much bigger story whose ramifications went well beyond their personal failings or ours.

Just as the ripples of a stone thrown into a pond will spread further and further away from the source, so the ripples of the disaster in 1948 hit my parents first and then spread to us and to our children long afterwards. Seeing only the ripples, it was easy to confuse the original cause with its effects.

CHAPTER 10

Evenings with My Father

I awoke the next morning to the sound of birdsong coming from the direction of Margo's room. She was in the habit of putting out stale bread on her windowsill for the sparrows in the garden each day. If she overslept, they would knock with their beaks against the window panes to wake her. I lay there in the quiet atmosphere of my father's flat and thought how far away occupied Palestine and its crises and dramas seemed. Israel, its soldiers, the checkpoints, the difficult crossings could have been on another planet for all their impact here. People in Amman were preoccupied with the problems of their own lives, high prices, little money, finding jobs, coping with unreliable services, dealing with unhelpful officials, and so on. There was often little sympathy to spare for their fellow Palestinians across the bridge labouring under a different yoke. I used to find this apparent indifference disconcerting and would try to break into banal conversations about the high cost of fuel or the problems of importing foreign cars with some shocking account of what I had seen in Jerusalem or Hebron.

Palestinian society in Jordan was markedly different from that in the West Bank. To a certain extent it was understandable, given the military occupation there and the relative freedom of life here. Nevertheless, that did not explain the parochial and often petty nature of people's preoccupations in Amman, their inability to look beyond their own lives and see a larger picture. They behaved as if the only issues that mattered were those concerning their families and daily lives. The political apathy they displayed towards events not far from their own doorsteps, and their inertia in the face of the often unfavourable political situation in Jordan itself were remarkable. It was not that they felt nothing for their fellow Palestinians, but rather that decades of living in a relatively stable Arab country where they had citizenship and a measure of rights had created a certain complacency and a desire to protect that status. It was as if they saw the depredations suffered by Palestinians at Israel's hands, the insecurity visited on them in many Arab countries from which they could be deported at will, and the struggle so many had had to survive in faraway places, not to speak of the refugees incarcerated in their camps, had made them decide they wanted no part of that misery and cling to what they had.

This bred a certain passivity of reaction in the face of Israel's repeated aggressions against the Palestinians under its control, a sense of resignation that nothing could be done. After all, no Arab state had been able to defeat Israel: in fact the Arabs were helpless against its power. How much less, therefore, could be expected of ordinary people like them? But in this stance there was also a weariness with the futility of past political struggle, the defeat of the PLO, the failure of Black September in 1970, when Jordanian forces quashed a Palestinian uprising in Amman, killing a large number of PLO fighters and refugees.[1] And worst of all, the Israeli takeover of the remnants of Palestine in 1967, which severed the direct connection across the Jordan River between the Palestinians of Jordan and those of Jerusalem and the West Bank. Perhaps it was not surprising after all that people concluded it was best to keep their heads down and get on with making their lives in Jordan.

---

1   In September 1970 a civil war erupted between the PLO, based in Jordan at the time, and King Hussein's forces which lasted for three weeks and led to the death of several thousand people. It was a devastating defeat for the PLO and led a year later to its expulsion from Jordan.

Many, however, continued to travel back and forth to see their families on the West Bank. They found a way of normalising the Israeli occupation by working around it, patiently submitting to the border restrictions, and focusing on their main aim of reaching the towns and villages where their relatives lived. Conversation about these visits was humdrum; no one complained about the injustice and the inconvenience of having to conform to Israeli rules despite the formal peace treaty concluded between Jordan and Israel in 1994, which should have led to the same ease of access for Jordanians going to the West Bank as for Israelis visiting Jordan. The Israeli occupation, like the refugee issue, had become a part of normal life, and Palestinian travellers endured the journey as best they could and did not question the difficulties.

Even though I knew that deep in their hearts no one had given up on the dream of regaining the homeland someday, I could see it had become a largely theoretical notion, to which many paid lip service, and which made no difference to the practicalities of everyday life. 'Inshallah,' people would say when asked about returning to their old homes in Palestine – literally meaning, 'If God wills it', but in common usage implying, 'Maybe. Who knows? Let's hope so.' Those lucky enough not to have ended up in refugee camps in 1948 or 1967 had little feeling for those who did. In 2005 there were some 338,000 refugees living in ten UN camps, since most had managed to find residence outside by then. The total refugee number in Jordan was in fact much larger, at nearly two million, and formed a sizeable percentage of Jordan's population of five and a half million.

I will never forget a visit I made to the largest of the camps, Baqa'a, some twelve miles north of Amman. It had a population of 100,000 and resembled a small town with its concrete houses, alleyways and shops. But nothing could disguise the poverty and overcrowding of the typical refugee camp, the piles of uncollected refuse, the high unemployment rate, especially amongst the young men hanging around, and the general state of disrepair. But yet there was in that camp an atmosphere I had not expected, a spirit of determination that transcended its shabby reality. To my surprise, people spoke not of their present hardship but of the return to the homeland, their right to reclaim their lost homes and lives there, and hoped it would not take too long to happen. To them it was no fantasy, but a solid belief in the inevitable recognition of the justice of their cause.

And I remember realising then what it was that distinguished this and all Palestinian refugee camps from their surroundings. On the outside, Baqa'a was a place in Jordan, but inside, it was a corner of Palestine that still lived on. No wonder the Israelis so hated the camps and attacked them at every opportunity. They too understood that, despite their poverty and marginalisation, the camps were islands of memory in an erased landscape, faithful repositories of a Palestinian history Israel had wanted obliterated. And for that Israel wanted them dismantled and their refugees turned into 'immigrants', scattered and dispersed in the various countries that would take them.

I was touched and uplifted by what I saw that day at Baqa'a, but when I later spoke of my experience to those other Palestinians living in Amman, it aroused little more than a passing interest. For them the refugees were neatly in their camps, out of sight and out of mind. That was especially true of the younger generations of Palestinians born in Jordan, who knew little of the history of Palestine or the dispossessions of 1948 and 1967. That story was not told to them at their schools, where Jordanian history, and in particular that of the Hashemite dynasty which ruled the country, was emphasised. It was little wonder they grew up with an indifferent attitude to their Palestinian origins.

Once, in the summer of 1970, just over twenty years after the Nakba, I happened to be on a visit to Amman and found myself briefly caught up in the skirmishes between the PLO and the Jordanian army that preceded Black September two months later. The Palestinian family I was staying with at the time was frustrated and frightened by what was happening, as indeed I was. We were all cooped up in their flat during the curfews imposed by the army, and the more dangerous the situation grew, the more their son, who was about twelve years old, called in panic on King Hussein, the reigning monarch at that time, to protect us. He would stand and make a military-style salute before the king's large portrait which had pride of place in their sitting room, while his older sister repeatedly cursed the Palestinian fighters for causing this conflict around us.

I knew few families that would have gone so far, and my father did not accord them much importance. 'What can you expect when the father works for Jordanian TV, and has been vetted by the security services a hundred times?' he had commented. But even in those families that did not take the same line, the children saw Palestine as predominantly an issue for their parents, not for them. It was a place their older relatives might visit, but they themselves had no plans to do the same.

I could not accept these positions. They filled me with dismay and disappointment. How could it be that so many of us in Britain, Palestinians and supporters alike, were passionately committed to the struggle against Israel, while the people closest to Palestine were this disengaged? How ironic that Israel, struggling to create an artificial social cohesion amongst its disparate immigrant groups where none had existed before, should have succeeded in breaking up our naturally cohesive society, separating us from one another until we neither knew nor cared how those not under our noses lived. Each of us had become wrapped up in our particular community, laden with its problems and unable to see beyond our immediate concerns.

* * *

Friday in Amman was quiet and for me, rather boring. But for my father it was the day on which he received his regular weekly visitors, all men and all devoted to him in their own way. The earliest of these were one or two unhappy people who came for morning coffee to tell my father about their problems. They were a collection of what I called no-hopers my father had somehow adopted, and whom I dubbed members of his 'Society of Poor Souls'. This amused him and we defined a variety of membership categories for the Society. Full members were the most miserable; others not so badly off became associate members; and a third category of honorary members was reserved for people on the way to becoming associate members and possibly full members later on. How my father managed to listen with such equanimity to variations of the same sad stories they related week after week baffled me.

After the Poor Souls had gone, the next wave of visitors appeared – men in their late seventies and older, though none as old as my father. He used to say afterwards he found them tedious, but they were cheerful and lively, talked about his favourite subject, politics, and he actually enjoyed their company. At the appropriate moment when he took the stage, so to speak, they quietened down and listened to him attentively and without interruption while he declaimed his views on Islam and the West as he invariably did. These meetings reminded me of similar gatherings in London when I was a child. Men friends of my father's would turn up at our house and talk politics, and my mother or I would serve them coffee and otherwise keep out of the way.

This time it was Margo who served the coffee while I slipped out through the back door and left them to it just as the Friday lunchtime sermon was getting under way, relayed in a booming reproving voice over the loudspeakers that were fitted to every mosque. There was no escape from it. I had learnt to ignore the calls to prayer in the daytime, but the dawn prayer woke me early every morning. It came from the mosque behind and uphill from my father's building and the sound was impossible to avoid. Amman was full of mosques; they were dotted about in every neighbourhood as if to remind people of their duty to worship God. I saw in it an insistent and oppressive religiosity which had crept in over recent years and was taking over the country in a conspicuous and tangible way that could not be ignored.

More women wore the hijab than I had ever seen in Amman before, and a growing minority covered their faces too. Feminine instinct being what it is, the younger women experimented with making their headscarves more alluring, sometimes two-tone in colour to match their clothes and consisting of a close-fitting cap in one colour overlaid by a longer head covering, resembling the chain-mail headdress of medieval European knights, in a different shade. Or sometimes they would affix a glittering brooch to the side of the headscarf, or wear tight trousers that outlined their every curve. An innovation was just coming in at the time, to place a large artificial bun on the back of the head that made the overlying scarf bulge becomingly. Long over-garments edged with silver or gold thread down the sleeves and bodices were a new feature, and sometimes the girls wore low-cut sun dresses in the Western style that would have been unacceptably revealing had it not been for the long-sleeved sweaters they wore underneath to cover their breast and arms. And in many cases, though the hair was covered, the face was heavily made up, kohl alluringly drawn around the eyes, lids painted with eye shadow of various hues, and distinctive lipstick.

At one time, when one got into a taxi, its radio would be turned on to the news or a music station; but that had given way to recitations of the Quran or to pious sermons. The latter were usually intoned in sonorous, reverential tones and took the form of questions and answers relating to matters of religious belief or practice. More often than not the drivers of such taxis were ostentatiously bearded and made sure that their radios were turned up loudly as if to make sure their passengers did not escape these improving broadcasts, whether they agreed or not. When I once asked the driver of such a taxi to reduce the volume on his radio, he stared at me in the rearview mirror and asked, 'Why, are you a Christian?'

I took a walk along the emptying streets as men headed slowly in groups of twos and threes uphill towards the mosque to perform the noon prayer. Although it was hot it was also pleasant; hardly a single car drove by; there was little activity around the supermarket, which looked closed although it was not; and a quiet settled over the city, rather like an English Sunday used to be before shopping was allowed and turned it into a day like any other. I walked on through the residential streets behind the main road. Having reached a parade of shops, all closed, some distance from the house I turned back and took a parallel road to the one I had used to get there. On this route I passed a modest building named the Palm Hotel on account of an old dusty palm tree that stood in its tiled forecourt. To my surprise I saw a couple seated on plastic chairs in the shady open space just outside the hotel's front door. The man had a great bushy beard, a three-quarter-length *dishdasheh* – a loose traditional caftan – that revealed a pair of hairy legs, and the woman was entirely covered in black. Nothing of her features could be discerned behind her face covering. They were evidently taking the air, though what air she could have breathed through her thick veil I could not imagine.

The picture they made as they sat there was so eloquent, so telling about the Arab world and what it had come to, it filled me with despair. The man, seeing me staring at them, smiled and beckoned me to come nearer with a wave of his hand. He was friendly and evidently curious about me. 'Welcome,' he said, 'please join us.' But I shook my head, afraid I would say something I might regret, and crossed the road away from where they were sitting. The thought arose irresistibly in my mind that had I been a Western journalist I could have had a field day photographing the two of them for my newspaper. The picture they made conformed to every cheap Western stereotype about Islam and appealed to every prejudice and sense of distaste the West felt for Muslims. I hurried away with a wave of farewell, no doubt leaving them mystified as to who I was and why I had been staring at them.

When I told my father about the encounter over lunch, he disagreed with my reaction, much to my surprise.

'What did they do wrong?' he asked. 'That's the way they dress in the Gulf. It's a tradition, no more than that.'

'But don't you see, it plays exactly into the hands of the West which you're always saying hates Muslims and Islam?'

He shook his head. 'No, no. Western attitudes to Islam go much deeper. They're about ideology and colonialism.' As he launched into his favourite topic with relish, I regretted I had said anything at all. But I could not leave it at that. When he paused in his exposé of the West's treachery against Islam, I jumped in.

'All of that does not explain the wave of religiosity that's sweeping through this country and the rest of the Arab world. That's what I saw in that couple. You can see it for yourself, and I know you don't think there's any actual religious basis to much of the behaviour of people around us.' He said nothing. 'Don't you see a terrible regression in it, a retreat into the past, back to – I don't know – seventh-century Arabia or something? I get the feeling that's more real for many people here than the present. Isn't that what's going on?'

He was looking at me intently. 'What I mean is,' I continued heatedly, 'it's safer living in the past, isn't it, rather than facing the present, having to do something about the awful situation we're in. For God's sake, Israel is on the doorstep. How's covering your hair and growing a beard going to help with that?'

My father spoke at last. 'But that's exactly the point. Who do you think planted Israel here in the first place and left the Arabs lumbered with it? Who arms Israel so that it will dominate a region which can't ever catch up, and who has kept the Arabs dependent and enslaved? How do you expect them to fight back?' He paused. 'Islam is all they have left. Would you take that away too?'

It was my turn to be silent. 'You need to think more about these things,' he admonished. 'People have reasons for what they do.' That particular explanation had occurred to me too, but it was strange how my father, even now, still had the knack of making me feel my ideas were somehow inferior and half-baked. No amount of cleverness or erudition on my part ever managed to impress him. He had made up his mind on the issue and his opinion must prevail: what I saw as a mass Arab retreat into religion, and from there into irrelevance, he saw as a defence against Western aggression.

'All right,' I said. 'I'll give you that it may be playing some part in this mess. But it's not the whole story.' I wanted to go on to say, using his earlier phrase to me, it went much deeper, that it was a form of escapism from intolerable helplessness – rather like the exaggerated responses to football matches against foreign teams that sent the whole of Amman into a frenzy of excitement, or the ubiquitous obsession with eating that made food the focus and centre of daily life and had caused an epidemic of obesity amongst the better-off. And perhaps, I thought, the same also went for the trivial preoccupations that engaged so many Palestinians and let them forget Palestine. But he plainly considered the matter closed, and when Margo appeared he went off for his siesta.

The next day, Saturday, was one of the high spots of my father's week, the occasion of the second of his regular rendezvous with his cronies. But these were different to the Friday gatherings, and he enjoyed them much more. I looked forward to the evening too, glad of the distraction from a depressing visit I had made earlier in the day that had left me even more disaffected with the state of Arab society than when I saw the couple outside the Palm Hotel on Friday.

I had gone to see Maha, a young woman I had known since she was a child, and whom I called on each time I was in Amman. Expecting to see her usual cheerful face and welcoming smile when she opened the door, I found instead a woman totally changed. When I had last seen her a year before, she was a happy and contented wife, busily running her household and caring for her husband and children. The person that faced me that morning when I knocked on her door was someone I hardly knew.

'What's happened?' I asked anxiously. 'Has someone died?'

'Oh yes, by God! You could say that!' she said vehemently. Taking my hand, she drew me into the house and, barely waiting for me to sit down, poured out her story. It related to events dating back to a year before, soon after I had last seen her, but it was clear they were as vivid to her as if they had just happened. She must have told the same story many times over, but I was a fresh arrival on the scene and a new listener to confide in. It seemed that her husband, to whom she was devoted and who she thought loved her equally in return, was leading a double life, with a second wife and family which he had kept totally secret from her and their children. I thought about the many times I had met him, a pleasant, ordinary man with unexceptional looks and polite manners. He did not strike me as a philanderer, and I found myself as astounded as Maha must have been to hear this story.

'I've wondered so often, why, why did he do it? Because I had no sons? Was that it?' Maha, a pampered daughter of a loving family, brought up to believe she was very special, had married young, when she was barely out of school. In the conventional way of such marriages, she had settled down to a life of wifedom and childbearing. But a string of daughters was the only result, not a happy situation for Arab women, whose husbands usually wanted sons. In such cases a man might well think of taking another wife, a position that society found understandable and did not discourage; not infrequently, it was the female relatives of such men who helped them to find the new woman. But despite the arrival of one daughter after another, Maha's husband showed no signs of straying, and she thought that all was well.

Like most other Arab states, Jordan was governed by shari'a law in all matters pertaining to the family and the position of women. Accordingly, polygamy was legal and Maha's husband was perfectly within his rights to marry a second, or even a third or a fourth woman, with no need to conceal it. In practice, though, taking a second wife was the most usual form of polygamy for financial reasons as much as anything else. Men with more than one wife were obliged to treat them equitably and support them financially, which was often beyond the means of most people.

The discovery of his duplicity had been like a thunderclap out of nowhere, and Maha could hardly take it in. She reacted with rage, disbelief and rejection of the new reality thrust upon her. She thought of vengeance, of flight from the family home, of setting her brothers on her husband and his family, of attacking the other woman. But her fury and distress soon gave way to the cold realisation that her freedom of action in such a situation was exceedingly limited. Having no formal training, she could not hope to find work if she struck out on her own. She could return to her parents' home, but they were elderly and she would only be a burden to them if she went to live there. Her brothers, all married with their own families, were likewise unable to take her in. Even worse, she could lose the custody of her children if she left the matrimonial home, and her daughters' chances of marriage might be impaired by their mother's divorce. They were badly traumatised as it was by their father's betrayal and the break-up of their previously harmonious home life.

Much against her will, Maha learnt to swallow her ire and tried to accustom herself to her new life. Now that things were out in the open, her husband spent some nights with her and others with his second family. Gradually the periods he spent with Maha got shorter, and he stayed most of the time with her rival.

'For me, I don't care if he never comes back here, ever!' she declared defiantly. 'But it's important for the girls.' That was not entirely true, and I could see that she still loved him; hardly surprising, since he was the first and only man she had ever known. In the face of the crisis in her life, she grew more religious, prayed and fasted regularly, which gave her comfort, and allowed her home to be used as a place for religious instruction to the children of her friends imparted by what were called religious guides, mostly women from Syria whose job it was to preach Islamic doctrine to gatherings of other women or their children. Well-meaning people respected these guides and opened their homes to them, though on what basis they could claim expertise in the teaching roles they professed was not clear. They usually charged a fee for their attendance and made a good living out of it.

Maha was not the first woman I had heard of to whom such a thing had happened, and her story was not unfamiliar in Arab society, but seeing its effects at close quarters on someone I cared for moved me ineffably. I later recounted it to Arab women friends in London, all firm Muslim believers.

'Yes, very sad,' they said. 'But what you're talking about is not Islam. It's what men like to do. They always interpret the Quran to their own advantage. The Quran says quite clearly that polygamy is only allowed on condition that the husband feels he can treat his wives equitably in every way. And the next verse goes on to say that men will never be able to do that, even if they wished to, and so, by implication, they should marry only one.'

'So, is polygamy allowed or not?'

'Let's say it's not recommended. And don't forget that Arabia at the time was full of widows and orphans left behind with no one to care for them when so many of the men died in battle. So permission for men to have more than one wife in those circumstances made polygamy a social necessity. But even then it was the exception, not the rule.'

'Be that as it may,' one of the other women summed up, 'I look at it like this. Polygamy isn't peculiar to Muslims, even if it's not called that in other cultures. How about all the women over here whose partners or husbands have mistresses they keep hidden until there's a showdown and people walk out, leaving the children. At least under shari'a law no one has to walk out. The husband is obliged to support both women, their children are all equally legitimate and have equal rights to support and inheritance, and both wives have recognised positions in society. Your friend's not going to lose her home or have to fend for her daughters on her own. You've got to look at it like that too.'

When I mentioned Maha's story to my father, who disapproved of the practice of polygamy and thought it destructive of family life, he shook his head regretfully. 'Poor woman,' he said. 'I know about her case. She asked for my help at the beginning. But what could I tell her? She didn't have much choice.'

The pattern of each Saturday was the same. After my father had had his siesta and afternoon coffee, he would prepare himself for the evening. Margo usually helped him to wash and shave, and he would put on a fresh dressing gown. In recent years he had taken to wearing a dressing gown all the time while at home, because he said he was more comfortable like that. On the occasions when he went out and had to wear a suit, the first thing he did on returning was to take it off and get back into his dressing gown.

The Saturday meetings always started promptly at eight in the evening, which was the hour when Dr Sami Khoury, the mainstay of the gathering, arrived. He was often joined by another regular, Mrs Rabiha Dajani, an eccentric, opinionated and imperious character in her eighties who was the nearest thing I knew to a Palestinian Grande Dame. I had met her originally in the early 1970s in Kuwait, where I had gone for a brief visit to stay with my cousins Zuhair and Aziza. While there, I was persuaded to be introduced in the Arab way to her eldest son with a view to making a match between us. I remember Rabiha at the time as a daunting but persuasive and charming woman, generous with the handsome, expensive presents she later sent me via her son in anticipation of a successful union. He was an engineer by profession, a nice enough young man and evidently the apple of her eye. But in those days I was wedded to the idea that I was more English than Arab and wanted to belong to English society. Although at first I was intrigued by the prospect of meeting a man who might become a future husband, I soon found that such Arab mating manoeuvres left me cold, and I suspected afterwards that even had Rabiha's son been a paragon of virtue, he would still have found no favour in my eyes. Inevitably, it never worked out and he went on to marry someone else.

How differently I came to see those Arab customs later, not only in the wreckage of my own unwise unions, but in the desperation of many a woman friend in England reaching middle age or beyond, alone and unpartnered, unable to meet a suitable or any man and fearful that she never would. Such could have been the fate of my friend Sumayya in English society had she lived there. She had reached her forties and still found no husband. In her youth she had turned down many a suitor who came forward in the usual way, through her parents, as not quite what she was looking for, until she was considered too old and no one asked for her hand any more. In an attempt to improve her chances she had travelled, worked in London where I first met her, but still her luck did not turn. Returning to her family in Amman, she finally asked her married sister and women friends for help. It was the accepted custom, and there was no shame in it. The sister and her friends asked around and soon came up with a recently widowed man who had a suitable job and reasonable means.

The only problem was that he had four children by his previous marriage for whom he was responsible. But Sumayya and he liked each other at first sight and got married soon thereafter. It was not the marriage she had dreamt about, and her new stepchildren were a hindrance, but she thought herself lucky not to have ended up with a much older man, as was the pattern for women of her age. The available men usually wanted much younger women, even when they themselves were getting on in age. However, she had few regrets: a married woman with a husband and her own home had a social status, and the alternative of becoming an ageing spinster caring for her elderly parents was unthinkable. Unappetising as her marriage seemed to me at first, I could think of many a lonely friend in England who would have been similarly tempted.

Rabiha was different. Widowed twice and living alone, she enjoyed her single life and had no wish to change it. She had aged well. Despite her slight figure – she was less than five feet in height – she was still handsome, with a striking presence, always colourfully dressed, carefully made up, and more often than not sporting a red flower in her hair. I had always admired her flair and forcefulness, never more so than when she flirted gently with my father, which rather tickled him and made us call her playfully his 'girlfriend'. With me, she behaved as if we had never met thirty years before and the marriage to her son had never been proposed.

Dr Sami was an altogether different sort. He was a retired Palestinian surgeon originally from Nablus, well known in Jordan for his medical work and the hospital he had established in Amman, which he had named the Palestine Hospital – against much initial Jordanian opposition to his using the word Palestine. He was widely respected and a man of eclectic tastes, well read, interested in opera and music, and enormously charming and warm. His long years in Amman and the success of his professional life in Jordan had done nothing to dim his passion for his original homeland or its cause. I used to love listening to him recount tales of his time as a young surgeon during the last years of the British Mandate in Palestine. He had a deep, resonant voice, at odds with his small stature, and a compelling way of retailing his experiences.

He once told me that sometime in 1947, one year before the Mandate ended, he had been on duty at the hospital in Jerusalem when British soldiers brought in a Jewish fighter, a terrorist as they called him, for emergency treatment. It was the time when Jewish militias in Palestine had turned against their British benefactors, attacking British targets in a ferocious bid to drive them from the country. The British authorities retaliated mercilessly, and Jewish terrorists guilty of killing soldiers were usually executed. Such a man was the Jewish fighter who confronted Dr Sami that day. He was asked to treat him and then return him to his British captors.

'What a dilemma,' I said, 'The man had presumably killed many Arabs too.' Dr Sami nodded. 'What did you do?'

'Well, of course I knew that he was our enemy before he was anything else. He and his kind wanted the British out so as to have a free hand to deal with us. By rights, I should have refused to help him. But, as a doctor and as a human being, I couldn't.'

'What was wrong with him?'

'It was a case of acute appendicitis and it was necessary to operate or he would have died. So I did, and it saved his life. As soon as he was well enough I handed him back to the soldiers as they had requested. But I never forgot him. While he was in the hospital he talked freely to me about his passion for his cause, his willingness to die for it, that he had a suicide pill on him which he would take unhesitatingly before the British executed him to rob them of the satisfaction of seeing him punished.'

'What was there to remember about him?'

'He was passionately, genuinely committed to what he believed in and ready to give it everything he had, including his life. Despite myself I could not help feeling a sort of admiration for him. If his cause had not been so unjust and so inimical to ours, I would have wished that such a man was one of our fighters and not theirs.'

My father and Dr Sami first got to know each other when my parents moved to Amman. Though he knew my father by reputation, they had never met until then. But having done so, and despite the apparent differences between them – the one a scholar and literary man, the other a surgeon and bon viveur – they went on to develop an unusual, deep friendship which endured until the end. When illness overtook my father, it was to the Palestine Hospital that he went, where Dr Sami tended to him and organised his care. There was something touching about the relationship between the two of them. Dr Sami, despite his achievements, looked up to my father as a mentor, a teacher almost, and a treasure-house of knowledge to be prized and admired; and my father saw in Dr Sami a man with a receptive, appreciative mind, eager for debate and yet prepared to listen and defer to the other's opinion. Even their body language when they got together reflected these dispositions. My father would sit in his customary place at one end of the sofa and Dr Sami would sit directly opposite, the coffee table between them. His armchair was at a slightly lower level to the sofa, so that he was looking up at my father.

No sooner was it eight o'clock than Dr Sami arrived at the door, punctual as ever, and came into the sitting room where my father waited. A look of pleasure spread all over my father's features in anticipation of the evening they were going to have. Rabiha, who arrived later, started off the gathering with a burst of light-hearted, teasing chatter mainly aimed at my father. But she soon gave way to the men, who were itching to engage in the conversation that really interested them. Everyone found these occasions enjoyable and instructive, so unusual in Amman society, where people tended to get together to gossip and exchange news about matters of the day rather than take part in discussions about ideas.

Word about these evenings soon got around. As a result, a number of hangers-on started to invite themselves and join in. One of these was Abu Firas, a building contractor with a good business sense but little education. He sat and smoked the whole time, but occasionally felt impelled to throw in his opinions as well, whether relevant or not. Fortunately, he never stayed long, which was more than could be said for another of the hangers-on, an ageing widow called Um Ahmad, who started to turn up though no one knew why. She never said anything; and her sole pretext for coming was based on a tenuous connection with our family through being a relative of a woman who knew my sister. She arrived every Saturday with the others or shortly afterwards, laden with heavy shopping bags from the Safeway supermarket opposite, and sat quietly through the whole evening until it was time to go home. It was as if her visits to us were an interlude between her weekly shop and the ride home in Dr Sami's car, which he inevitably had to offer her each time.

Rabiha, as was her wont, had made an elaborate cake which was served with coffee. Dr Sami preferred it that way; he ate little at night, and never accepted a dinner invitation from us. The conversation turned to the favourite topic of religion, on which my father dilated, discussing the differences between Christianity and Islam. It did not bother him that Dr Sami was a Christian, and the latter took no offence at my father's often critical opinions. On that evening, it was the subject of miracles that preoccupied him.

'Miracles,' my father asserted, 'are essential to Christianity. Without them there would be no Christianity. Take the many miracles enacted by Jesus Christ, turning water into wine, walking on water, healing the leper, and the greatest miracles of them all, the virgin birth and the resurrection.'

'I agree,' responded Dr Sami mildly.

'The problem is you have to suspend disbelief in order to be a Christian at all,' continued my father. 'It's the essential basis of Christianity. Whereas in Islam everything that happened was factual, historical, and needed no magic. Muhammad was a man with no divinity attached to him at all.'

I thought my father had gone too far, but Dr Sami did not seem at all put out. He merely looked attentive. 'Fine. But let me in my turn ask you why you think it matters.'

'You mean you don't mind if your religion is all a myth?'

Dr Sami laughed. 'I mean, it doesn't bother me. I take no account of these stories. For me, God is nothing to do with them because he is about something else: love, pure love, the love between men and women, of parents for their children, of friends for each other, for the wonders of this world, beautiful music, the glories of nature. That's God. He's not "up there". He's down here, amongst us.'

I could see this did not satisfy my father, who had been put off course by Dr Sami's response. He paused politely to let the moment pass, and then resumed developing his previous theme, that concrete reality and documented history were essential to religion; without them, it might as well be Greek mythology.

'The point here is that believing in miracles encourages magical thinking, and from that type of thinking it's an easy step to superstition and fear. If you can't understand what's around you through your reason, you will become irrational and dangerous. You only have to think of the European witch hunts in the Middle Ages or the people burnt at the stake for so-called heresies to see the truth of this.'

They talked on amiably about this point, but I was no longer listening. My thoughts had left the gathering and turned to the anticipation of what lay before me the next morning when this restful interlude with my father and his friends would end and I would have to make my way back to Ramallah: to Dr Farid and his hostile deputy, to the office and its unhappy workers, to the pointless conference I had temporarily escaped from, to Israel's overarching, menacing presence, and most of all to my lonely flat and its echoing rooms where I did not feel at home. It was not a pleasant prospect and I did not want to go.

CHAPTER 11

Gaza

Israel's preparations for disengaging from Gaza were growing apace, and the evacuation of Jewish settlers would soon begin. The Palestinians were jubilant and had planned celebrations for the big day with flags and placards. The head of UNDP was to be in Gaza for these events, and I found myself infected by people's enthusiasm. I wanted to be there too, and it rankled with me that Dr Farid had refused to let me go. Palestinians believed that it was the brave resistance of Gaza's people that had made Israel's occupation of the Strip too onerous and finally persuaded its army and settlers to leave with their proverbial tails between their legs. Oblivious to such inter-pretations, Ariel Sharon was being internationally praised for his Disengagement Plan, which President Bush, who had met him earlier in Washington, described as 'historic and coura-geous', while other Western leaders were hailing Sharon as a 'man of peace'.

When I said goodbye to my father at breakfast, he looked crestfallen and so forlorn that I longed for one of my siblings to come to his aid. But it was not yet time for their visits and I did not think they would agree. His sad expression stayed with me, and I often wondered afterwards how it was that, when all of us prized our father so much, were proud to be his children and basked in other people's admiration for him, none was prepared to interrupt the humdrum routine of their lives to come to his rescue. Nor could I congratulate myself on my own better record in that regard, since I was in the region already for other reasons. Perhaps, looking back, I should have insisted that the three of us work out a rota of visits to ensure he was not left alone in the short time left to him. But we were not that sort of family, and each of us had worked out a convenient routine that was not easily broken. He asked when I would be back, and I promised that I would not stay away for long.

The crossing over the King Hussein Bridge, as the Allenby Bridge was called on the Jordanian side, took over four hours of hold-ups and inspections by Israeli border officials. But I was finally on my way back to Ramallah and the ministry, where I went straight away for fear of being too late. Amin was back using his desk, but I had been given another in what had become a crowded office. Dr Farid was in his room, I was told, and had asked to see me. My immediate fear was that he would ask for news of progress on the conference, which I had managed to forget about while in Amman. He greeted me with his usual effusiveness.

'Please sit down. I have some good news for you. You'll be glad to hear that the Israelis have given permission for you to visit Gaza.' For a minute I thought he had relented and that I would be covering the disengagement after all. But he went on, 'UNDP is sending a group to Gaza tomorrow morning on one of their regular visits and you can join them. I will tell our office to expect you when you get to Gaza and give you what assistance you need. I shall follow on and will hope to see you there.'

He asked Adel, who had come into the room, to give me the telephone numbers of the PA's Gaza office and of several people who would be there to help me. 'We've booked you into the Beach Hotel and you will be able to return with the UNDP car when they've finished their work.' This was a routine work trip for UNDP staff who coordinated projects in Gaza and, as I later learnt, it was the UNDP office that had applied for my visa and got clearance from the Israeli authorities. Israel required all visitors to Gaza to obtain entry visas. I knew Dr Farid's chances of effecting the same result were limited even though he was a senior Palestinian Authority figure. The Israelis could and frequently did turn down requests from PA officials on a whim; the UN was more difficult to resist. Still, I thought, who cares, as long as I get there. To my relief there was no mention of the conference, only that I would have use of a mobile phone while in Gaza.

Preparations for the conference, however, had not been shelved as I had hoped. In my absence Amin had been given the task of making contact with potential participants. He had not liked that and confined his communications to those from Arab countries; visitors from the West, even if Arabs, were left to me. Ilan Halevi, whom Dr Farid respected and liked, had been asked to advise on the conference. He had proffered a number of ideas, but they would need to be implemented by someone else. I wondered hopefully if he had drawn up the conference statement or any of the other conference papers, but his contribution had been mainly verbal and I was still saddled with those tasks.

I spent the rest of the day in the office and went home early to make ready for the trip to Gaza the next day. I looked for Annetta, but she was not around, and the gatekeeper told me she had been out all day. René was in his flat, but I did not feel like seeing his mournful face. Ever since he lost the water engineering contract with the PA, he had gone around moping and aggrieved at his unfair treatment and complaining that it had ruined his whole experience with the Palestinians. In happier days he would cheerfully have kept calling me (and every other Palestinian woman he knew) his 'Arabian princess', and declaiming that we were 'friends forever'. But no more; all that was gone in the general gloom that engulfed him.

The next morning I made my way to the Qalandia checkpoint to await the UNDP car that would pick me up to go to

Jerusalem. The sun was not yet hot as I stood on the other side of the checkpoint amidst the Pepsi sellers and men touting for taxis, with the Israeli watchtower high above. From it unseen voices yelled out every now and then through loudspeakers, ordering people below to hurry along. 'Get going, you dogs! Move!' More expletives followed but, unruffled by it, a taxi tout came up to me and asked, '*Hajjeh*! Need a car to Jerusalem?' I looked at him in astonishment: anything less like a *hajjeh* than myself that morning, in jeans and T-shirt, my linen hat on my head and huge, fashionable sunglasses perched over my nose, could not be imagined. I felt like protesting, but the UN car arrived at that moment to pick me up and we drove off to Jerusalem.

The party that finally set off from Jerusalem consisted of myself and four UNDP workers, with Ayman, whom I had met at Maher's dinner party, in charge. They were all young people who had made the trip to Gaza several times before. Gaza was forty-eight miles away from Jerusalem and it took us nearly two hours to reach the Erez checkpoint marking the 'border' with Israel. Absurd to call it that, as if Gaza were another country and not merely the coastal extension of the same land. But the sight of the crossing, a formidable series of concrete buildings set into a high metal perimeter fence, reinforced the idea of a border terminal between two countries. Only internationals, officials and people governed by the PA could use the crossing. In practice and since Israel increased its restrictions on the movement of Palestinians after the Second Intifada, the Erez crossing was much less used. But that did nothing to lessen the military character of the place which was bristling with soldiers, security cameras and multiple types of surveillance equipment. High above the ground in offices overlooking the checkpoint, armed soldiers watched proceedings below through closed-circuit TV. From time to time they barked out orders through loudspeakers, and once again the image sprang into my mind – as it had when I stood before the separation wall at Abu Dis – of a horde of crazed, bloodthirsty Palestinians straining to get at Israel from behind the barricades.

As a UN party we were spared the treatment meted out to ordinary Palestinians and other visitors, including journalists. They had to cross Erez on foot through a kilometre-long labyrinth of high concrete walls and corrugated metal roof. It was closed at both ends by heavy steel doors; once through the first door, pedestrians walked along a narrow, dingy tunnel fitted with cameras and punctuated by a series of tall turnstiles that could suddenly lock, trapping the person inside until the soldiers gave the order to open them. In this section of the crossing, no actual soldiers were to be seen; their presence could only be discerned by the eerie sound of their disembodied voices coming through loudspeakers from somewhere above, giving commands to those inside the passage. People might be told to lay down their bags on the ground, turn slowly around before the cameras, take off their coats or jackets, and the like.

I had passed through a similar passageway at the checkpoint outside Bethlehem. It had been the stuff of nightmares, tortuous, poorly lit and frightening, and I remember wondering how a child would feel, trapped in such a place. This crossing, though, was much worse, and on that sweltering August day I could only imagine the horror of the furnace inside the airless tunnels under their oven-hot metal roof. A year before, a Palestinian worker trying to go through the same passageway crowded with others had suffocated to death. For these reasons the Erez checkpoint had a fearsome reputation among Palestinians. By contrast, the Israeli officials on our side of the crossing were relaxed and quite friendly. Such behaviour was clearly reserved for people like us and, had it not been for the caged passageway on the other side of the air-conditioned checkpoint building where we waited for our passports to be cleared, one could almost be persuaded that Erez was a normal crossing point with ordinary, polite officials carrying out their routine duties.

Going across to the Gaza side of the checkpoint we drove through the security zone created by Israel on what had been Gaza farmland, and to which no Gazan was allowed access thereafter; at the end of the zone Palestinian border officials checked us again, as was the protocol. Driving towards Gaza City, it was as if we had indeed crossed into another country: a third-world place of dusty uneven roads and litter, unimaginably different to the ultra-modern Israel we had left a short while before. It had been much worse when I was there in 1993, just before Arafat and the PLO made Gaza their headquarters, when half-demolished buildings with gaping holes for walls and twisted metal and wire everywhere were commonplace in the aftermath of several recent Israeli bombings.

In amongst the old dilapidated houses stood incongruous, freshly constructed white buildings, said to belong to a new, moneyed class of PLO officials who had accompanied Arafat on his return from exile in Tunis. The city was full of noisy traffic, cars, trucks and the occasional donkey cart. Several streets were blocked off by sandbags or petrol barrels, set up by the Israeli army to control the city. One or two Israeli military jeeps with bars over their windscreens drove past. But people went about their business as if the Israelis did not exist, and despite the poverty evident everywhere there was a striking buzz and vibrancy to the atmosphere I had not expected.

The Beach Hotel I had been booked into was a modest place by the sea, and the rest of our party was in the next building. As I arrived I found a young man called Tariq waiting for me in the foyer, apparently assigned by Dr Farid's office to be my companion and driver during my stay. I wondered if Dr Farid were trying to compensate me for not being allowed to attend the Gaza disengagement, but I was grateful for the use of Tariq's car, decrepit and ancient though it was. Walking any distance in that hot and humid weather would have been impossible. It was by then nearly lunchtime, but I thought it best to call in on the Ministry of Media and Communications to register my arrival. It was housed in a building shared by the offices of Muhammad Dahlan, the man I had briefly seen at the American Colony Hotel in Jerusalem with Tim Rothermell a few weeks back. Dahlan represented the PA in Gaza as a member of the Palestinian National Council and commander of the largest military force in the Strip. He wielded much power and, it was said, ruled almost independently of Mahmoud Abbas and the PA in Ramallah.

When Rami, the man in charge of the Gaza ministry office, invited me to lunch, he explained something of the situation. The crowded, popular restaurant he took me to was famous for its food, in particular its fish, freshly caught from the sea and prepared in a variety of delicious ways. It was normally open to the air, but during the day was roofed over like a tent to protect against the baking sun. Despite the excellent cuisine it was a shabby, homely place, teeming with young waiters and full of noise. We had no sooner sat down than there was a commotion at the door and a group of armed men in uniform muscled their way past the waiters. With them was a thick-set, bearded young man with a red kuffiya wound around his head and a gun sticking out from its holster in the belt of his trousers. He had a swaggering walk and made his way with his companions past our table and into the centre of the res-taurant as if he owned it, calling loudly for the owner. As soon as his voice rang out, several waiters rushed over in effusive greeting and obsequiously escorted the group to a table.

'Who are they?'

Rami smiled. 'They're members of our security services. Haven't you ever seen them before? The man in the red kuffiya is Dahlan's personal bodyguard.'

'I don't mean to be offensive,' I said, 'but he looks like a thug. Why does Dahlan need guards anyway?'

'Shh. Please keep your voice down. There's a power struggle here between different sides, and Dahlan has enemies.' It seemed to me that he did not care for Dahlan either. 'So he keeps this "thug", as you call him, because he's a good bodyguard.'

Hamas, many of whose members could be counted amongst Dahlan's most serious enemies, was growing in strength as Fateh officials flaunted their power and wealth, relative though it was to the poverty all around. Resentments appeared and there was much talk of the financial corruption in the PA that had created this wealth. This inevitably led to increasing support for Hamas, and I wondered how Dahlan and his superiors could ignore this changing situation and the danger they were in; or did their remedy for it lie in security men and bodyguards? What a sad decline for Fateh, the first Palestinian resistance movement since 1948 to stand up proudly and fight Israel, to give up its young men and women to that struggle, to reclaim Palestinian independence and the right to autonomous decision-making. How had its ideals been so degraded to nothing more than this empty, posturing display of power?

I looked over at the PA security men. They were talking loudly and laughing, oblivious to the rest of us. I wondered who they thought they were lording it over: the poor waiters in that restaurant or the even poorer refugees outside, who made up most of Gaza's population and from whose ranks they were almost certainly recruited?

'Do they behave like this all the time?' I asked, still watching them being hovered over by a group of eager waiters, whom they ignored.

'I don't know what you mean,' he answered impassively. 'Our security forces are there to protect us and to keep order.'

Dr Farid arrived that afternoon, but I had no wish to see him. My time in Gaza was limited, and I knew I could not easily return to meet people I was unlikely to come across outside. I had entered Gaza this time only because of UN help; without it, I doubt I would have been able to. Israel had turned this small strip of land into a fortress, virtually impenetrable to the outside world and quite often to relatives wishing to see their families. There was many a story of such people turning up at the Erez checkpoint with their painstakingly acquired entry permits that had taken months to be granted, only to be rejected by the checkpoint officials; many subsequently re-applied and returned with new permits, but were still denied entry. And sure enough I was never able to visit Gaza again. When I tried in 2008, in company with a large group of Western psychiatrists invited to a mental health conference there, all armed with our official invitations and World Health Organisation sponsorship, we were turned back at Erez. There was never any logic to this behaviour; it was random, and seemed to depend on unknown factors or simply on momentary impulse. Gazans wanting to go the opposite way to reach the West Bank were likewise often prevented from getting through.

Tariq took me for a drive along the seafront. The route was marked by Israeli watchtowers with a clear view of our car, but my companion ignored them as if they had been a natural part of the scenery. He stopped at a café by the sea, a shabby place with metal tables under faded umbrellas and cracked plastic chairs of various colours and designs. A thin boy who was hanging about under one of the sunshades showed us to a table and took our order for soft drinks, which he brought over in paper cups on an old and stained metal tray. He served Tariq first and then me as an afterthought. I must have looked odd to him, a woman alone with a man, not wearing hijab and looking foreign though seeming to be Arab.

No one but us was about, and for a moment it was peaceful and quiet. I looked out at the glittering azure sea, so calm, so beautiful, its graceful waves, as if unaware of the encaged, tormented place they touched, gently lapping against the shore in languid succession. The sky overhead was a crystal-clear blue as far as the eye could see, and the sandy beach that fell away from the edge of the café was pale and smooth, sloping quietly into the water. It was a view from the best travel brochure, the perfect holiday beach. With its natural beauty, Gaza would have been a paradise, a place for artists and holidaymakers, of fun and relaxation. Only this was no Riviera and no one here, except perhaps the Israeli settlers, was on holiday. The air had a pungent stench of seaweed mixed with raw sewage discharged from the Jewish settlements on to Gaza, and thence into the sea.

'How can that be allowed to happen?' I demanded of Tariq, as if he were to blame.

'We've got used to it,' he said. 'We can't do anything about it anyway. They won't let us work the sewage plant, so our sewage and theirs just goes on pouring down. Though, to be honest with you, it's the last thing on people's minds. So much else to worry about.' I could see that also included him.

Tariq was born in Beach refugee camp in Gaza City not far from my hotel, one of thirteen children. This camp was one of the most crowded in the Strip, with 87,000 residents. Over 80 per cent of Gaza's population were refugees, people who had fled in 1948 from the towns and villages to the north of the Strip, under attack from the Jewish armies. UNRWA had looked after them and their descendants ever since.[1] For a time Tariq's father and brothers, like many other Gaza refugees, had made a living by working in construction and various menial jobs in Israel. But after the Second Intifada in 2000, Israel imposed a ban on the entry of Palestinian workers and Tariq's family was forced to find something else. They got by

---

[1] UNRWA stands for the UN Relief and Works Agency, set up in 1949 specifically to provide assistance and protection for the Palestinian refugees. It caters for their social and educational needs, running schools and heath clinics inside the camps of which there were in 2005 fifty-nine in Jordan, Syria, Lebanon and the West Bank and Gaza.

eventually through fishing and a bit of farming, and Tariq had been bright enough to excel at school and go to college afterwards. His job with the PA as a gofer and part-time driver earned him enough to marry and have a family of his own.

Looking at him, a handsome young man in his twenties, slim and neatly dressed, no one would have guessed at his poor background and his struggle to make something of himself.

'You live in London, don't you?' he asked, eyes shining. 'You teach students there. Tell me about London. I wish I could go there.'

'What would you do if you went?'

'Oh, lots and lots. I would go to university. I would look around. I'd learn things. Maybe make a bit of money.' The look in his dark eyes was one of quiet pleading, as if it had been in my power to fulfil any of his wishes. Like most Arabs who had never been there, he probably had little idea about London. Such people would often ask me if I knew their cousin or friend in London and look disappointed if I didn't. 'Strange,' they'd say suspiciously, 'because my cousin's lived there for years.' Born under Israeli occupation as Tariq was, he had never travelled anywhere in his life, perhaps not even to Israel. Within Gaza itself, Israeli checkpoints made passage between one part and another difficult, and there were people who had not visited relatives living only a few miles away for months on end. In theory, travellers could leave Gaza via the Rafah crossing to Egypt in the south. But in practice, the crossing was subject to arbitrary closure by the Egyptian authorities, or, when open, travellers were frequently held up for days and passage could not be guaranteed. Without some sweeping change in Gaza's strangulated situation, I did not think Tariq's chances of seeing the outside world were good.

'If you went to London you'd have to leave your family behind. How would you feel about that?'

'It wouldn't be a problem,' he responded eagerly, as if I were indeed offering him the chance of going to London but just

needed to clarify a few details. 'You see, my wife is the daughter of my uncle. She'd understand. They married us off far too
young. I want to do things with my life. Marriage makes you
stick where you are. You can't move on.' There was a desperation in his voice to which I wanted to respond. But I could
think of nothing to say that would change his circumstances.
In that regard, we were both as helpless as each other.

'Listen, Tariq,' I said. 'I understand how you feel, or at least
I can imagine it. I know how hard life is here. And as things
are, there's nothing I can do to help. I wish there were. But
don't give up. You must never give up. It won't always be like
this. It can't last, and you'll be able to do a lot with your life.'
Even as I spoke I felt that my voice lacked conviction. I had no
more hope than he that anything would improve. Gaza had
been abandoned by everyone, left to endure or fight Israel on
its own. And in that unequal contest the winner was a fore-
gone conclusion.

As we drove back to the city and to my next appointment,
Tariq was silent. I could see he had not been convinced by
my avowal of impotence to help him and thought that I just
needed more persuading of his merits to change my mind. I
was silent too, wondering how the rest of my time in Gaza
would work out with him. Once we reached the city, he
took me to a building on a side street where I was to meet
Mahmoud al-Zahhar, a senior Hamas leader. A friend, Ziyad
Abu Amer, whom I knew from London where he was studying at one time, had made the arrangement. After returning to
Gaza he had become a well-known political figure and was
able to connect me to al-Zahhar, whom I would have been
unlikely to meet otherwise.

Ziyad was waiting for me inside the building when I arrived.
Several guards, who knew him, waved us through. He looked
as energetic and alert as I remembered, and a memory came
back of my asking him once if he intended to learn Hebrew.
It was only sensible to learn the language of the enemy, I had

argued. 'Why should I?' he had demanded. 'Why waste my time learning the language of people who're not going to be around here for much longer?' His calm self-assurance in saying this had struck me at the time. I wondered if he still thought the same.

'This is the Doctora I told you about,' he said as we went into al-Zahhar's office. Al-Zahhar was sitting behind a desk and rose at our entrance. I found myself looking at a shortish man in his late fifties who reminded me disconcertingly of a Jewish American professor I knew. Although the latter was of Russian-Polish origin, the resemblance was uncanny. He was stockily built and had a broad, flat, bearded face with small, sharp eyes, very like my friend. I shook the thought off and returned his greeting. Even in that short time I saw he had considerable presence and a quiet self-confidence that commanded respect.

His life had been full of activism. He co-founded the Hamas movement in 1989 and became a top member of its leadership. In the Palestinian Legislative Council elections, he had been considered as a possible prime minister for the Palestinian Authority. When, in 2004, the Israelis assassinated the spiritual leader of Hamas, Sheikh Ahmad Yassin, it was rumoured that he would replace him. At all events he was an important enough figure for the Israelis to try to kill him too. In 2003 an Israeli F-16 plane dropped a huge bomb on his house in which one of his sons was killed and his daughter wounded along with twenty others. But he himself was unharmed, and it confirmed in his view that the only way to deal with Israel was through war. He did not believe that Israelis understood any other language.

Ziyad, having introduced us, excused himself and left; I found myself alone with al-Zahhar. He had a reputation for being an uncompromising hardliner and a hawk who formulated Hamas policy behind the scenes. I found him relaxed and easy to talk to, and not at all put out by sitting with a bare-headed woman who wanted to discuss politics. It occurred to me that he was often interviewed by foreign journalists, and, though we were speaking in Arabic, I may have struck him as similar to one of those. We established a bond early on when we discovered that we were both doctors of medicine, he a surgeon who had qualified in Cairo.

'But your life is politics now, isn't it?' I said.

'It's not possible to be a Palestinian and be any different.' He smiled. 'In any case, the Israelis don't let us do anything else.'

We talked about his views on the current situation, on Gaza and the struggle against Israel.

'Unfortunately not many of our people really understand Israel.' He pushed his chair back, resting his palms against the edge of the desk. 'I hear people talking these days about a peace agreement where we would accept a two-state solution. What that means to me is they take most of our country and we get what they leave behind.'

There was at the time much talk of a Hamas readiness to accept the proposal of two states – Israel and a Palestinian state alongside with East Jerusalem as its capital – contrary to Israeli assertions that Hamas rejected 'peace' and was a bunch of terrorists who only wanted to destroy Israel.

'And you don't agree with the two-state solution?'

'That's what I mean about people not understanding. To reach such an agreement, even if we really did think it was good, we need to have two sides acting in good faith, isn't that right? But Israel does nothing in good faith. If our people haven't learnt that yet, there's no hope for them.'

'But if you think the two-state idea is not good, what do you think the solution should be?'

He took a deep breath. 'Let me explain. Jews are not our enemies. They are People of the Book.[2] We respect them as

2 *Ahl al-kitab* in Arabic, referring to the Quranic designation of Christians and Jews as fellow religionists and, unlike pagans, part of the community of believers.

we do our Christian brethren and mean them no harm. So we have no problem in living together with them, and they should have none with us. It was always so throughout history when they lived under our Muslim rule. And so it will be again. We would establish a state in which we could all live together in peace and friendship.'

'That's a beautiful vision. But isn't there a problem? In the past, Jews were a minority in these lands. Today many Israeli Jews live here. How would this state you propose deal with them? They're used to power and privilege, so how would it work?'

He regarded me with a mixture of surprise and impatience, as if I should have known better. 'Do you imagine that any harm would come to the Jews because they are here?' (I noticed he never used the terms Israel or Israelis). 'They will not be expelled or made to suffer as they fear and as the world accuses us of aiming for. But they have to learn their place and understand they are in our region, not the other way around. They will live under our rule and find peace and contentment, never fear. Islam is a religion of tolerance and justice. Look at what they've created in our country left to themselves: misery, oppression and injustice. We will never be like that. Our religion, our God, would never allow it. These Jews have strayed from their God and made him evil and cruel like them, incapable of compassion. Under our rule it will be different.'

I could see he was serious and spoke out of a sincere piety; he believed wholeheartedly in what he was saying.

'Yet you have a reputation for being a hardliner and warlike, not peaceable and tolerant. How does that fit in with the vision you describe?'

'Please be clear. I advocate force only against those who use force against us. We never started any war against them, yet they have fought us from the beginning. What have our babies, our children, done to them that they kill them without mercy? By what right do they bomb us and put us in prison for wanting our freedom? What we do is in self-defence only. We are not the aggressors. It is the Islamic way, to defend against aggression, not to start it.'

'And suicide operations? Where do they fit into all this?'

He frowned, not liking the term I used. 'Look, we Palestinians are in a war not of our making. Israel has been at war with us from the first moment of its existence. It has big guns, cluster bombs, F-16s, Apache helicopters, tanks, and uses them all against us. We have none of these things, so should we do nothing? No. We use what weapons we have in return. Our martyrs sow terror in their hearts. The Jews have no defence against fear; they are a fearful people because they have no morals. Our operations have wrecked their tourism and their economy.'

His assertions were borne out by the facts, as I later discovered. Between 2000 and 2003, when the Israeli army was battling against the Palestinian uprising and the growing number of suicide operations, the International Monetary Fund noted that Israel's economy experienced its worst recession since the founding of the state. Tourism declined sharply, reflecting widespread nervousness about the security situation; people described seeing Tel Aviv's ghost beaches and deserted holiday resorts. The construction industry, heavily reliant on Palestinian labour which was banned after the start of the Intifada, also declined. Foreign investment fell due to lack of confidence in Israel's stability, and unemployment rose to 10 per cent. Inflation was high, and the shekel had to be devalued by nearly a fifth. This dire situation was not all due to the Intifada; it coincided with a fall in high-technology exports to the US, vital for Israel's economy. But the impact of the Palestinian uprising, and especially of the suicide bombings, coming on top of these developments, threatened Israel's financial stability as never before. It was a heavy economic blow from which the country struggled to recover.

'We hit them where it hurt,' said al-Zahhar with satisfaction. For him suicide bombing was a legitimate weapon of war, no more nor less.

'I see that,' I persisted, 'but isn't the problem that these operations target civilians? One can understand attacks on military targets, but ordinary people?'

'Do you think we do this out of choice? That we wouldn't prefer to strike at their soldiers and their war machines? But we can't reach them. Their men hide inside tanks with metal grills over their windows when they come to face us, or they bomb us from the air where they're safe. It is they who have imposed this choice on us because they have stripped us of any other way to defend ourselves. Why don't you ask about *our* civilians? Does Israel avoid killing *our* women, *our* children, *our* innocent people? Do you think their bombs distinguish between fighter and non-fighter when they drop them on us without mercy?'

He paused for a moment. 'Israel will not last. Its power comes only from America, and who says America will be there forever? Will Arab weakness in the face of Israel also last forever? No, it will not. So our duty while we wait is to remain steadfast, never to give in to them, never to accept their colonisation, never to make deals or compromises. They are uncivilised people and so is the West that supports them. True civilisation means compassion, caring for your fellow man, building, not destroying. They have done nothing but destroy since they came, just as America destroyed Iraq.'

His logic was simple and clear. He exuded an air of quiet certainty, as if he spoke from a position of strength and not the opposite that was the reality. For him the universe was ordered and secure under God's command. Justice was inevitable, and Israel, discordant and at odds with this natural order, was doomed and would wither away. The Jews it left behind in Palestine would come under Islamic rule and that would be the end of the conflict. I wondered what his timeframe for such a scenario was and how he could be so sanguine under an occupation that showed no sign of fatigue and when no external power had been willing to end it. Perhaps, like many other Hamas members, he thought that it was their struggle against Israel that had succeeded in 'liberating' Gaza, as would happen shortly. But perhaps also his optimism was born out of that very occupation and the captivity it imposed on Gaza, whose people had scarcely any interaction with the outside world. Apart from a minority of leaders and public figures, the majority lived in abnormal isolation. In the small, over-crowded area that was Gaza, devoid of contact with other communities and even its own, denied travel to other places, there was little room for news or fresh ideas. The result of what could only be called a cruel social experiment in how to isolate a community and observe the effects was a closed society, religious and conservative. Extremism, illusion, con-spiracy theories and suspicion thrive in such environments, and Gaza was prey to all of these.

I saw how such phenomena worked in practice when later that evening I went to visit Maliha's family. Maliha worked for a German-funded NGO in Ramallah and was originally from Gaza. She and I had become friends, and when she heard of my visit to Gaza she asked me to drop in on her family whom she had not seen for a year or more. Her many attempts to visit them had all failed, even when she begged to see her mother who was seriously ill at the time. The Israelis had turned her down repeatedly and she had given up. Like many in Gaza, hers was a large family; they made me welcome and insisted that I stay and eat with them. There must have been a dozen family members, some with their spouses, and several children, all congregated in the family's sitting room. A few of the younger ones were openly staring at me, and I real-ised how odd I must have looked amongst the other women who were all in hijab and long robes. The mother, clearly the central figure in the family, was wearing a caftan and slippers.

She was shy and had little to say to me. Despite their friendliness, I could see they felt awkward and I guessed that they hardly ever had visitors from the outside world, which in their case meant anywhere beyond Gaza. They asked about Maliha and if she was happy and in good health. Other than that, they had no questions and showed no curiosity about me or about Ramallah or anything else. Tea in small glasses, black and very sweet, was brought in, and after that the conversation dried up. I asked them about themselves and life in Gaza, which they answered in vague generalities.

'Are you glad that the Israelis will be pulling out soon from around you?'

No one answered. After a while, one of the men asked why I wanted to know.

'I just wondered. It's quite an event, isn't it? They've been here for nearly forty years, maybe as long as many people can remember. And now they're going away. That's something, surely?'

They looked at each other uneasily and a couple of the women fussed with their children. The mother spoke. 'We don't bother with that sort of thing. We leave it to others who might know better than us, and to God, who knows all. We just get on with every day.'

'But weren't the settlers unpleasant to have around?' I persisted, unwilling to believe they had no view on something so important.

A younger man, Maliha's brother I presumed, answered me. 'We have nothing to do with the Jews. They do not fear God and have no morals. We do not speak to them and keep our children away from them. We cannot punish them, but God has prepared a mighty punishment for them. May that day come soon!'

'Amen!' said the rest. The call to the evening prayer sounded out from the nearby mosque, at which all excused themselves to go and pray. The mother and the man who had answered my first question stayed behind. 'Why do you want to know all those things?' he asked guardedly.

'Only curiosity, I assure you. I didn't mean any harm.' He and the mother looked unconvinced. I should have realised they knew little about me; I came across as foreign and Westernised, and that implied possible connections with their enemies, whether Americans, Europeans or Israelis, for whom I may even have been spying. My questions were too direct and too political, and they could think of no other reason for my asking them. There was little more to be said between us. I thanked the mother for her offer of dinner, which I declined, and when the rest came back from their prayers, I took my leave.

What had Gaza come to? I had gone there first in 1991, in the aftermath of the First Intifada which had erupted as a protest against Israel's occupation; the bravery of Gaza's unarmed people standing up to Israeli tanks and guns had set a proud example for others to follow. The Intifada scared Israel and its Western allies and led to the first serious search for a peace settlement. I went again in 1996, after the Oslo Accords and Arafat's return which were the consequence of that search. There was an exciting atmosphere at the time, one of hopefulness and optimism about the future. I remembered people's generosity and open-heartedness, how engaged and responsive they were, and, despite the poverty and oppression that had not subsided in the wake of the new Israeli–Palestinian rapprochement, were unafraid of contact with Israelis. Secular figures such as Eyad al-Sarraj, the outstanding psychiatrist who set up a modern, world-famous mental health service for traumatised Gazans, Haidar Abd al-Shafi, the physician, PLO nationalist leader and Gaza's major political figure, and many others who flourished at that time.

But all that seemed a world away now. What I saw in Gaza that day was nothing but a spectrum of despair: at one end,

Maliha's family, suspicious, inward-looking and averse to strangers; at the other, Mahmoud al-Zahhar, enveloped in his cosy vision of a triumphant Islam that would overcome his enemies and bring them back to the true path. How could I blame any of them for finding solace where they could?

Gaza was a place of Israel's making, created out of deliberate impoverishment and violence. The wonder was not that it was caving in to narrow-mindedness and extreme religiosity, but that, despite its depredations, it was still on its feet and still fighting to stay alive.

CHAPTER 12

A Gaza Kidnapping

The next morning I awoke early and decided to take a walk along the empty streets around the hotel while it was still relatively cool. Since arriving in Gaza I had seen little of the UNDP party I had come with. They were busy with their projects and had picked up two more workers who had been in Jerusalem and would return with us. Looking at the scenes around me I might have been in a poor Indian city: cracked pavements, mounds of rubble and sand, overflowing rubbish bins. A young boy passed by me, barefoot, sooty black with dirt, his blue eyes and fairish hair suggesting his normal complexion underneath was also fair; a grubby T-shirt and short trousers clothed his angular frame. The beaches were deserted; no throngs of skinny boys like him splashing and running in and out of the waves.

The Israeli soldiers in their watchtower were awake like me, and I wondered how they felt as they watched the people below living in such dilapidation and poverty just a few miles from their own modern, prosperous towns. Did they think those people wanted to live like that? For one mad moment I wanted to shout up at them to come and talk to me, to drag them down from their watchtower by their bullet-proof vests and their guns and their walkie-talkies. I wanted to push my face up against theirs and shout, 'Look around you! Properly! These are human beings here, not beasts, not vermin. They want to live decent lives like you. Understand?'

The power of the image I had conjured up made me so shake with agitation I had to walk on quickly to dissipate the feeling and after a while calm down. The deputy director of the Palestinian Centre for Human Rights,[1] Jaber Wishah, whom I had met briefly the day before, had invited me for breakfast with his family and was due to pick me up at the hotel. He was a genial, happy-looking middle-aged man with an air of optimism and purpose, though the hard life he had led should have made him exactly the opposite. His home where we would join his family for breakfast was in Bureij refugee camp, to which the family had moved from the nearby Nusseirat camp, his birthplace. As with most refugees in Gaza, his parents had fled their village in 1948 and ended up in the Gaza camps where they had lived ever since. Like other refugee children, Jaber was educated by UNRWA, and later became a physics lecturer. With his peers he soon became involved in resistance activities against the Israeli occupation. There were no suicide bombers in those days and violence was unusual, but young men used every other tactic they could think of in their struggle. Inevitably, he was caught, and in 1985, two years before the outbreak of the First Intifada, the army came for him in the night and he was committed to an Israeli jail, where he remained for the next fifteen years. He did not tell me what he was accused of, but such harsh punishments were not usual for relatively minor acts against Israel as a deterrent.

There he joined the many thousands of other 'security prisoners', Israel's designation for those carrying out what the Palestinians would have called acts of resistance against its occupation: stone-throwing, distributing revolutionary leaflets, holding secret meetings of activists to plan possible operations. Israeli law had no category of prisoners of war or

---

1 The Palestinian Centre for Human Rights, an NGO based in Gaza City, was established in 1995 and headed by Raji Sourani, an internationally reputed Gazan lawyer. It fights for Palestinian rights in accordance with international law, and its human rights work is widely respected. Israel has frequently denied Raji Sourani exit from Gaza to engage in international conferences and meetings.

political prisoners as applied to Palestinians. Along with other inmates accused of planning hostile acts against Israel, Jaber was tortured and kept in handcuffs and leg shackles. It was a terrible, unspeakable time during which his daughter was born, never to set eyes on him until she was five. But it was in that dark and rotten cell, as he described it, where he was kept in solitary confinement, that something important happened to him.

'A man from the International Red Cross finally got to see me. They kept moving us to different jails, so it was difficult for the Red Cross to find us. But he did and I thought what a marvellous man he was for devoting his life to human rights. And it was then that I decided I would do that too. Don't get me wrong. I will always hate the Israelis for what they did to me and all the friends I met in prison. They ruined my career and my family life for years, but they didn't win. I resolved to fight them, not with violence, but through the struggle for human rights and the rule of law. That is what I have done ever since, and *inshallah*, we will succeed.'

I looked at him as he recounted his harrowing story; despite his ordeal, he had an air of inner peace as if he had indeed found his way. He chatted amiably as he drove me to the camp, telling me about Gaza, his work and his family, and stopping briefly to pick up fresh-baked *mana'ish*, flatbread covered in olive oil and *za'tar* (thyme), a typical breakfast dish in Palestine, Syria and Lebanon. Bureij camp was situated in the centre of Gaza and had about 35,000 inhabitants. In 1949 it had been nothing but an emergency collection of hastily erected tents and abandoned British army barracks to house the flood of refugees pouring in from the east of Gaza. But UNRWA later replaced the tents with concrete houses, and the camp became more firmly established. It looked more like a crowded small village than a refugee camp when I saw it, its dwellings set close together, trees and bushes growing amongst them.

I was struck by its peaceful, friendly air on that quiet Friday morning, and as we made our way through the narrow alleyways everyone we passed knew Jaber and greeted him warmly. No one would have guessed at Bureij's turbulent history, how in 1953, when it had barely come into existence, an Israeli army unit under the command of Ariel Sharon – the same 'man of peace' being lauded by President George Bush – opened fire on the camp as people slept and killed forty-three of them; how when Sharon became Israel's prime minister in 2002, his army raided the camp again, killing ten people, two of them UN employees; and how it attacked again in 2003, demolishing the camp's mosques and fourteen of its homes.

'Yes,' said Jaber when I mentioned this. 'Bureij has had many a blow. But we never took it lying down. We fought back. That's why they hate us, why they keep coming back.'

His house was larger than most I had seen in the camp. It was spotlessly clean and welcoming, full of family members, including his old mother. She was waiting for us in their best room in her embroidered *thobe*, the full-length caftan typically worn by Palestinian peasants, a white scarf loosely covering her hair. She was slight and had a warm, smiling face rather like her son's. He introduced me, raising his voice for her to hear, and said I was interested in her memories of the past. He had earlier told me something about her, and I was eager to hear her story first-hand.

A young girl came in with a tray of coffee, and Um Jaber settled herself in her chair and looked at me expectantly. It turned out that she was used to telling the story of her family's expulsion from their village near Asdud (renamed Ashdod by the Israelis) to journalists and foreign visitors who were curious to hear it. The memory of 1948 was still fresh in her mind, she said, and as she started her account without prompting from me, she spoke fluently and without hesitation. I could not help wondering how much her story had been shaped by hindsight and in response to what she sensed different questioners wanted to hear. I could understand that, for I had felt something of the same myself when faced with Western sympathisers eager to hear the Palestinian narrative.

But I was more than happy to listen to her. The events surrounding the Nakba had fascinated me for years, not least because they were never fully documented. The Nakba was a seminal event in every Palestinian's life, the root of all the sufferings that followed, and I hungered to reach back for its elusive history through first-hand accounts of that time; how else to unseal its memory, so dim and unattainable, and draw it back into a communal space that could be shared, examined and compared? So I listened to Um Jaber recounting how she and her husband and small children had been forced out at gunpoint by Jewish fighters who invaded their village in the night. All the neighbours were driven out with them and all fled. They walked, half carrying the children, half dragging them, through fields and orchards until exhaustion forced them to stop. They found concealment among the trees and survived on what fruit they could pick. Everyone was afraid the fighters would find them and so kept on moving until finally they reached Gaza where there was no fighting. Abu Jaber wanted to return to the village with the other men once she and the children were safe, but they heard that the Jewish militias fired on anyone trying to come back, and so they resigned themselves to waiting for the time they could return.

That time never came, and every day brought greater numbers of fleeing villagers like themselves to be housed in tents and army barracks. Um Jaber did not look unhappy telling this story, and I doubted that it connected with her emotions any longer, the blind panic and terror she must have felt at the time. Whatever spontaneity there had once been in the telling of it had long gone and robbed that terrible experience of its power.

'Would you like to know anything else, Doctora?' Jaber asked. I shook my head and thanked them. He helped his mother out of the chair and we all went in to breakfast in the kitchen. The table was laid with a generous spread of typical Palestinian food: falafel, *fatta*, (made with pieces of bread and topped with hummus and pine nuts), cracked, bitter olives, *zeit* and *za'tar* (olive oil and dried thyme, eaten by dipping bread in the oil and then coating it with the thyme), and freshly baked flatbread, added to the still warm *mana'ish* we had brought. As we ate I could see the family was close and harmonious; clearly, Jaber, whatever the hardships in his life, had managed to create a happy home.

After breakfast he suggested we drive to what he called the worst spot in Gaza, the Abu Holy checkpoint. 'You must see this,' he said and the others all nodded. 'You will not understand how hard it is here until you do.' I wanted to say that I did understand already, but I could see he was anxious to show me these horrors in the hope I would spread the word about them abroad, where he thought it mattered. The checkpoint stood on the main north–south highway running thorough Gaza – and an essential thoroughfare for people and goods. Each time the Israeli army closed it, Gaza was split in two and all through-traffic was paralysed. It had been erected to enable the Jewish settlements nearby to connect directly with Israel; the settlers used an overpass to drive there, and whenever they did so, the Gaza traffic below was closed off to prevent contact between them and the Palestinians. By such devices the settlers were enabled to live entirely separate lives from those around them. As with all checkpoints, Abu Holy (cruelly named after the farmer on whose land it stood) was built on confiscated farmland, a cause of much bitterness to him and the other dispossessed farmers. Ever since it was erected in 2001 as a punishment for the Second Intifada, journeys that used to take thirty minutes could take ten hours or more.

When we approached I could see why. A queue of cars stretching for as far as the eye could see was ahead of us as we joined the highway. By order of the army, only cars could pass through the checkpoint; no pedestrians were allowed, not even animals, and as I looked about me I saw a car in front with a donkey on the back seat, its head hanging dolefully out of the window. 'What else could the poor man do?' commented Jaber, seeing my stare. 'It's either that or leave the animal behind.' There were three of us in Jaber's car, to comply with another army rule: that all cars must have no less than three occupants, on the grounds that terrorists usually travelled alone or in pairs at most. If it happened that the requisite number of people was not available, one or two of the boys hanging around amongst the trees by the roadside would oblige for a few coins. A small trade in hiring out such children as companions for the ride had grown up, as had also a soft drinks and food business selling provisions for the journey. Many people brought their own sandwiches and coffee in thermos flasks, and even blankets and towels, expecting a long wait in their cars.

The heat was stifling as we crawled along; not a whiff of air passed through the open windows to cool us down, and I started to feel faint. Jaber gave me a bottle of water which had been cold when we set out, but was now warm. The road seemed endless and the ordeal of waiting to reach the checkpoint almost unendurable. Yet people took it stoically enough, leaning out of their car windows to chat to those in front; some joked and laughed or shouted out some piece of news, and everyone seemed to take the whole thing philosophically. It reminded me of the approach to the checkpoint on the way to Nablus. The hold-up on that road was nowhere near as bad as this, but there also people seemed to accept their situation with quiet patience. They got out of their vehicles as they waited and stood around talking to each other, or strolled about to buy drinks from the roadside vendors.

'This wait is dreadful. How can people take it so passively?' I asked Jaber.

'Passively? We're not passive. But you don't argue with a machine gun in your face. And believe me, we're counting the hours and the minutes until they leave and take their hellish checkpoints with them.'

It was certainly true that the soldiers at both these checkpoints were particularly aggressive, and it struck me that it was perhaps the very patience and stoicism of the people waiting to cross which maddened them. Far better if the crowd had turned violent and tried to attack them: their assault rifles and armed patrols were always at the ready for such a thing, and could act at a moment's notice. But against this submissiveness they had no weaponry. Looking at the two sides, as I had done at the Nablus checkpoint – the nervy, helmeted soldiers shouting at the queue of cars, and the docile drivers obeying them – I had no doubt which would last the longer in this land.

If I had felt uplifted and encouraged by what I saw at Bureij camp, those feelings were soon dissipated by my next visit that day. Jabaliya, the largest of Gaza's eight refugee camps and of all the camps in the Palestinian territory, was one of the unhappiest places I had ever seen. It came into being soon after 1948 and was given the name of the nearby town of Jabaliya, a place of lush citrus groves and fertile soil. Lying some two miles north of Gaza City, the camp was close to the border with Israel and so within easy reach of the army's tanks and helicopters. It had been arranged that Mansour, a Palestinian UNRWA field officer, would take me there. UNRWA had a policy of employing Palestinians in all its operations, often recruited from the camps where they were born. As we drove into the wide road that led into Jabaliya, it looked like any shanty town one might see on the outskirts of some large cities.

On our right was the large UNRWA school, a building that catered for several thousand camp children, and opposite I

could see houses closely packed together in rows barely separated from each other by narrow alleys. And no wonder: this
camp was the most crowded place on earth. Over 100,000
people lived inside its tiny area of 1.4 square kilometres. Half
of them were children under the age of fifteen, descendants of
the villagers who had fled from the south of Palestine in 1948,
and their presence was ubiquitous, peering at us from alleyways, playing on the main street, fetching and carrying bags
that looked too heavy for them.

This camp was more urban than Bureij camp, with little
greenery to be seen amongst the concrete and asphalt. It was in
a dilapidated state with an inadequate drinking water supply
(and what was available was expensively bought from Israel,
which had extracted it from Gaza's aquifers in the first place),
and an equally deficient electricity supply. Its thirty-seven
schools and one health clinic could hardly cope with its large
population. Unemployment was high, and the majority were
so poor they were dependent on UN and other international
agencies for food. I had visited Jabaliya briefly once before in
1993 with a group of Arab Americans during a conference. At
that time traces of the First Intifada, which had first erupted in
that camp and spread from there to the West Bank, were still
visible. The kids who came up to us fearlessly then were full
of defiance and pride in what their camp fighters had achieved
against the might of the Israeli army as it tried to crush the
uprising.

'We threw stones at them and they were scared!' cried one
bold young boy, and the smaller children, who had not even
been born then, clustered around him and echoed, 'Really
scared, they were!' Many of them had fair hair and light-
coloured eyes, the typical looks of people from certain parts
of pre-1967 Palestine, traditionally believed to be the result
of contact with European crusaders in the Middle Ages and
blond Circassians who came to Palestine under the Ottoman
Empire. 'We showed them and they ran away!' chimed in

another boy. A big crowd of children soon gathered around us, curious and friendly, and my companions, mostly new to this part of the world and so Americanised that they regarded the children with a sort of gawping orientalism, were enchanted. The walls of houses and public buildings were painted with colourful slogans proclaiming victory and the triumph of the resistance. The older children's grasp of political events and their confidence in the rightness of their parents' struggle were striking. Tomorrow's fighters, I remember thinking. Israel should beware.

Seeing Jabaliya again in 2005, I found it greatly changed. It had always been a place of resistance to Israel, which drew upon its head recurrent bouts of violent retaliation from its earliest days. In 1955 Ariel Sharon's army attacked the camp, ignoring the fact that refugee camps were protected places in international law. Many similar assaults followed, culminating with the attempted crushing by Israel of the First Intifada in 1987. After 1989 it became a Hamas stronghold, for which its population again paid a heavy price. As Hamas started to fire home-made rockets at southern Israel after 2001 in a futile attempt to fight off Israel's assaults, the latter intensified its shelling and bombing of Gaza.[2] Jabaliya camp became a particular target, with frequent army raids and arrests of what Israel called 'terrorist suspects'. Parts of the camp were flattened by the army to clear a route for Israeli tanks to invade it more effectively. The assaults and house demolitions led to enormous suffering and disruption of daily life.

I was taken on a walk into the crowded camp, picking my way through the narrow alleyways full of puddles of muddy water mixed with sewage, and stopping at one or two houses.

2 In 2003 the Israeli army raided Gaza daily and Jabaliya was attacked three times in one week, leaving eleven people dead and eight houses demolished. A year later the army destroyed many more houses in the camp on the pretext that they belonged to families of fighters who had planned or carried out attacks against Israeli targets.

People were welcoming and hospitable, but the poverty they were living in was evident everywhere. We finally entered one of the houses, the home of a family that my companions had stopped by to visit. The woman of the house bade us enter, motioning with her arm towards a man in a wheelchair who hovered silently in the shadows behind her. Several children of different ages came to join them, staring at us unsmilingly.

'How are you today, Um Sufyan?' asked the UNRWA woman worker who had come with us. The man in the wheelchair, having looked us over, wheeled himself back into an inner room. Um Sufyan ignored him and smiled welcomingly. She seemed pleased to see us and shouted to one of the children to get us a drink. The shack we were in, for there was no other way to describe it, was dark and none too clean. From what I could see it had only two rooms and a small kitchen at the end of a short, dingy corridor. The child did nothing and we followed Um Sufyan as she looked for a few glasses and some cans of Seven-Up to give us. The kitchen sink was piled high with dirty plates and pans, and the floor was sticky with grease. A baby's wail went up from somewhere and Um Sufyan dropped what she was doing and pushed past us into the second room. I followed her and nearly fell over a bundle on a floor mat just inside the door, her newest baby as she explained and just a few weeks old. The wail had not come from this infant, but from another who looked to be less than a year older. Both babies were wrapped in dirty sheets.

The place was a scene of hopelessness and squalor. 'I hope you'll excuse me,' said Um Sufyan in a flustered way. 'But you know how it is, the little ones always need seeing to, and with Abu Sufyan disabled, he can't help.' I asked what was wrong with him, and she said he had been injured when he fell off a building site while working in Israel a few years before. Accidents were common amongst Palestinian workers in Israel's construction industry, where they were usually given the most dangerous jobs with few health and safety measures provided for them. If they were injured at work they were not normally offered treatment at Israeli hospitals, and several deaths of such workers had occurred.

'He hasn't been able to work since,' the UNRWA woman told me, 'and his brother stays here as well from time to time while trying to find work. So their home gets even more crowded.' She looked sympathetically at Um Sufyan. 'It's very difficult for her, and we try to help as much as we can. Don't we, Um Sufyan?'

'You do, God bless you. I don't know what we'd do without you,' said Um Sufyan ingratiatingly. 'Abu Sufyan always says the same.' The latter, who had come out again from his room to observe us, looked as if he did nothing of the sort. The expression on his pallid, unshaven face was querulous and disgruntled. He started to complain that no one from the Agency (as UNRWA was known amongst the refugees) had helped him to get back on his feet. He'd been abandoned, he said; the medical clinic was no good and neither were the doctors.

'Now don't start that again, Abu Sufyan,' butted in Mansour firmly but not unkindly. 'You know what we always tell you. You've got to help yourselves as well. How about cleaning the place up for a start, Um Sufyan? The children can help, can't they?' He put his hand on the head of the boy nearest to him. I could see the children, I counted some five or six, did no such thing. They hung about still staring at us, and the two eldest boys looked surly. When we finally left, one of them walked out with us silently. Recalling those other camp children I had seen in 1993, full of life and defiance, I tried to talk to him. What did he want to do when he grew up? He shrugged, looking at the ground, and mumbled something. I tried again, and asked if he would like to be a fighter perhaps. He looked at me with a dull expression and shook his head.

'Well, what would you like to be?'

'Nothing,' he answered. Two other boys, as unfriendly as he, came out of an alleyway to our left and joined him, ignoring me, at which he walked off with them without saying goodbye.

That visit to Jabaliya depressed me immeasurably. I had seen such places before in the worst of Lebanon's Palestinian camps, Shatila in Beirut and Ein al-Hilweh outside Sidon, whose refugees were the victims not only of Israel's original evictions in 1948 but also of Lebanon's neglect and refusal to give them assistance. Yet I remembered more the many houses I had visited in other Palestinian refugee camps, including this one, and how often I had been struck by their internal cleanliness, whatever the state of the alleyways outside. The mothers in the camps never failed to astonish me by their strength and resilience, the way they managed to bring up children who were normal and sane and many of whom grew up to be teachers and doctors or other professionals.[3] These refugee mothers were legendary in Palestinian folklore. It was they who kept the family together after the massive dislocation of 1948 and sustained it through the many depredations thereafter, often by themselves when their menfolk were sent to Israeli jails. It was no exaggeration to say that without them, the family unit which was the bedrock of Palestinian endurance through decades of dashed hopes and suspended lives, would not have survived. It was indeed those very qualities, inspiring and heroic, that endeared Palestinians to foreigners and earned their admiration.

Would they feel the same seeing this place now, with its abject despair and poverty where domestic violence afflicted over two-thirds of households, the inevitable result of overcrowding and unemployment, and where more than half the children were so traumatised and disturbed that some of them spoke of wanting to die because life had nothing to offer them?

---

3 Abd al-Bari Atwan, the founder and editor for many years of *al-Quds al-Arabi*, a well-regarded London-based Arabic newspaper, was a product of Jabaliya camp. Izz al-Din Abulaish, a gynaecologist and internationally known peace campaigner, was another.

If I had been shocked by the conditions at Jabaliya that day, what would I have made of it three years later when Israel launched its most ferocious assault ever, 'Operation Cast Lead', on Gaza? Israel's army used its most sophisticated weaponry in that attack which it said was in response to the firing of rockets from Gaza, although in fact Israel provoked it by breaking a ceasefire agreement with Hamas. The result was a death toll of over 1,400 Gazans and the extensive destruction of Gaza's infrastructure. The UNRWA school I had seen at the camp entrance was bombed in the assault and forty of the 350 people sheltering inside to escape the shelling were killed.[4]

That evening, my last in Gaza, Dr Farid invited a number of us to dinner. The restaurant was by the sea and full of people enjoying themselves. It was a mixed crowd, many of the women not wearing hijab, and the atmosphere was lively. People were smoking hubble-bubbles, including the women, and some were drinking beer. When I joined Dr Farid, I found him with his wife, a handsome woman in her fifties, and a group of their friends that included two PA diplomats posted in foreign countries. His guards hovered nearby and everyone was chatting and laughing. I could smell barbecues grilling meat and fish. The sea was a black mass stretched out before us, and the air was humid but much cooler than it had been during the day. On the horizon, and not much further along the coast from where we sat, the lights of the huge Nezarim Israeli settlement glinted in the darkness.

'Welcome to the Doctora!' Dr Farid called out, rising as I approached the table. He was in his element I could see, social-ising among friends and being affable to all around him. He told jokes and anecdotes at which he laughed more heartily

---

4 In the summer of 2014 during a yet more vicious Israeli assault on Gaza, the Jabaliya school, as before sheltering hundreds of people fleeing the war, was bombed again with the death of at least nineteen people.

than anyone. By his side was his wife, chatting vivaciously, and they seemed well suited.

'And what have you been up to, Doctora?' Dr Farid asked. 'I hope Tariq has been a good boy and looked after you.'

'Oh, he has, and very well. Thank you for sending him to me. Actually I was in Jabaliya camp today.'

A shadow crossed over Dr Farid's face. He fell silent, but the conversation amongst some of the guests at the opposite end of the table continued. 'I suppose you met some of our good friends at UNRWA,' he said after a pause.

'I did, and I could see they were doing their best. But the place was quite awful. I can't forget what I saw there.'

Dr Farid looked reluctant to pursue the subject. He shrugged, and his wife stopped talking and looked at me expression-lessly. 'Of course it's awful, all our camps are. But what can any of us do?' He did not comment further and turned back to the others to rejoin the conversation that I felt I had so tastelessly interrupted with my sombre interjection. No one said any more about it, and we passed a convivial evening of excellent food and light-hearted chitchat as if we had not been in Gaza at all. No matter how anomalous I thought it, it was nothing more than the natural human wish to be 'normal', if only for that evening, and to take a break from the grim reality I had witnessed. And for that I could not find it in my heart to blame Dr Farid or anyone in that restaurant seeking a temporary escape.

Our party was due to return to Jerusalem the next day. It was still the Jewish Sabbath, which was rigorously observed in all public places, and the Erez crossing operated a limited service after dark on Fridays and most of Saturdays. We would need to make sure we were able to leave, and it had been arranged that I would be picked up from the hotel early that afternoon. I put my few things in the bag I had brought and was ready in good time. I went to the hotel lobby to wait for the others, feeling almost impatient to leave Gaza and its misery. But no one came. I telephoned the hotel next door, to be told the UN party had still not come back to check out. Time was passing but still nothing happened. I went outside to see if anyone was coming for me and as I did so a car drove up at great speed and abruptly halted at the hotel door inches from where I was standing. I could see Tariq inside with a group of young Palestinian security men. Hardly had the car stopped than he ran out towards me. He was breathless and excited.

'Something's happened, Doctora. Let's get inside.'

'Look, I'm supposed to be leaving Gaza now. I'm waiting for the other UNDP people to pick me up.'

'I know. That's the problem,' he answered urgently. 'Two of your friends have been kidnapped. You're going to have to make other arrangements. That's why we're here.'

I could hardly take in what he was saying and was about to ask for more detail when the man from the hotel reception, visibly curious, came out to say there was a phone call for me at the desk. It was Abbas, one of the UNDP officers who had driven us to Gaza. He sounded tense.

'I can't talk much. But we're held up trying to get Sally and Ramzi out.' There was interference on the line and I could hear raised voices in the background. He obviously assumed that I knew what had happened. 'Can't tell you when we'll be finished. Sorry.' The call ended.

So it had been Sally Roberts, a pretty blonde English girl who worked part-tine at the UNDP office, and Ramzi al-Souri, a half-Spanish, half-Palestinian artist in Gaza to work on a photographic exhibition, who had been kidnapped. Both of them were foreign to look at, and it must have been that which had made them targets. In Gaza at that time, capture of foreigners, particularly Europeans and Americans, was rife for a variety of reasons: most often to force the release of Palestinian prisoners held by Israel or by the PA, to secure jobs for the kidnappers, or to settle some dispute with another

family or political faction. The idea was that Western countries of which the victims were nationals would accede to the
kidnappers' demands by putting pressure on Israel to comply,
or forcing the PA to do the same. The ploy hardly ever succeeded, and most of the hostages were released within a day
or so, but still it went on happening.

'Do you know anything about it?' I asked Tariq.

Some of the men with him answered me. 'We know who's
behind it. It's a family quarrel and your friends are caught in
the middle.'

It seemed that Ayman and the others had gone out in the
UN jeep to finish off some business before leaving Gaza and
had stopped momentarily on an empty side street. Suddenly
two cars appeared from behind driving fast and swerving to a
halt alongside the jeep. With lightning speed some half-dozen
men spilled out, brandishing machine guns and Kalashnikovs
and pointing them at the jeep. They were dishevelled and
dressed in PA traffic police uniform, which confused Ayman
and the others until they realised from their behaviour these
were no policemen. Wrenching open the jeep's back door, they
dragged Ramzi and Sally out and shoved them into one of the
cars. Then they pushed Ayman and the UNDP driver out on to
the street. In the commotion Sally tried to escape, but the men
caught her and pushed her back roughly inside the second car,
separating her from Ramzi.

They drove off at great speed, leaving Ayman and the UNDP
driver looking after them helplessly.

'But Ayman managed to catch up with them and then followed them to a house in Beit Lahiya,' said Tariq, 'and that's
where he is now, trying to negotiate with them.'

'How do you know? Do you have something to do with it?'

'The family that's holding them and my family are related,'
Tariq explained, 'and I've become involved in trying to get
your friends out.' He had talked to one of the uncles at the
house in Beit Lahiya and begged him to let Sally and Ramzi

go, but to no avail. Many others who knew the family had already tried to intercede, but likewise without success. The young men holding the two hostages then fell to arguing with each other and nearly coming to blows. But that did not release the UNDP people either. In that small part of Gaza it seemed that everyone knew everyone else in the case or was related to them.

'How long is this likely to take?' They shrugged.

'Who knows? *Inshallah*, not too long.'

I started to panic. Everything suddenly felt hostile around me. I did not know the rules here and had no one to turn to. I spoke to my nephew, Omar, who was working as a journalist in Jerusalem and told him my predicament. He suggested I get a taxi to Erez there and then, and he would meet me on the other side. The hotel manager, openly listening in on the conversation, offered a taxi firm he knew. 'My cousin runs it. He'll look after you. But you've got to go soon.' He quoted me an unreasonably large sum of money for the service.

Overhearing this, Tariq said, 'Don't worry, Doctora. Dr Farid is sending someone especially to escort you to the crossing, and there'll be another car coming from Jerusalem to pick you up on the other side.'

Dr Farid had been meant to return at the same time as we were, but had become embroiled in the negotiations to free Sally and Ramzi, which only made matters worse. The kidnappers, having started to show signs of flexibility, instantly hardened their positions at his intervention; they held a grudge against the Palestinian Authority and against President Mahmoud Abbas in particular. His minister was the last person they would have responded to, and no one knew how it would all end.

Dr Farid was as good as his word. Two men driving a comfortable, air-conditioned car belonging to him came to the hotel to take me to the Erez crossing. It was quite deserted and I seemed to be the only traveller there. The car drew right up to the demarcation line and a couple of Israeli officials came towards us. The PA men helped me out of the car and greeted the Israelis with a great show of camaraderie. They stood exchanging friendly remarks, as if for all the world this was a normal situation and theirs was a normal relationship. The Palestinians were markedly warmer and more effusive, slapping the Israelis on the back and clasping their hands in hearty handshakes. There was in it the same ingratiating desire to please I had seen years before during the lunch I had attended at Arafat's compound in Gaza.

As I waited for my passport to be cleared, one or two of the Israeli officers asked me for details of the kidnapping, which their intelligence services had evidently not succeeded in probing. I gave them only the vaguest of answers which left them unsatisfied, and walked with relief to the white Mercedes waiting for me on the Israeli side of the crossing.

I spent that night regaling Omar and his flatmate, another journalist, with what I knew of the kidnapping story. Had I known its full content at the time, it would have been a good scoop for the papers they worked for.

It turned out that the issue, as one of the PA security men told me earlier that day, was to do with a feud between two large Gaza clans. One clan, to which the kidnappers belonged, had a grievance against the other, which they believed the PA favoured over theirs. Hostility on the part of the favoured clan had led to the imprisonment of several members of the aggrieved kidnappers' clan, and the aim of hijacking the two foreigners had been to put pressure on the authorities to release their relatives from prison. In addition, they wanted the PA to end its favouritism of the rival clan. Negotiations and intercessions from family and friends, in addition to a promise by the authorities to look into the matter, did not succeed in ending the crisis. The Arab way of reconciliation, relying on appeals for calm, and exhortations to fear God, to observe social propriety, to feel with others, and respect the ties of brotherhood, tended to be the most successful in such cases, although not in this one.

The story was that, after being dragged from the UNDP car, Ramzi and Sally were driven through a maze of winding back streets with such reckless speed it looked as if they must crash at any moment. And sure enough the driver of Sally's car who seemed especially agitated, almost manic, and she thought afterwards was 'on something', smashed the car into a wall. His companions had to get out and push it away with much puffing and cursing while trying to keep their guns trained on Sally. It would have been comical, she said later, had it not been so frightening. Once they had freed the car, which was miraculously still functioning, they drove on to their final destination, a house on the outskirts of Beit Lahiya village north of Gaza City.

Inside was an unexpectedly homely scene: a woman cooking in the kitchen and a number of young children playing; a baby was asleep on a mattress in the corner. The woman showed no alarm at the arrival of the two foreigners and did not interfere as they were taken to an upstairs room where they were locked in with two of the kidnappers. One of these was the manic driver who kept waving his gun about wildly or pointing it at Sally, vowing to keep her and Ramzi imprisoned for days. His mood swings were terrifying and his companion kept trying to calm him down. It emerged later that he was a refugee from Beach camp and an orphan who had got by doing odd jobs. Now that Ramzi could see them properly they were no more than kids, both under twenty, and obviously novices at this kidnapping adventure. He tried to talk to them in a friendly way, but they did not respond and only kept up their threats. And all the time, they had an eye out for the television in the room, watching for a mention of the kidnapping on the news.

They were eventually rewarded when Al Jazeera reported the incident, at which both were as delighted as if they had become instant celebrities. And with that, their mood visibly relaxed. The excitable kidnapper calmed down and told Sally that he was at the university in Gaza doing business studies and wanted to get a proper job afterwards. As he spoke of his hopes she found herself pitying him and his fellow kidnapper. After a while the children brought up a tray of food, and as everyone ate, the kidnappers expressed their disgust at the PA government which, they said, existed only to protect Israel. Meanwhile, they could hear what seemed like a multitude of people, Tariq among them, coming to the house and trying to intercede, which agitated the two young men all over again.

In the end, PA security forces surrounded the house, shooting into the air, and the kidnappers, having first threatened to kill the hostages, saw the game was up and released them. They brought their captives downstairs and delivered them to the policemen, who escorted them away under special guard. As they drove through Jabaliya village, a huge crowd of people, including PA police and many journalists, were waiting to see them. They were treated like VIPs, crossing into Israel without a hitch at the border, as if the Israeli border guards had decided to leave the Palestinians to fight it out amongst themselves. At a ceremony in Ramallah President Abbas welcomed Sally and Ramzi back and congratulated them on their freedom. Muhammad Dahlan was also present and indicated it was his armed forces who had secured their release. There were press photographs of the hostages shaking hands with various PA dignitaries, and Sally and Ramzi acquired the status of heroes. But some people muttered that, had the hostages been mere Palestinians, there would never have been half so much publicity.

The captors, meanwhile, were promised that their relatives would be let out of prison. Whether it actually happened we never heard, and they may have ended up with little more than a public airing of their grievances. These would no doubt surface again before long, and the young men would be left to foment more plots in Gaza's stifling, overheated atmosphere from which there was no escape.

CHAPTER 13

Qalqilya, the Walled City

Talk of the kidnapping went on for several days after my return to Ramallah. I gave a small party at my flat to which I invited Sally. Ramzi was in Jerusalem, still recovering from their ordeal which had affected him deeply; he was not sleeping or working and had been seeing a psychologist. Sally had taken it better, but she was still shocked by the kidnapping and did not stay long after telling us the story of what had happened. The people in Dr Farid's office wanted to know all the details. But in the other ministry no one mentioned it and life seemed to be the same as when I left, everyone focused on their day-to-day problems and frustrations. Hanan was no nearer getting her back pay, and neither was Muhammad.

I too resumed where I left off, wrestling with the preparations for the media conference that soon chased the memory of Gaza from my mind. Dr Farid was still not back from there, but any thought that I could forget the conference until his return was not to be. My desk at the ministry, which someone had been using, was littered with scrunched-up balls of paper on which I could discern some writing connected to the conference. Amin, not looking at me and apparently concentrating on the computer in front of him, spoke without turning his head.

'Very glad you're back, Doctora. We had a meeting here yesterday with Ilan about the conference, as Dr Farid has asked him to take charge of preparations while you were both away.'

'Oh yes? What came out of it?'

He sat back and swivelled his chair round to face me. 'A few suggestions and recommendations for you. I've made a list here.' He rifled through the papers on his desk and passed me a sheet with some English writing on it which I took to be in Ilan's hand. It looked sketchy and vague.

'That's it? Did Ilan say which of the things he's written here he would do?' Amin shook his head.

'Why don't you phone him? I'm sure he'll explain,' he said impassively and turned back to his computer as if no longer concerned with the matter. Adel dropped in with a note for me from Dr Farid to the effect that the perfunctory conference statement and outline programme I had sent to mollify him before leaving for Amman were fine, and I could continue with the work. When Ilan Halevi breezed into the office later that morning, he was as affable and friendly as ever, but obviously disinclined to do any more than give advice about the conference over a cup of coffee.

Dr Farid telephoned me at home that evening, anxious to know how I was getting on with the programme. It was clear that he still set great store by the success of this project, and it was not the time to tell him that he needed to find someone else to work on it.

'Please get a full programme ready for when I'm back and a guest list,' he said in a businesslike voice. 'I have a number of names I want added as soon as possible. Have invitations gone out to those on the list we had drawn up already?' I knew that no one had done anything so far and no one had any idea who was in charge. Since nothing ever happened without the threat of repercussions from someone in authority, work on the conference had been ignored. Only my mysterious sense of obligation to Dr Farid kept me trying to do something about it.

'What did you say this conference was about?' asked my dinner companion that evening, Michel Habibi. We were at Pronto, a popular bistro-style café-restaurant in the centre of Ramallah, which I liked and whose friendly young waiters were pleasant to deal with. Michel was a lawyer of Palestinian parentage who had been brought up in the US and lived in

Washington DC, where he normally had his practice. He spoke little Arabic and his manner was even more American than Samir's, but he was a clever, articulate man who presented the Palestine case effectively in American circles and on American TV and was disliked by many Zionists for that reason. Much like myself, he was in Ramallah to work as a consultant, in his case at the prime minister's office which was in the same building as Dr Farid's ministry.

Things had gone well for him at first, and his legal reports and analyses, including several high-level TV interviews he gave, were received with admiration. But increasingly he found himself frustrated by an obtuse bureaucracy at the office which was reluctant to consider his ideas about the PA's political strategy. The officials he dealt with were mostly senior members of Mahmoud Abbas's government and considered themselves experienced enough to dispense with his advice.

'They haven't got a clue!' he would complain to me over coffee in his office, which was small but he had sole use of it. 'I watched a TV interview with one guy who really fancies himself, and he kept calling the presenter "Sir" or "my dear friend" and quoting from French writers I never heard of, for Christ's sake! I think he was educated in France or something, as if anyone cared. Or another guy whose idea of being smart was to reel out a load of statistics about settlements, refugees, UN resolutions, you name it! It bored the pants off the presenter and everyone else.'

When Michel suggested a different approach to interviews, one that had served him well in the US where it really mattered, he said, his advice was politely dismissed. Having quite an ego himself from what I had seen, this did not go down well with him. He was rumoured to be on the point of leaving, partly for that reason, but more immediately because the funding for his post, which came mostly from British sources, was under threat. He had heard that Zionist pressure on the British funders had brought this about. I did not doubt that it might be true, since Palestinians who became effective in public life were unwelcome to Israel and its supporters. I had recently seen such an example in the case of Raji Sourani, the well-regarded head of the Palestinian Centre for Human Rights in Gaza, whose travel to attend foreign conferences and meetings was repeatedly blocked by the Israeli authorities in an attempt to silence him.

'A conference on media strategy for Palestine, you say?' He burst out laughing. 'What, another one? I don't believe it! Do you know how many of those things they have around here? Workshops, seminars, conferences and Christ knows what else. It's like there's nothing else to do. Crazy!'

'Maybe, but it's still going ahead.'

'You shouldn't take it so seriously. You can bet no one else does.' He put down his wine glass and looked at me. 'Don't be a sucker, Ghada, they'll just use you, although I must say I'm a little surprised at Dr Farid. I thought he was better than the rest. At least he's one guy who does know how to talk to the Western media.'

'That's just it,' I said. 'I used to know Dr Farid many years ago, and he always struck me as a genuine, civilised and sophisticated man, and very pleasant with it. We were really quite friendly, and when I applied to come here through UNDP, they told me he was thrilled and insisted I work with him. But I hardly recognise him here, or maybe I never really knew him. He's like a caricature, shallow and silly. I can't take him seriously.'

'Well, don't try. Most of these guys take themselves seriously enough without your help. It's like they believe this stuff about statehood. Like they think it's just around the corner. Bunch of clowns!' There was not a trace of sympathy in his voice. 'Think they're a match for Israel? What a joke!'

His harshness and scorn put me somehow on the defensive. 'Oh come on, they're not all like that. There are decent hardworking people among them trying to do their best in a terrible situation.' And to be fair, I told him, who on earth *was* a match for Israel? We were very unlucky to have such an enemy. Israel was an advanced Western country which knew all the tricks, could get its friends to manipulate the US Congress, make and unmake US politicians. It scared US presidents, forced Europe to fund its occupation of our country and got away literally with murder.

Michel nodded and was about to say something, but I was in full flow now. 'Against that, who did we have? People who mostly haven't lived in the West and aren't familiar with the way Westerners, including Israelis, think, and simply don't have the deviousness or the sophistication to play the game as they should.

'Like you, I find them pretty annoying, but aren't they just people who're not up to the job because it's a hell of a difficult one, rather than villains or fools?' I had never expected this defence of the PA and its officials to escape my lips. But his disdain and condemnation stirred a sort of pity for them in me.

'Sorry, that's no excuse,' he retorted vehemently. 'If they can't do the job, then they should move aside for someone who can. Or at least they should listen to those who can guide them' – like himself, I presumed – 'but no, they think they're just perfect, you see, they don't need any improvement and they patronise you if you try to help. That's why there's no excuse.'

'You don't think the occupation makes them like that? It wouldn't be the first time an occupying power has deliberately cultivated a special class of ineffective leaders and given them special privileges so they can all squabble and compete with each other.'

'Sure,' he said, 'but those set-ups never lasted. Nationalist movements always forced them out. Look at the ANC in South Africa: they didn't collaborate with the apartheid government or make compromises with it; they didn't fall for stupid bribes like VIP status or get themselves fobbed off with some pseudo-"authority" and phoney statehood. They didn't do deals with white businessmen. Compare them to our people, with their joint entrepreneurial projects and "security cooperation".'

After the signing of the Oslo Accords, a thriving economic sector had grown up linking Israeli and Palestinian businessmen. This relationship had become established and operated largely behind the scenes. Palestinian proponents of this phenomenon believed it would bring about a peaceful coexistence with Israel. But the vested interests that resulted from these activities went a long way towards preserving the status quo and countered efforts towards reaching a just settlement of the conflict.

Palestinians greatly admired the ANC's struggle against apartheid and saw in it a model for their own against Israel. The PLO had had close ties with the ANC from the 1960s onwards, and in the era when both espoused the armed struggle they had engaged in joint military training. Relations between Yasser Arafat and Nelson Mandela were especially close. Mandela saw his commitment to the Palestinians as both personal and moral and he was a loyal champion of Palestinian rights throughout his life. In 1997 he made a famous statement ever after treasured by Palestinians: 'We know too well that our freedom is incomplete without the freedom of the Palestinians!'

Perhaps it was thinking about the huge change that had overtaken the Palestinian struggle since those heady days that made Michel so angry and disillusioned. But it was not so simple, and I did not want to leave it at that. 'It's not quite as you say. I can think of many colonial situations where the same thing happened as here. In fact it's the norm.' Anyone who had read Franz Fanon knew how that sort of thing worked, I said. To be sure he was writing about the French in Algeria, but the essentials were the same. The colonisers did everything they could to stop any form of resistance against them. They set leaders over the people they colonised who could be bribed to care more about the privileges of office than the welfare of the community they represented. Anyone who threatened to upset this arrangement was killed or put in prison, making it impossible to change them for better leaders, and so it went on.

'In the end, everyone gets so demoralised they learn to live with the situation. And as for the ANC,' I said, 'the two situations are not the same. Don't forget black South Africans were in the majority and living inside their country, whereas most of us are outside. Apartheid exploited blacks and moved them off their lands when it wanted to, but it wasn't primarily about expelling them outside the country and taking their place, as Israel did to us. And white South Africans didn't have the influential and powerful friends all over the world that Israel has. These are huge differences and you can't discount them.'

He looked at me with pained surprise. 'So, now you're an apologist for these people, are you?'

'What do you mean, "these people"? You might not like it, and I don't much either, but we're all the same people. And how do we know that we would have been so different had we been in their place?'

Michel was not alone in feeling the way he did; other talented young Palestinians trained abroad who had come, fired by patriotism, to offer the PA their skills were just as disappointed and wanted to leave.

He was not convinced by my words. 'Look, I know where you're coming from, but I don't buy it. These people are no good no matter what the reason, and they need to go.'

He had struck a sensitive chord. There was a growing debate in Palestinian circles that had begun to question the role of the PA. The idea of removing the Palestinian leadership, of actually dissolving the PA, was being increasingly voiced, albeit hesitantly and privately, amongst intellectuals; it was still being discussed years later. An academic at Bir Zeit University, Ali Jarbawi, had been the first to publish an article in 1999 unapologetically calling for the PA's dismantlement. His argument was that the PA's main function was in effect to provide cover for the occupation, absolving Israel of its legal responsibilities for the territories it occupied. By presenting a picture of a false parity between the government of Israel and that of 'Palestine', as if they were equivalent in power and resources, it absolved the world of its responsibilities towards the Palestinians too. And so long as that travesty of the true situation was allowed to go on, there would be no chance of an end to Israel's occupation. On the other hand, removing the 'middleman' that the PA had become would force Israel into direct contact with the people it occupied and compel them to take charge of their affairs. Only then would the world understand the true situation in 'Palestine'.

But that was all very well, people argued back. If the PA disappeared, who would pay its employees their salaries, and how would they feed their families? Whatever else it was, the PA was an employer and a source of livelihood for a million people. Nor was that all. Despite its shortcomings, its existence had also given people a national identity and a channel for their national aspirations. There was support for the president amongst a minority of people, even if not actual enthusiasm. And as long as no one came up with an alternative leadership, not least because Israel had eliminated any potential candidates who could have replaced the current PA officials, people were reluctant to give up the status quo.

Michel sighed. 'It's a goddamn mess. They should never have started down this road in the first place. Arafat should never have accepted the Oslo Agreement. It was a trap, a lousy deal, and this is what it's led to.'

We went on talking in the same vein. Nabil, another US-trained Palestinian working for the Negotiations Support Unit, who was at another table in the restaurant, joined us with much the same views and complaints as Michel. Neither could find any sympathy or excuse for the people they worked for, and nothing I said made any difference. In the end I fell silent, aware that I too scoffed at and disparaged the men I worked with and was no less critical than they of our sorry situation.

The next day I decided to follow Michel's advice and stop taking Dr Farid and his conference so seriously. Recalling my more sympathetic attitude towards him and his colleagues during our conversation over dinner, I tried to think kindly of him but could not bring myself to do so whilst I was struggling to work on the dreary conference programme and workshops, expanding the vacuous themes of each and appending an up-to-date guest list. Every topic I thought up was hackneyed and repeatedly used in all such meetings, and every workshop description was a virtual replica of what I had already written in my media strategy for the ministry. Had Dr Farid bothered to read that, he would have recognised the almost identical content and wording. The 'new' programme I drew up ran to several pages which I passed by Aref for comment. He suggested a few amendments, and I then handed the papers on to Adel for Dr Farid when he returned. When the latter telephoned me yet again that evening, anxious for news of my progress, I was able to reassure him that the conference preparations were going forward and the documents were ready, awaiting his attention.

The next morning he was in touch again to give me more names of participants to be invited. I was at Dr Sabah's ministry to get away from Adel and his nervous habit of rushing about looking worried and everyone else's studied indifference to the conference. Even the dingy office I occupied and the unfriendly atmosphere was preferable to that. Taking the *servisse* to the ministry earlier on, I heard one or two people talking about an Israeli dawn raid on a house in al-Bireh, two young men taken away by soldiers without explanation. No one said anything about the likely fate of the men, who would very likely end up in prison with no one to defend them. I sat thinking about this and trying to summon up the energy to examine Dr Farid's guest names. But my heart was not in it and I put the papers back in their file.

What I really wanted was to get right away from the tedium of the conference, and from Ramallah as well. I was very glad that I had earlier arranged to see Salim, a friend who worked in London but whose home was in the village of Taybeh in what was called 'The Triangle', a collection of small Arab towns in northern Israel close to the Green Line that divided pre-1967 Israel from the West Bank. He happened to be visiting his family there at the time that I was in Ramallah and had invited me to join them.

The next day was a Friday and he had proposed that we first visit Qalqilya, a Palestinian town straddling the Green Line, before going on to his home. Taybeh was a little to the north of Qalqilya and close to Tulkarm, but, being on the Israeli side of the Green Line, its people had Israeli citizenship. The other two towns were in the West Bank and not in the same position; no one there in fact had any form of recognised citizenship. All three were agricultural places, but Taybeh still retained its farmlands and its people could move around freely, while Qalqilya's lands had been confiscated by the state, and what was left of the town was totally encircled by the separation wall which cut off nearly all movement to the outside world. Nowhere in the West Bank was as tightly encaged as Qalqilya, and I wanted to see it for myself.

I met Salim on the main road close to the huge checkpoint that blocked access to the town. Looking at it from there, all I could see was the twenty-five-foot-high wall that shielded it from view, like some mysterious medieval fortress. We were stopped at the checkpoint, but once through we soon reached the walled town. Entry was afforded by its one gate, which was open that morning. The army often closed it quite arbitrarily, and even when it was open the townspeople needed an Israeli permit to use it. This was especially hard for those farmers who still had lands to tend outside the wall and were frequently prevented from reaching. As a result of these restrictions, what had been a prosperous town became impoverished; the Qalqilya peasants who used to work the land became labourers in Israel; and when that was no longer permitted following the Second Intifada, they turned to construction work in the settlements springing up on the land they had lost.

Qalqilya was about ten miles to the south-west of Tulkarm and had the same rich agricultural soil, but its farms benefited from the plentiful water of the huge aquifer beneath its land, one of the largest in the West Bank. When my father was a boy he would often go with my grandfather and uncles to visit 'Qalqili', as it was affectionately known. But those happy times did not last. The war of 1967 put an end to Qalqilya's independence when Israel occupied it and immediately confiscated its land for settlement-building. Its people were evicted and many of its buildings were demolished. They were later allowed back, only to endure further land losses during the mid-1990s for use as Israeli security roads and military bases.

By the time of my visit, there were nine Jewish settlements ringing the town, using its farming lands and sucking the water from its aquifer. Salim related its sad history as we passed through the sentried gate and walked towards the main street. It was a quiet Friday morning and the town had a strangely tranquil atmosphere, at odds with the grim sight that awaited us. As I looked around me the only thing I could see was the huge, dark wall reaching upwards to the sky and shutting out the light. There, like a slap in the face, it took my breath away. This was infinitely worse than anything I had seen at Abu Dis. There was not a single point in the town from which the wall was hidden, no road I walked along which did not stop dead against its slate-grey slabs. I had never seen such a place before and it gave me a feeling of dread, as if I were inside a prison without hope of escape.

And yet, with all that, Qalqilya had the familiar, reassuring hallmarks of the traditional Arab town: the central souk with its colourful stalls, crowded with early shoppers and throngs of small boys, some riding donkeys; and the main mosque preparing for the noonday prayer and Friday sermon. Most of the men wore the typical dress of Palestinian peasants, a white skullcap or a *hatta* and '*igal* on their heads, and every woman I saw was in hijab. A few boys came up and asked cheekily if we were tourists; they offered to show us around for a few shekels. But when we declined they went off without rancour. Seen like that, it should have been a normal Friday in any ordinary Arab town. One might even have forgotten Israel's existence for a while, except that in Qalqilya no such escape from reality was possible. The wall with its razor wire on top and its watchtowers monitoring everything below were constant reminders that normality was the last thing that poor town could dream of.

Salim greeted a number of people as we walked along; he told me he often came to Qalqilya out of a feeling of solidarity, but also because he had made friends there. In the old days it would not have taken long to reach Qalqilya from Taybeh and people got to know each other well. But all that was over, and, cut off as Qalqilya was when I saw it, it was a wonder there still lingered in it the remnants of a strong and steadfast society that, despite a myriad depredations, had not lost its old kindness and warmth. Salim took me to a restaurant in the souk whose owner he knew, and said it served the best breakfast in the world. And so it turned out: fresh food, warm bread, grilled meats. When I protested that it was too early for these, Salim said, 'There is no way you can come to Abu Hasan's and not eat his kebab. The meat is like butter. You will never taste anything better in your life!'

When we had breakfasted and taken our leave of Abu Hasan and his friends, who had all come in to greet Salim while we were at table, I said,

'Why has this place been so punished? What on earth could justify making it into such a prison?'

'The Israelis don't see it as a punishment,' he said. 'They make out it's a security issue because of the settlements they've built around the town. You see, to them Palestinians are very dangerous and liable to attack any Israeli they see. At least, the settlers all believe that and it makes them nervous. So, the army protects the settlers and solves the problem by shutting the Palestinians away behind the wall.' I marvelled he could speak with such equanimity, as if delivering a factual report about something to which he was indifferent.

'And of course Qalqilya is right on the frontier between Israel and the West Bank, and they say it's a place from which suicide bombers can easily cross over to attack them.'

I mulled this over as we walked. Away from the souk, the streets became ever quieter and emptier. I noticed that many of the houses were shuttered and not even a stray dog or cat could be seen. Perhaps it was because of the approaching noonday prayer and people might have been indoors or at the mosque, but yet the silence did not seem right. As we walked on towards the exit to leave the town, I realised that what I had taken for the peace of tranquillity when I first saw Qalqilya was more like the silence of death.

Once in Salim's car and driving towards Taybeh, he gave free rein to his feelings. 'You asked me about Qalqilya being punished. I didn't want to say too much when we were inside the town; they have enough problems without overhearing me talking about them.' I could sense the suppressed anger inside him. He went on: 'Of course they're being punished! Just as we all are, aren't we? It's a pity you saw Qalqilya on a Friday, it's not that quiet on weekdays, more lively. But even so, you can see what a terrible situation they're in. Most of those who can afford it are leaving. It's a place without a future.'

I looked at his profile as he drove. Salim was a strikingly handsome man with a strong face, blue eyes and black hair, and I judged him to be in his late thirties. He had been born in Israel, had studied medicine there and was fluent in Hebrew and familiar with Israeli society. Apart from a few professional colleagues, however, neither he nor his family socialised with Israelis. This was not unusual amongst the older generation of so-called Israeli Arabs – Palestinians with Israeli citizenship – who had not forgotten the harsh military rule imposed on them by the Israeli state in its early years; many had been evicted from their villages and lost their land to the new Israeli farmers.

Most of Salim's generation were much the same, alienated by the daily discrimination they suffered at the hands of Jewish Israelis. This showed itself in numerous ways, both subtle and crude. On paper, Israeli Arabs were supposed to have many rights equal with Jews. But the reality was different: only a small number of Arabs could hope to attain high office in the Israeli government, business or the professions, and most ended up employed in middle-ranking or lower occupations. All menial jobs traditionally went to Arabs until the Ethiopians, who came to Israel after 1984 and were considered almost as inferior as Arabs by the Jewish Israeli elite, started to compete for the same jobs. Despite their lowly status, it did not take the Ethiopians long to affect the same supremacist Israeli attitudes and start to look down on Arabs as well.

But none of this was frozen in time. The youngest generation of Palestinian Israelis were mixing socially with their Jewish counterparts, and aspired to be like them. Some even felt a loyalty to the Jewish state and admired its prominent people and its way of life. Older Palestinians regarded this behaviour with dismay and put it down to a confusion of identity, a sign that the young people had lost their way. No such ambiguities afflicted life in Taybeh as far as I could see. It was a strongly conservative, overwhelmingly Muslim place, its atmosphere like that of many traditional Muslim Arab towns. But for the Hebrew lettering on its billboards and in its public places, no one would have guessed it had any connection with Israel or that it lay next door to modern Israeli towns. Israeli Jews regarded places like Taybeh with distaste, thought them backward and inward-looking and kept away from them. The distinction between two such communities inhabiting the same land could not have been sharper, and each considered the other as an alien anomaly.

Finding myself in Taybeh, I remembered the story of Mr Tibi and the mulberry tree. The Tibis were old friends of my family whom I had known since childhood. Mr Tibi was a foremost scholar and expert on Islamic Spain whose erudition my father much respected. Taybeh was Mr Tibi's village of origin and his family still had land there. After many years of living in exile abroad, he had settled with his wife and grown-up children in England, where he seemed happy enough. But then, in his eighties, he began to talk about returning to Taybeh, to his land, with mounting insistence. 'I want to go back and sit under the mulberry tree in my garden,' was all the explanation he would give. It was a typically Palestinian sentiment: mulberry trees were native to Palestine and Lebanon and were widely cultivated in the Taybeh and Tulkarm area. They usually grew in proximity to fig trees and vines, and their gnarled and twisted trunks and branches gave them a distinctive appearance. Mulberry trees could reach a great height, up to seventy-five feet, and the extensive spread of their branches made a roof in the sky beneath which the ground was shady and cool.

People pointed out to Mr Tibi that it was not a practical idea. Neither he nor his wife or children would be allowed to take up residence in Israel, since only Jews had that privilege.

Everyone else needed a visitor's visa that did not exceed three months. But he persisted. They would build a house on the land, he said, and then he could satisfy his urge to sit under his tree. Appeals to the Israeli authorities to make an exception for elderly people like the Tibis and allow them to stay for longer than three months were rejected.

He was undeterred by that show of Israeli meanness and ill grace and would not give up. If it meant staying in Taybeh for just the allotted three months and then leaving the country to renew the visa for a further three months, then so be it, he said. And so indeed it was. He and his old wife went on shuffling in and out of Israel every three months until the house was built, and, though they grew older and more frail, they kept up the cycle of travel from England to Israel and then out again. Each time they went they hoped the Israelis at the border, who had got to know them through these recurrent visits, would relent and grant them a longer stay, and each time they were disappointed.

They were not in Taybeh at the time of my visit, and I asked Salim to show me their land. It was not my business to look over their property or pry into their affairs and I probably should not have gone. But I was curious to see what had drawn Mr Tibi to endure such travails. Salim, who knew all the major families of Taybeh and their land, showed no surprise at my request. He took me to a large orchard full of vines and fruit trees, one among many such orchards and testimony to the richness of Taybeh's soil.

And there was the mulberry tree, dark and tall against the sky. I walked up to it and circled around it, and in my mind's eye, I could see Mr Tibi sitting contentedly on his chair under its leaves, his wish fulfilled. He knew he could not stay and it was not ideal, but for him to go there, however interruptedly, was to be reunited with a part of the old Palestine and a sort of return.

CHAPTER 14

The City of David

The road back to Ramallah would have been shorter if I had gone there directly from Taybeh. But the day was not yet over, and there was another place I wanted to see before it ended. Salim had arranged for a family friend to drive me back, but I asked this man to make a detour by way of Jerusalem in order to reach Silwan. I had heard much about this village, which lay on the outskirts of East Jerusalem immediately to the south of the Old City walls. Until the war of 1967 it had been a quiet, rural place, unremarkable and much like any other in its vicinity. But when the victorious Israelis took over East Jerusalem in that war and later annexed it to Israel, Silwan's fortunes took a dramatic turn.

It became the pivot and focus of an impassioned Israeli archaeological hunt for the biblical past. Religious Jewish settlers had associated it with the biblical King David, and from then on it was doomed. Israelis viewed archaeology as less a scholarly pursuit for its own sake than a battleground in which to promote Jewish history as they saw it, at the expense of any other kind. The imperative was to find proof of an ancient Jewish presence in Palestine's modern land that would show the world how justified, indeed how natural, was the modern Jewish desire to reconnect with those imagined Israelite ancestors the Bible spoke of in such realistic and concrete terms. If the evidence could be found, it would give their presence in Palestine a legitimacy they still felt they lacked. It was the self-same impulse that animated the Jewish worshippers I had seen in Hebron's Ibrahimi mosque, praying at Islamic tombs they had reconfigured in their minds to be the repositories of their Hebrew patriarchs' remains.

Faced with this frenetic archaeological activity, many Arabs would say in wonderment, 'What on earth is the matter with these people? They've taken the whole damn country. Why isn't that enough?'

But it was not enough and, unluckily for Silwan, Hebrew legend identified it with the original site of Jerusalem at the time of King David. It was accordingly dubbed the 'City of David', '*Ir David*' in Hebrew, and ultra-religious Jewish settlers started to move in soon after 1967, installing themselves in homes among Silwan's Arab houses and in the spaces created by bulldozing some of them. A particular focus of this Jewish settlement was the Bustan area at the northern end of the village, allegedly the site of the biblical 'Garden of the King' where supposedly David and Solomon walked. Israeli religious organisations, headed by the especially fanatical Elad, offered generous funding, thought to be from American sources, and spurred forward the archaeological excavations designed to validate the biblical claims to Silwan. The Israeli government, the Israeli Department of Antiquities and the Jerusalem municipality all gave these groups free rein, and much of the village land right up to the southern wall of the Old City was cleared of Palestinian housing to make room for a massive National Biblical Park intended for Jewish visitors and tourists.

At the time of my visit, a demolition order had been issued for a further eighty-eight Palestinian houses still standing in the area designated for the national park. Their owners, desperate to have the order withdrawn, had managed to delay the decision for the time being. But it remained an imminent threat hovering over them like an executioner's sword. Israeli soldiers harassed them constantly with night raids and hold-ups at impromptu military checkpoints and, along with the settlers, kept up an unrelenting campaign of intimidation and attack.

There was no clear entrance to Silwan. Since Israel took it over it looked like a seamless continuation of East Jerusalem, as if it had always been a part of the city. It was a hilly place with a deep central valley, its traditional white, flat-roofed houses built picturesquely into the hillsides. Looking at them from above one could see in and amongst them the settler houses flying the blue and white Israeli flag, incongruous enclaves pointedly fenced off from their neighbours. To the right was a huge gash in the ground like a giant bomb crater. This was the major archaeological excavation site, where the search for biblical authenticity was conducted. It was massive, stretching over an area of more than one acre and sinking to a depth of twenty metres; to my mind, the ground exposed by the excavation looked violated, as if it had been forced to yield up its entrails for inspection.

The heat of the day having subsided, I could see several men at the bottom of the shaft working with chisels and hammers. Thick plastic sheeting roofed over parts of the site, and steps went down into it. My companion and I climbed down led by an elderly Palestinian who offered us coffee. He greeted a thickset, fair-haired European-looking man, an Israeli archaeologist I presumed, overseeing the Palestinian workers chiselling into the walls. Not a single Palestinian archaeologist was in sight, but I did not mention it and the Israeli obviously took me for a sympathetic visitor. I asked him what they were excavating.

'We're doing some important work on the Jewish heritage here,' he explained. His manner was pleasant and friendly, and he seemed to assume that I shared his views. 'You see these stone structures,' he said, blithely pointing to the largest which, according to what I had read, dated from the Roman period, 'they're almost certainly from the biblical age.' He must have known better, but chose to conceal it. 'We're connecting this dig with the tunnels under the southern end of the Temple Mount.' Israeli archaeologists had excavated a network of deep tunnels, which they found under the Haram al-Sharif (the Noble Sanctuary) in the area of the western wall and extending to the Via Dolorosa, against strong international protestations that such digs could undermine the foundations of the eighth-century Islamic buildings and the fourth-century Church of the Holy Sepulchre above; if not halted, they could ultimately lead to their collapse, they warned. A year or so earlier an UNRWA school in Silwan had partially fallen down because of the damage to its foundations caused by the digging.

But nothing could be allowed to stop the archaeological search for the Jewish past. As the excavations continued, any layers of history that came after the biblical age were demolished in the process of reaching back to it. Hellenistic, Roman, Byzantine and Islamic remains were cut through and forever lost to archaeology. The remnants of an eighth- to ninth-century Abbasid building were dismantled in this manner, and the tunnels uncovered by the excavations under the Old City walls passed beneath Roman, Crusader and Mamluk historical layers that no longer existed as a result. I pointed this out to the archaeologist.

He shrugged. 'I don't know about that, but the search for truth must go on,' he said firmly.

I pressed him further, making much the same point. But he remained confident of his position and serenely indifferent to what I had to say. It was the same with the Israeli guide in the City of David tourist centre above ground, which had been built in the open area opposite to the excavation site and close to Silwan's ancient cistern, a source of water the villagers had used for centuries, but now renamed 'Jeremiah's Cistern'. The guide, who was eager to tell us about the biblical marvels that had been unearthed, pointed to a structure labelled 'Bathsheba's Bath'. Did he really believe it was Bathsheba's bath, I asked? He nodded vigorously and indicated the tourist shop behind him with a broad sweep of his arm, as if the historical proof lay there; it contained a rich collection of biblical pamphlets, books on Ancient Israel and posters of how the biblical park would look, once completed.

'This is where it all began!' he proclaimed proudly, 'from King David, all down the ages, and on to us today. Isn't it wonderful? When the digging is finished and the tunnels are all connected up, visitors will be able to go down and walk underground all the way from here to the Mount of Olives and to Mount Zion.' From his enthusiastic description, it seemed that an entire underground city was in the making to create the 'Biblical Experience', as he called it, and I had no doubt that, when completed, it would feel more real to the Jewish faithful who flocked there than the concrete Islamic structures on top. And perhaps that was the aim of the project.

Near to the Israeli tourist centre and standing bravely on its own was a small Arab shop, selling what it advertised as antiquities from the archaeological site. The shopkeeper showed me Roman coins with the emperor's head on one side, and claimed they were genuine. To my untrained eye they looked authentic enough; some had been mounted on gold frames to make tasteful articles of jewellery, which he tried to sell me. There were cracked glass jars and broken pottery, all allegedly from the excavation site too, though how they had come into his possession was not clear. I felt sorry for him in his dusty, empty shop, and I doubted he did much business there.

What did the local people who watched their village being torn up and reshaped according to this historical Jewish fantasy think about it all, I wondered? From what I could see they had got used to it and went resignedly about their business, their main anxiety that the houses they lived in would escape demolition. Before leaving Silwan, I was taken to see a place in which just such a calamity had occurred, a rubble-strewn patch of ground where the house that had previously stood there was bulldozed by the army. Groups of international volunteers sympathetic to Palestinian suffering were working to clear the area prior to helping the owner rebuild his house, although there was the constant danger that the authorities would demolish it again as had happened repeatedly after many such brave endeavours. The owners of houses thus destroyed were usually required to pay the authorities for the costs of demolition.

Sometimes, driving along a beautiful road like the one going north from Ramallah as the sun was setting on the horizon I would gaze at the long shadows of ancient trees slanting down on to the quiet hillsides and imagine how it must have been before anyone was here, before modern Israel and its soldiers and bulldozers arrived, before its settlers, religious zealots and military checkpoints disrupted that gentle harmony. In these imaginings I knew I was not alone; I had a rival in every religious Jew who saw the same landscape and fancied it came straight out of the Hebrew Bible, just as the Christian travellers who came to what they called the Holy Land thought themselves to be walking 'in the footsteps of Jesus'.

It was Palestine's great misfortune that it fed so many fantasies and answered to so many emotional needs. For centuries people had pinned their dreams and delusions on its land, seen it as their salvation, and tried to make it exclusively their own. If only it had been an ordinary place, without a special history or a sacred geography, without religion or scripture, then perhaps we, its people, might have been left in peace.

'You know, being here is getting me down,' I said. 'Since I came every place I've seen is blighted in one way or another. Sometimes I feel I can hardly bear it. Is there nothing to lift the spirits?'

Hanna Nasser, to whom these remarks were addressed, looked at me in surprise and dismay.

'What are you saying?' he demanded. 'Of course there is! Have you looked about you properly? Seen our young people, our students, our clever entrepreneurs, all working in

impossible conditions? Aren't they something to be proud of?'
I started to protest that I had not meant that, but he pressed
on. 'Do you see how this society is – full of life, unstoppable,
determined? We're not giving in!'

'Look, I didn't mean *everything* was hopeless,' I said. 'You
know what I'm talking about: Israel and what it has done to
this country.'

He paused, considering me slowly, and then said, 'I tell you
what I'm going to do. I'm going to take you somewhere that
will change your mind. You'll meet someone great who will
never let you think like that again!'

I did not know who this was, but it struck me that he himself
was such a person, a local hero in a society that desperately
needed them. I had first met him after he returned to Ramallah
from a long exile. He was the president of Bir Zeit University
at the time, and much admired for his achievement in trans-
forming what had been a community college founded by his
father into Palestine's first university. It stood in attractive leafy
grounds on top of a hill near the village of Bir Zeit just outside
Ramallah. His patriotism, self-confidence and independent
thinking soon aroused Israeli hostility, and in 1974 he was
deported to Amman where he remained until 1993. In that
time he became a member of the PLO's Executive Committee
and later head of another organ of the PLO, the Palestine
National Fund. Shortly before Nasser retired, Arafat appointed
him director of the Central Elections Commission, a body that
oversaw elections to the Palestinian Legislative Council, which
post he still held when he came to see me that morning.

'Apart from anything else, what're you doing sitting in this
dark office on such a beautiful morning? Is this where they've
stuck you? No wonder you feel so gloomy.' I had gone to my
office at Dr Sabah's ministry with the intention of lying low
and avoiding the conference preparations at the other ministry a little longer. Nasser had found me there after visiting
Dr Sabah.

'Hey, Esperance!' he called out sharply through my open office door. She ran over with more alacrity than I had ever seen her show before and stood in the doorway smiling at him. He was an attractive, boyish-looking man with an American crew-cut, and his manner was so playful and charming that no one could have taken offence at his peremptory tone. And evidently Esperance did not, as she beamed at him playfully. 'Why d'you put the Doctora in the back like this? It's a wonder I found her!' She looked flustered but was still smiling.

'You haven't visited us for ages, Dr Hanna,' she said archly. 'Can I bring you some coffee?'

'Thank you, I'd love to, but another time. For now I'm taking the Doctora away to somewhere more cheerful.'

'Where are we going?' I asked, rather taken with him myself.

'You'll see. Just get yourself ready and let's go.'

There was a cooling breeze outside and a brilliant blue sky. Once we got into his car, he was more serious. 'I must apologise for not coming to see you before. I knew you were here, but we're so busy getting everything set up for the coming elections, I just didn't get around to it. I'm sorry.' Elections for the Palestinian Legislative Council were due early in the New Year, and preparations for them had already started. An extensive training programme for people in the rural areas unfamiliar with such procedures was under way, to enable their participation in the vote. It was no easy matter to organise a national plebiscite in a situation of restricted movement and barriers separating one locality from another, as was the case in the West Bank and Gaza.

Getting around those hurdles and Israel's extreme hostility to the whole process so as to ensure that voters could reach their ballot stations required no little ingenuity. Israeli obstructions were everywhere, and in Jerusalem the authorities insisted on dividing Palestinians according to voting districts inside or outside the eastern half of the city. Those inside were allowed a postal vote only, and voters living in the central area, that is, in and around the Old City, were forbidden from voting altogether. As for Gaza, contact with the election committee had to be done by video-conferencing, since no one from the West Bank was allowed to go there.

It was a brave effort and I could see why Arafat had put a capable man like Hanna Nasser in charge; if only it were not happening under military occupation, I thought. When the elections finally took place in January 2006, the international observers overseeing the process pronounced them free and fair. It was unfortunate for the winners that the results were not to the liking of Israel or its Western allies, and they and the voters were made to pay a heavy price.

The new Palestinian Legislative Council was dominated by Hamas members rather than by Fateh, which the US and its allies considered more amenable to Israel's interests. Strenuous US interference in the form of threats and bribes in the run-up to the elections to ensure a Fateh victory were unsuccessful, and the popular vote brought in a Hamas government. As soon as this took power in January 2006, an immediate and total blockade that paralysed its ability to operate was imposed by the US, the EU and Israel, all of which made determined efforts to topple the new government. All contacts with it were suspended, gas and fuel supplies were halted, and soon afterwards all Western financial aid was stopped with grave humanitarian consequences for the Palestinian population.

'I was on my way to see Mahmoud Darwish, and thought you'd like to say hello to him. Now there's a man to raise anyone's spirits!'

'Indeed I would,' I assured him. 'It would be a great privilege.'

It was an exciting prospect to visit this great man, whom I had met in the past but always briefly and at a distance. He had an office in the Sakakini Cultural Centre, a beautiful old Ramallah house that had once belonged to a mayor of the town and subsequently sold on to the Palestinian Ministry of Culture. The ministry set up the Centre to promote Palestinian culture and the arts, and it had a rich programme of musical and literary events. Seeing it that morning I could not help thinking about the man after whom it was named, Khalil Sakakini, who before 1948 had lived two streets below us in Qatamon. He had been a great Palestinian educationalist, a committed nationalist and a prolific writer; he and my father had been friends and sometime colleagues. His splendid house, which had taken three years to build to his exact specifications, used to be a meeting place for writers and intellectuals, and held a large and valuable collection of Arabic books and beautifully ornamented Qurans which he had assembled over many years.

In 1948, not long after the Sakakini family, which had held out against leaving our war-torn area until the very end, was forced out, the house was ransacked by Israeli soldiers. In their wake experts from the Hebrew University library turned up in vans, carted off Sakakini's most valuable books and placed them in the Israeli National Library at the university, where they were classified under the designation of 'Abandoned Property'. Many other Palestinian book collections held in private homes in Jerusalem, Jaffa, Haifa and Nazareth met the same fate, and no doubt my father's library was one of those likewise removed from our house at about the same time. All the books seized in this way went to the Israeli National Library and were kept there from then on, to this day unclaimed by their owners, most of whom knew nothing of the looting.[1]

Mahmoud Darwish's office was on the first floor of the Cultural Centre, a large sunny room where we found him sitting at his desk reading. He was a slim, elegant-looking man

---

1 The story came to light through the researches of Gish Amit, an Israeli PhD student, who estimated that 30,000 books, many of them irreplaceable treasures of historical and religious significance, had been pillaged in this way as part of a systematic assault on the Palestinian cultural heritage. His findings were made into a documentary, *The Great Book Robbery*, by the Israeli filmmaker Benny Brunner in 2011.

in his mid-sixties with a thin, sensitive face and large-framed glasses. He hardly said a word to me or looked me straight in the eye after we were introduced, and I wasn't sure if he remembered who I was, even though we had once been at the same conference in Abu Dhabi for two days in the mid-1990s.

'Doctora Ghada is here at the Ministry of Media and Communications,' said Hanna Nasser, 'where she's giving them help with ... their strategy, I believe?' He looked inquiringly at me and laughed. Darwish said nothing. 'You know who she is, surely? Her uncle was Abu Salma.'

'Of course I know her.' Darwish looked at me for the first time and smiled. 'And who could ever forget Abu Salma, our great teacher?'

The atmosphere had lightened somewhat at mention of my uncle, and we all sat down. Darwish's reticence and modest demeanour belied his great fame in the world of poetry and his high standing among Palestinians, for whom he was a source of immense pride. He belonged to a generation of political poets that sprang up after the creation of the Israeli state and the Palestinian suffering it led to. The resistance poetry they wrote was full of anger at what had happened, of longing and nostalgia for the usurped homeland, of Palestine's essence, its scents and flowers, its thyme and olives. Many of the poems expressed defiance and a determination to resist oblivion.

In that, they were inheritors of an older tradition amongst Palestinian poets writing before 1948, when Palestine was under the British Mandate. Reflecting the concerns of that time, they had voiced their refusal to accept British domination of their land and anger at British complicity in the Zionist plan to take it over. My uncle, who was my father's half-brother and whose real name was Abdul-Karim al-Karmi, was an arch-example of these poets, and as such soon came to the unfavourable attention of the British authorities. While employed as a teacher by the department of education along with my father, he published a poem called 'Jabal al-Mukabbir' about the famous hill outside East Jerusalem. In the 1930s Jabal al-Mukabbir became the site of the British High Commissioner's residence, and my uncle, using historical and allegorical allusions to conceal the poem's real intent, wrote of the determination to bring down this seat of power on Jabal al-Mukabbir. The British authorities were not fooled by the symbolism and he was dismissed from his job.

But his poems, like those of his equally prominent contemporary, Ibrahim Tuqan, were eagerly received by Palestinians at the time and widely read. They went on to be taught in schools throughout the Arab world for long after his death. Just as his poetry had struck a chord in people's hearts, that of Mahmoud Darwish followed in the same vein. Many of his lines so memorably fitted the Palestinian condition in its various aspects that they were often quoted or used as titles of stories and plays. They gave a vivid flavour of what exile meant, and especially for someone displaced like me. I felt him speaking directly to me in such lines as, 'I am from there, I am from here, I am neither there nor here'; or again, 'I come from there and I remember'; 'We have a country of words'; and especially when he wrote, 'We travel like other people, but we return to nowhere.' His words resonated with all Palestinians wherever they were, for they reflected the multiple experiences that were the lot of so many, whether refugees, exiles, or unequal citizens in Israel.

Born in Palestine in 1941 in a village near Acre, he and his family had fled during the Nakba to become refugees in Lebanon before returning to what had become Israel and to his village, which he found razed to the ground and replaced by two Jewish settlements. He had then lived as a second-class Israeli citizen until his citizenship was revoked by reason of his political activism; he was exiled once again to Lebanon where he witnessed the siege of Beirut and the Sabra and Shatila massacres in 1982, commemorated in his long and vivid prose poem, 'Memory for Forgetfulness'. Being a member of the PLO's executive committee, he was evacuated at the time along with other PLO members to Tunis and later left for Paris. He spent the last years of his life in Amman and Ramallah, where I saw him.

Darwish was a remarkable figure, not least in his refusal, despite everything, to dehumanise the Israelis of whom he said, 'I will continue to humanise the enemy. The first love affair in my life was with a Jewish girl.' He sought reconciliation between the two sides, asserting that when that happened, 'The Jew will not be ashamed to find an Arab element in himself, and the Arab will be content to declare that he incorporates Jewish elements.'

It was thrilling to be face-to-face with him, and I wished I could have appreciated his poetry more fully. But my Arabic was not good enough, since I had been schooled from a young age in England where no Arabic tuition was available in those days. And it would certainly have taken considerable proficiency to understand his poems as they later developed to encompass themes drawn from ancient religion, mythology, philosophy and history; his allusions were often obscure to those not knowledgeable in these disciplines. But he also wrote much that people could identify with. As his fame grew, he became a household name for Palestinians everywhere and the recipient of many prestigious international literary awards and prizes. His poetry, like my uncle's, came to be read in schools all over the Arab world. In 2010 there was even an Israeli proposal by the minister of education, the head of the Meretz party, for it to be included in the curricula of Israeli schools. But the then prime minister, Ehud Barak, opposed the idea and it was never adopted. Even so, four volumes of his poetry were translated into Hebrew.

As it turned out, very little came of my meeting with Darwish. Hanna Nasser left us alone after a while to return to his work, and in the awkward silence that ensued I did not know what to talk to him about and his shyness did not help.

When I saw him again in Ramallah at a ceremony to mark the launch of his newest poetry collection, the organisers asked me to come on to the platform with him. I presented him with my memoir, *In Search of Fatima*, which he seemed pleased to receive although I knew his English was not good, and he gave me a copy of his new book in return. I thought I would try to visit him again before I left Ramallah, but it never happened, and three years later almost to the day he died in a US hospital, still in exile and far from home.

Looking back on that encounter with him, I wished fervently I had made more of it. What an opportunity I had lost to talk to him about the past and our shared experience of exile and rootlessness. I should have asked him about his memories of the Nakba when he fled with his family at about the same age as I did, and told him mine; how, so many years later, the feeling of loss had never gone, nor the longing for the home that had been there. And how there was a particular loss that I could not forget.

Even though my individual story might have meant nothing to him, I was sure he would recognise its theme, one he wrote about in one form or another for most of his life; and I had an intuition that I could have told him about the loss of Fatima; the secret Fatima who lived in my heart and was the embodiment of my dimly remembered childhood. Fatima, swallowed up, as so many were, in the abyss of 1948, when women lost their children and old men fell by the wayside, left behind in the stampede of people fleeing for their lives.

We never heard of or from her again, knew nothing of her fate, when she died or where, until she became a distant memory, a faint ephemeral presence that lingered only in my mind and whom no one mentioned any more. Although Mahmoud Darwish and I did not really know each other and I could not presume on a friendship with him that did not exist, I had a strong sense that of all people he would have understood about Fatima and why I could not let go her memory.

CHAPTER 15

Fatima

The woman called Fatima al-Basha came into my life during that fateful time before 1948. She was what townspeople would have called a *fallaha*, a village woman, who lived in al-Maliha village about three miles south-west of Jerusalem. My mother found her honest and hardworking, and so took her on to clean the house and help with the cooking a couple of times a week. Following the unexpected death on Christmas Eve of my uncle Mahmoud, assassinated in Beirut by a rival Palestinian political faction, my parents had to attend his funeral in Tulkarm and I was left behind as an infant with Fatima to look after me during my mother's absence.[1] Palestine had recently come out of a three-year general strike and mass revolt against British rule, and it was an unstable and uncertain period. The British, accused of complicity in enabling the immigration into Palestine of Jews from Europe whom Palestinians feared were there to set up a Jewish state, were the main target of people's anger, in addition to the Zionists working assiduously to build that state.

The General Strike was a great rebellion whose intensity so shocked the British authorities that they were forced to recruit extra troops in order to quell the unrest. Assisted by the nascent 15,000-strong Jewish army that the British had trained and which the Jews named the Haganah, they put down the revolt

---

1   Much political infighting took place in Palestine during the 1930s between supporters of the Grand Mufti of Jerusalem, Hajj Amin al-Husseini, and those of the mayor of Jerusalem, Raghib al-Nashashibi. It led to several assassinations of members of the rival camps.

with brutal harshness. Thousands of Palestinians, most of them peasants, were killed, their leaders executed or imprisoned, and many homes were demolished – a practice faithfully emulated by Israel against the Palestinians today. Because Palestine's main port of Jaffa was closed during the strike, the British retaliated by encouraging the Zionists to build a rival one in Tel Aviv. British conduct throughout the revolt was one of ruthless opposition to the demands of the strikers and full determination to support the Zionist enterprise in the country, whatever the cost to the native population. By the time the strike ended in 1939, the Palestinians were left leaderless and demoralised. My father could never speak of those events without anger and bitterness at the great sacrifices he saw ordinary people make trying to attain their rights and the failure of their leaders to take proper charge of the uprising and gain them some reward for those sacrifices.

Fatima's life had been a difficult one, married off at a young age to a man who treated her so badly as to make her escape back to her parents' house. Her two daughters by the marriage remained with her, and her husband seemed subsequently to have disappeared; we never knew whether he had died or abandoned them, and never heard any more about him. By the time we met her, Fatima was living with her daughters in a house in al-Maliha near her brother, Muhammad, who also came to work for us as gardener and odd-job man. Soon she was coming daily to our house, but never stayed the night except when my mother asked her to.

I remember her as a gentle, kind presence who never lost her temper or got flustered. My mother was a sociable, gregarious woman and was often out to see her friends during the day, leaving Fatima at home with us. We were living in Qatamon, and I was about two years old, my sister and brother a few years older. In no time I became deeply attached to her, followed her about everywhere as she worked, and talked to her incessantly about whatever came into my head. Even when she tried to sleep during the siesta hour in the afternoon, I would sit beside her, telling her stories and wanting to keep her awake. She would lie on the mosaic floor of the veranda in front of the house with her veil half covering her face, her eyes closed but nodding at me occasionally to make me feel she was listening. I have no doubt that she slept through most of my chatter, and after a while I would give up and lie down beside her, looking up at the underside of the veranda roof and hoping she would soon wake up.

When I saw our house again after the passage of many years and when it had passed through many hands, it was standing in the same street but on a new map; the tiled veranda was still there with its mosaic floor preserved. Seeing it instantly conjured up that image of a sleeping Fatima and the child that was me beside her. I used to make a point of eating my lunch with her in the kitchen, while the rest of the family ate in the dining room. I somehow identified with her, did not want her to eat alone having no one to talk to and trying to finish her meal quickly so she could clear up the dishes from our table. Her brother sometimes joined us, and I remember him too as kind and always ready to help. I saw Fatima as my special person, devoted only to me, but when I grew up and thought back on that time, I realised that she had cared for us all in equal measure.

We loved going to her house in the village and would walk there all the way with her, Muhammad sometimes coming along as well. It took us a good hour to get there, but when we reached the outskirts of the village with its white peasant mud houses clustered close together and the Omar ibn al-Khattab mosque in the village centre whose tall minaret could be seen from miles around, our tiredness would vanish. In those days al-Maliha had a population of about 2,000 and its rich agricultural land grew wheat, barley, olives and fruit. A freshwater spring on the periphery served the whole village, a water trough beside it for the animals.

Fatima's house was small and square-shaped with a wooden roof. Inside it was cool and homely, its one room the place where everyone sat, ate and slept. Fatima's family was poor and just managed to make ends meet, but in my memory it could not have been richer. Fatima's daughters were warm and affectionate and it seemed to me everyone loved and cared for each other. We relished the simple peasant food she gave us – homemade bread – local black and green olives, fresh spring onions, olive oil and thyme, and it was as if we had eaten the best food in the world.

Fatima was with us from 1939 until our departure in 1948, years that should have been happy ones for an ordinary family like ours had they not been overshadowed by the encroaching Zionist presence in the country. Our innocent pleasures became increasingly curtailed as more Jewish immigrants entered Palestine and the intention to elbow out those in the way, that is, us, became ever clearer. British policy in Palestine in those years, affected as it was by the Second World War, was inchoate and paradoxical. The Jews, having enjoyed a favoured staus under the British Mandate from 1922 until 1948, went on the offensive in the 1940s against their British benefactors whom they had begun to see as the major obstacle in their path towards statehood. Faced with this unexpected development, the British reacted against those they called 'Jewish terrorists' and tried to limit further Jewish immigration into Palestine. But at no time did they turn their backs wholeheartedly on Zionism, and we ended up the unlucky victims of this favouritism. By 1947, the situation having become untenable, the British decided to shed the burden of Palestine that they themselves had created and, to Jewish jubilation, announced the ending of the Mandate.

As a child I understood nothing of these events or of the massive upheaval they heralded. But ordinary life around us began to change, subtly at first, and then more dramatically. The number of Jewish families in our area, all European immigrants, increased, although they were not unpleasant at first and kept themselves to themselves. My father knew one or two of them and, as the persecution of Jews in Germany grew and the German armies began to advance on North Africa, a few of them even started to speak of converting to Islam.

In 1946, Jewish terrorists blew up the King David Hotel in the centre of Jerusalem, the headquarters of the Mandate government, and killed over ninety people. Thereafter matters deteriorated rapidly, and by 1947 the British decided to throw the problem at the United Nations. In November of that year the UN voted to partition Palestine between Jews and Arabs. The Palestinians reacted to this extraordinary decision, taken without their permission or participation, with rage and disbelief; the Jews were overjoyed, and we were caught in the middle of the fighting that erupted between the two sides. Yet for a while life at home remained the same, our father going to work every day, our mother socialising as was her wont, and Fatima staying with us as she always had throughout my young life.

Like all children, I went on playing heedlessly with my friend Randa and doing all the things that were a normal part of life. But at the beginning of 1948, that normal life suddenly ceased. My school and that of my brother closed, as it became too dangerous for pupils to get there. My sister became a temporary boarder at her school to avoid having to make the perilous daily journey to reach it. Above all, I started to feel an atmosphere of tension and anxiety hanging over our parents, though I did not exactly know why. Throughout that time, Fatima remained a steadying, reassuring influence in our home, and sometimes and to our great delight stayed overnight.

The situation did not hold like that for long. As from January 1948, we became aware of an intense push by Jewish militias to take over our part of West Jerusalem. Several Jewish settlements already existed in our neighbourhood and the Zionists had earmarked it to be part of their future state.

Their plan was to empty Qatamon and the nearby parts of West Jerusalem of their Arab residents and replace them with Jews. It was in the drive to chase us out of Qatamon that our departure finally took place in April 1948. Many families had already fled, but my mother hung on, refusing to leave her home. And Fatima and her brother stayed on too. Our street became an eerie place; the houses were empty of the people we knew and hardly anyone walked outside for fear of the Jewish snipers shooting from the upper windows. I still played in our garden, but had no one to play with.

Finally the day came when we too had to leave. It was an April morning full of spring, trees in blossom in the garden, a bracing chill in the air but the sun already shining from a deep blue sky. We were headed for my grandparents' house in Damascus and would take a taxi from the central bus station to get there. My parents had worked out that this was the best plan, since, like all the Palestinians who had been forced to leave at that time, they believed our departure to be a temporary one, undertaken at a time of war, and that we would be back as soon as the situation calmed down. They did not suspect that we were leaving for good, our return impossible once the new Jewish immigrants had taken over our homes.

Whatever my sister, who was nearly eighteen at the time, or my eleven-year-old brother made of our precipitate departure that morning, I could only feel bewildered and alarmed, sensing rather than knowing that something disastrous was happening all around me. A taxi, obtained with great difficulty, since our area of Jerusalem had become dangerous, took us to the bus station. Muhammad and Fatima came to see us off, but they were to stay behind: Fatima returning to Qatamon as my father had instructed, to look after the house until we came back – 'very soon', as he told her – and Muhammad continuing his gardening and other caretaker duties. Since they did not live in Jerusalem, he thought they would be safe enough just calling in on our house.

As it transpired, we had managed to leave in the nick of time, for Qatamon fell to the Zionists not long after. People said it had been a wise decision to escape from Jerusalem when we did, given the political situation. But what did I know of wisdom or politics? I only knew that saying goodbye to Fatima at the bus station that morning was like setting the seal on a living nightmare. I clung to her by the taxi, unwilling to let go or accept that she would come no further with us. To leave her was to leave all that I knew as home, its comfort and security, and for what? A journey to an unfamiliar place and unfamiliar people I did not want to see. When I was eventually persuaded to let her go and made to settle back into the taxi, a silent emptiness descended on me, as if my whole life had ended on that terrible day.

Al-Maliha's fate after we left was a sad one. As the battle for Palestine intensified, the village came under the protection of a truce drawn up between the villagers and the Haganah to spare it from attack. But in spite of this agreement, from May 1948 onwards it became a target for Jewish forces fighting to take over West Jerusalem and its environs. By the middle of July al-Maliha was totally overrun following a fierce battle with Arab troops from the surrounding countries trying to defend it. It was emptied of its inhabitants, most of whom had already fled in the waves of Israeli attack before this last battle. Their homes were subsequently taken over by Jewish immigrants predominantly from Arab countries, and the name of al-Maliha was dropped in favour of 'Manahath', said by Israeli scholars to be the name of the biblical place with which they had identified the village. But Israelis went on calling it by its old name, modified to 'Malha'.

Under its new keepers it was extensively modernised; a housing development and shopping mall were built, but a number of the original two-storey houses which had belonged to the better-off Palestinian inhabitants of al-Maliha remained, as Israelis found them picturesque and desirable. The mosque in the centre was also allowed to remain, but it was shut up and neglected. In time a basketball arena was added to the new Israeli Malha and a 'Biblical Zoo', stocked with wild-life said to be mentioned in the Bible, became a main tourist attraction. By the time the Israelis were done with it, the old village had been effectively obliterated. Only the mosque's tall round minaret, which could be seen from Jerusalem high up on the hill where al-Maliha stood, remained to mark that it had once been a very different place.

In the turbulent years that followed our flight from Jerusalem, spent first in Damascus where we jostled with my aunt's family also seeking refuge in my grandfather's house, and then in London where we went next, my father having found work there, no one spoke about what had been left behind, nor of Fatima. Bewildered by our new lives and struggling to adjust, my siblings and I hardly ever mentioned Palestine. Learning to settle in post-war London for us, who had never travelled anywhere in our lives, was daunting and all-consuming. We never formed the habit of recalling the past in those early years and I do not remember that we ever discussed what had happened to us or how we had felt during those last terrifying months in Jerusalem. Our parents rarely spoke of it; it was as if the door had been firmly shut on Palestine, and only what was happening to us in England mattered.

It did not occur to me for years how odd this was, how different from the experience of many other Palestinians – particularly those in the refugee camps where generations passed down to each other the stories of how they had left Palestine, from what village or town, and what they had endured. When I visited some of the camps in Lebanon in 1998, I was struck by the small children reciting the names of the places 'they' came from in Palestine, as handed down by their grandparents and reiterated by their parents. Yet in our home it was as if there were a taboo on such rumination. No one said as much, but there was a distinct reluctance to reflect on what had befallen us. We took our cue from our parents' silence on the subject and focused on the present, our education and how to live in the society around us. Our father threw himself into his job as language supervisor at the BBC Arabic Service, and our mother tried to make a home for us in the new environment.

Slowly the memories of Jerusalem faded and retreated to some dark corner of my mind that was out of reach. My parents, despite their unwillingness to dwell on the past, had not forgotten, but I suspect they could not encompass the pain of remembering. They were both still young when Palestine was 'ruined', as my mother always referred to the time of the Nakba:, my father then forty-three years old and my mother thirty-six. They must have looked forward to spending the rest of their lives secure in their home and in their city, seeing us grow up, marry and give them grandchildren. The assault on their lives that robbed them of everything in a few months was too violent, too final for them to digest, and so they put the memories away. And for the rest of their lives they never returned to visit the old homeland. I imagined that to see the Palestine they remembered in alien custody, its new occupiers strutting about the streets and orchards as if they had a valid title to them, was unthinkable. For them Palestine had died in 1948, 'it's gone,' my mother would often say. 'Palestine is gone.'

And Fatima was a part of that death. We never tried to find her after our departure. But we heard that she had continued to check up on our house for a while after we left, and then her visits stopped, presumably when the area came under full Israeli control. We heard nothing more and did not know what had happened, nor did she have a way of contacting us. So she melted into the darkness of that unmentionable time, and no one asked about her or the neighbours we had known. Indeed, if we heard about any of them it was merely by accident. Such disconnections were not unusual in the exodus of

1948. Friends and relatives were separated and lost to each other; some were reunited, but not all. It was a tragic consequence of the chaos and panic that the flights and forced evacuations had occasioned and whose details were not recorded. No follow-up service was ever set up to help people trace their missing loved ones, and it went down as one more trauma in an avalanche of distress.

For decades I carried my parents' attitudes unthinkingly, but then began gradually to reject them. It was not true that Palestine had gone: it was still there, albeit in others' hands, and to banish it from our lives was to accept the Zionist claim to its ownership. In 1991, forty-three years after we left Jerusalem, I finally took the plunge and travelled to the forbidden land, Israel. My sister followed suit some years later, but my brother could not bring himself to do the same and never went. Searching for our old house in Qatamon, which I did not find on that first journey, the thought of Fatima came back. But it was not until I had visited Jerusalem several times that I began to feel the urge to look for her. Even though I had broken the taboo and taken the fearful step of seeing the country that was mine but now belonged to others, I had still not completed the task. The ends of the chain that was broken in April 1948 were still hanging loose, and I had to find the missing pieces to link them up again.

'You know, you Palestinians have got to learn to let go,' a Jewish psychiatrist I knew in London once told me. He was something of a friend and, like many Jews, was intrigued by the Palestine issue. 'It was all a long time ago, and you're here now in this wonderful country. Why not be glad of that? Let go the past, you can't change it.' He was what one might call a liberal Zionist, sympathetic to Palestinian suffering, but a firm believer in the right of Jews to a state of their own in their ancestral land as he put it.

'Look at the Jews. Many of us came from Lithuania or Latvia or Poland, but we've made good lives here in England.

Or take me. We came from Lithuania without a penny. We were so poor, I had only one pair of shoes full of holes. But we worked hard and settled down, and now I'm reasonably happy. England's given me chances I never would have had where I came from. I've learnt to forget, and so should you.'

I knew that he had gone to live on an Israeli kibbutz in the early 1950s and been enthralled by its socialist ideals. Discovering then that he had been given a new homeland, Israel, to make up for being driven out of Lithuania, and that he could choose to live either there or in England, must have been gratifying.

'If only I could,' I answered. 'But you see, for us the past is still the present.' I realized he did not know what I meant and understood nothing of our predicament.

'Well it shouldn't be. Look,' he said in a gentler voice, 'you have to accept Israel is there to stay. It's our homeland too. We've all got to learn to tolerate each other and get over the bitterness and anger.'

The quest for Fatima took place during the time I was in Ramallah in 2005. I was determined to find out what had become of her. The more I thought about it the more inexplicable it seemed that I could have waited for so long to do that. I did not know where to start and tried to recall what had been said about her after we left Palestine. There had been talk of her ending up in a refugee camp, like so many Palestinians in 1948, but we did not know where. It never occurred to me to tell anyone of the family what I was doing. None of them was given to 'sentimentality', which is almost certainly how they would have designated my search for Fatima. So I started off by talking to Sharif Kanaaneh, a respected professor of sociology at Bir Zeit University and a veteran of Palestinian history and folklore. His first suggestion was to assign the search to a young student he knew who was working on

Palestinian traditions and customs. She was a refugee herself, from Jalazoun camp to the north of Ramallah.

Rabi'a, as she was called, had been born in the camp, and was a fresh-looking, tidily dressed and intelligent young woman. I found her a willing collaborator, interested in the project and, having heard about my memoir with Fatima's name in its title, was keen to do the research with me. Once she understood what I needed, she started to make her investigations in a practical and methodical way. In no time she was able to establish that there was a small group of refugees originally from al-Maliha living in the al-Am'ari refugee camp in al-Bireh. Like Jalazoun, this camp had been established in 1949, but it was smaller, with about 5,000 residents who had come mostly from Jaffa, Lydda, Ramla and their associated villages. It was not as crowded as the other camps and looked more like a poor neighbourhood than a refugee camp of the type I was used to seeing, with brick and concrete houses built on several levels, narrow alleys and a rural atmosphere. Like many such longstanding camps, it had acquired an air of permanence and appeared like a natural part of the town around it.

We visited there one afternoon. People sat chatting in the shade outside their houses. They were friendly and helpful, directing us to the homes of people who they thought had come from al-Maliha. We went to talk to a number of these, mostly elderly men and women. But after a few hours of interviews we had drawn a blank. And then someone mentioned an old woman from al-Maliha by the name of Fatima whom we had missed. Going to see her raised my hopes again, and I hardly dared believe I had been lucky enough to locate my Fatima so quickly. When we found her small house, two women welcomed us into the front room where she sat. They explained they were not relatives, but looked in on her regularly. I could see that she was very old, at least ninety by her own reckoning, and her eyesight was poor. Her name was Fatima Ibrahim, and although she used to live in al-Maliha, she did not recall anyone with the surname of al-Basha and there was no other Fatima from the village in the camp. I asked her if she had ever worked for a family in Qatamon, told her my name and that of my parents, but she did not know us.

No one else had anything more to offer, and in the end we gave up and left, disappointed. 'Never mind, Doctora,' said Rabi'a sympathetically. 'It's only the beginning, and I won't stop looking for you. With God's will, we will find her.'

The search and the memories it evoked pervaded my mind. It was as if my quest for Fatima had opened up a magic chest that transported me to the Palestine of those days, brought back its colours and smells and the whole feel of it. So powerful was the effect that I could scarcely wrench myself away from it back to my daily life in Ramallah, the ministry, Dr Farid and his conference. It was like watching a flashback in a film, the people looking younger and wearing different clothes, the sights and sounds of another age. I did not want to leave this vanished place that held the memories I had forgotten, would show me my childhood, my friends, my house as it had been, and bring back the elusive Fatima whose features I could no longer recall.

I wandered around in this semi-haunted state for days. And then Rabi'a got in touch. It seemed that following our visit to al-Am'ari camp, she had decided to return in case she could find anyone we had not managed to talk to when we were there. Sure enough, she found one or two such people, and one contact led to another until she was finally directed to a man they believed was related to the woman we were seeking. He lived in al-Bireh, and after more investigation she found the house where he lived and went to visit him on her own.

'He's Fatima's nephew, I'm fairly sure,' she said excitedly, 'and when he heard about you he invited you to meet him.'

Would it be another disappointment, I wondered? I trusted Rabi'a's good intentions but was unsure how rigorous her research was. Dr Kannaneh, on the other hand, was emphatic about her skills. He insisted she knew what she was doing and had never failed him in any research she had carried out for him. He urged me to follow her lead and let him know the outcome. He had read my book and was just as intrigued as the rest of us. So I met Rabi'a in front of the municipality building in al-Bireh and we walked towards our destination from there.

The house was in a side street. It was modest but well kept, and when we arrived a man who looked to be in his fifties opened the door and welcomed us in. His wife and another couple were also there, and what I presumed were his children came forward to greet us.

'This is Doctora Ghada,' said Rabi'a, and we all shook hands. I was indeed in the house of Fatima's nephew, Muhammad's son, an engineer by profession and, from the look of his home, a successful one. He was warm and forthcoming and knew why I was there. It did not take long for the story to be told. Fatima and her daughters had fled al-Maliha in the summer of 1948. They had gone, not into a refugee camp as we had supposed, but to Bethlehem. It was a short distance from al-Maliha and most villagers had gone in the same direction. Fatima's brother, Muhammad, who had been with them, eventually settled in Ramallah where he lived out his days.

'I don't know too much about it because it happened before I was born,' he said. 'But I remember my aunt, who came to stay with us many times. I really loved her. We all did.'

'So, she is dead?' I asked. That she should still have been alive was too much to hope for. I did not know how old she had been when we knew her, but she had not been a young woman.

'She died in 1987,' he said. 'I wasn't there when it happened, but I heard that she went on wishing she could see you all again until the end. When your father used to come on the BBC, she would listen to him on the radio and then start to talk about him.'

'Do you know if she ever mentioned any of us children, me in particular?' I could not stop myself from wanting to know. 'I'm not sure, but I don't remember that she did.'

I digested this. 'Do you have any photographs?' I asked.

He nodded and went over to a table in the corner. Inside one of the drawers was an envelope which he took out. While he was looking through it his wife offered us a cup of coffee. The woman of the other couple, who had been listening avidly to the conversation, got up to help. Rabi'a was looking at me with an intense expression.

'Here we are,' Fatima's nephew said, holding a photograph in his hand. He came over and gave it to me. 'If you look, you will see my father and aunt side by side. They must have gone to a studio to have this picture taken, although I don't know when and for what reason.'

It was a black-and-white photograph, its edges a pale ochre colour due to its age. Looking straight at the camera were a man and a woman, he with a white *hatta* and black *'igal* on his head and wearing a Western-style jacket over his long striped tunic such as peasants wore. That was Muhammad, his face smooth and youthful, the skin polished and shiny in the studio light, and his light-coloured eyes bright and alert. He was half-smiling at the camera and exuded an air of friendliness and warmth. Next to him was Fatima. I stared and stared at her face, avidly searching her features for familiar traces that would evoke my memory of her. I could not believe I had finally recovered her elusive image, so hidden and unreachable for years, and could see her at last. Her expression was serious and unsmiling. She wore a loose head covering under which her dark hairline was visible, and her features were fine, with an aquiline nose and thinnish lips. Her eyes were dark and soft as they looked into the camera. From her face it was impossible to know what sort of a person she was beyond the fact that she looked kind, but purposeful and mature.

Seeing my reaction, her nephew said, 'The man who'll be

able to tell you much more than I can is her grandson in Bethlehem. That is where she used to live. You should talk to him or visit him.' He got up. 'I can phone him now. Would you like me to? He knows you're here and wants to talk to you anyway.'

Fatima's grandson was called Muhammad al-Helou. He was the son of her eldest daughter, and they had all lived together. The phone call I made to him, followed by a visit to his house in Bethlehem, finally filled in the gaps of Fatima's life after we left in April 1948. From then onwards al-Maliha had been repeatedly attacked by Jewish forces: in April, again at the beginning of May and finally in the middle of July when it was completely depopulated. It was in one of those assaults, he was not sure which, that Fatima and the rest of the family fled their homes. They half-walked, half-ran with what they could carry of their belongings and took the road to Bethlehem. Knowing no one there and having nowhere to stay, they sought out a cave in the hills where they could take temporary shelter. The hills around Bethlehem were famous for their ancient limestone caves that were frequently interconnected. Legend has it that Jesus was born in such a cave, misleadingly described as a 'manger'. The Church of the Nativity and several other churches in the Bethlehem area were built over caves.

Many had more than one chamber and were traditionally used to shelter livestock in winter. Families often shared the caves with their animals in separate chambers. The cave Fatima's family lived in remained their home for a long while after 1948, possibly years, her grandson could not remember. In that time they learnt that not only their village but more than half of Palestine was permanently lost to them. With hard work and patience they made a modest living and eventually moved out of the cave and into a small house, also in the hills above Bethlehem. And there Fatima stayed, going to see her brother Muhammad in Ramallah from time to time, until her death.

Her grandson remembered that she once said she wanted to see my father again. It was sometime in the 1980s after one of his BBC broadcasts.

'What did you say?' I asked.

'I wished I could have done what she wanted,' he answered. 'I knew what seeing your family again meant to her. But how could we have managed it?'

He sighed and shook his head regretfully, and all I could think was how terrible it was that for all those years and unbeknown to us, there we were and there she was, both alive at the same time, albeit in different countries but accessible to each other, and yet we never met. How different it would have been if I could have seen her again, could have asked her a myriad questions to summon back my childhood, to look it full in the face and dispel forever the phantoms of the past.

As if he read my mind, he said gently, 'Never mind. It was not meant to be. But we will both always remember her.'

CHAPTER 16

Motherhood

When I finally forced myself to return to the ministry I found that Dr Farid was back, looking vigorous and refreshed. He had stayed on after 15 August to witness the dramatic Israeli withdrawal from Gaza. With remarkable efficiency, Israeli troops evacuated the 8,000 Gaza settlers in a few days and bulldozed their buildings and other installations inside the settlements. Everything was quickly reduced to rubble, which the army promised to remove after its departure but never did, leaving the hapless Gazans to clear it up. Anything that could be of use to them was smashed up. Half of the greenhouses which had been erecetd for settler farmers to carry on a thriving trade with the outside world were destroyed by their owners before they left.

Despite the speed of the operation, it was not until 12 September that Israel finally completed its withdrawal of every last soldier and military installation it had held in Gaza. Dr Farid did not stay on to see it, for, as he told us, it was enough to have enjoyed the spectacle of cheering crowds of Gazans rushing in to raise the Palestinian flag over every evacuated settlement. For a short while, Gaza experienced a euphoria and sense of optimism and hope for the future similar to that which had followed the signing of the Oslo Accords. As if anticipating the Palestinian mood, the US secretary of state, Condoleezza Rice, declared at a press conference in late July: 'When the Israelis withdraw from Gaza it cannot be sealed or isolated over with the Palestinian people closed in after withdrawal ... We are committed to openness and freedom of movement for the Palestinian people.'

Heedless of these words and to widespread dismay, the Israeli army, far from leaving Gaza alone, proceeded to cordon off the land adjoining the Erez checkpoint for a 'buffer zone' to protect Israelis against what it called 'terrorist attacks'. All Gaza's borders by air, sea and land would remain under Israel's control, and the Rafah border with Egypt was closed. Two years later, in 2007, Israel went further and declared Gaza a 'hostile entity' with which it was in a state of war. The very fate that Condoleezza Rice had determined should not befall the people of Gaza was precisely what happened to them, and their incarceration continues to this day.

When my father telephoned again with his usual complaint about being alone and no one to visit him, it crossed my mind to tell him about my discovery of Fatima, but I decided against it. He probably would not have been able to hear me on the phone, and even if he had, I did not know if mention of it would upset him. It was not Fatima, who had not meant that much to him, but thought of the past that it might evoke. My family chiefly remembered Fatima as a maid who had served us for a while when we lived in Qatamon. They thought kindly of her, but she was not important to any of them in the way she was to me, and they would have been surprised at the significance I accorded her in my life.

My father asked when Salma was due to come. I had told him that she would soon be arriving to visit me in Ramallah and would pass by to see him on her way. Speaking of her reminded me how much I had missed my daughter, left behind at home in London. Ramallah's hectic atmosphere and the pace of events had taken all my attention. I had not consulted her when I decided to take up the appointment with UNDP for fear she would object. It upset her and I had felt badly about it since, as I did about so many of my maternal failings towards her. Since I never discussed it with anyone else, I was the sole judge of these maternal misdemeanours and did not know how serious or not they were.

Salma was an only child, whom I had late in life in circumstances I had not anticipated. The tiny family she and I made up was very different from the one I used to dream about, and I would torment myself wondering how much that was due to chance and bad luck and how much was my own fault. She had no siblings, no father living with us, and no one to fall back on except me, all of which misfortunes I felt somehow responsible for. I should have made a better marriage and given her a sister or a brother to share her life, since my siblings and I were not close enough for me to rely on them. Only my mother and father gave her their unconditional love, but they were quite old by the time that she was born. My father in particular held a special place for her in his heart, wanting to compensate her for not having her own father close at hand.

How had it happened that I ended up a single mother, something I never expected or wanted? For most of my life I had had no interest in motherhood or babies, and if I ever met a single mother I usually regarded her with pity. Motherhood did not form part of my self-image or my aim in life, and if truth be told I rather disdained the whole business which I thought a poor alternative to the really important pursuit of a career and making a mark in the world. I suspected these attitudes were Arab male views of women I had internalised during my early childhood in Palestine and from my parents and their friends. As a child I could already see that real power lay with men; they made the significant decisions that affected our lives. Women had no power, they had children instead. And I knew which side I wanted to be on.

And yet at the same time I passionately believed in a woman's right to be the equal of men in every sphere. My mother, following the norms of the Arab society she had grown up in, fuelled these feelings by favouring my brother over us girls. I remember the rage I would feel as a child when he was let off the housework, trivial matters in reality, but of great importance to me.

'Silly girl!' my mother would scoff at me laughingly. 'You're not going to die if you clear up the lunch table.'

'But it's not fair, it's his turn!' I would insist, close to tears, while my brother ran off to play. 'I laid the table and he must clear it up, that's the arrangement.'

My father's ambivalence only added to these inner contradictions. He was an educated and enlightened man, but he was also a product of his upbringing in the male-dominated, rural and conservative society of Tulkarm, where women had a subordinate role. He would often define a conversation he thought nonsensical or trivial as 'women's talk', while insisting on a university education for me and my sister at a time – the late 1950s in England – when most girls settled for secretarial college or similar as they awaited marriage.

By the end of my thirties, I found myself to my dismay still unmarried and unpartnered. A short-lived marriage during my twenties and several relationships that followed had all come to nothing. As I grew older I felt myself increasingly anomalous in a society where couples were the norm, whether in England or the Arab world, and my single state was becoming a burden. People did not care for unmarried women; they were either a problem at social gatherings where the hosts had to 'balance the numbers' between their male and female guests, or, as in Arab society, where they were regarded with pity as social failures. I put a brave face on things, but it baffled me that something so natural, so commonplace and so normal as a committed relationship should be enjoyed by millions except me, and I worried that I was heading for a lonely old age.

In 1979 I went to work at Yarmouk University, a newly built establishment close to the city of Irbid in northern Jordan. This was at the time when I first went in search of my Arab roots, reasoning that Jordan was close to Palestine and most of its people were Palestinians. Growing up in a traditional Arab home in the middle of London, as I had done, with nothing to connect the two and with a mother who made no attempt to adjust to the society around her, I found myself landed with an unenviable dichotomy of identity that dogged me for most of my life. Unlike my parents and older sister whose sense of self was firmly rooted in the Muslim, Arab world, I had been too young to be similarly influenced. So I struggled to accommodate my two selves, the one Arab and the other English, and failed. It had to be one identity, not two, and so I attempted to be English, discarding my Arab origins. But this decision brought only temporary relief; it broke down in the end, and I was back with the original quandary.

It was then that I turned to the Arab world for a solution. I went to Yarmouk University to teach the history of medieval Arabic science and medicine, a subject I had taken up after leaving my hospital appointment in London. It had been my form of escape from clinical practice, which I had longed to abandon ever since qualifying in medicine. And it was at Yarmouk University that I met Salma's future father. He was a Tunisian lecturer in Arabic literature by the name of Abd al-Rahman Ayyoub. I was attracted to him from the first, a slim, dark-haired man with fine North African features and a charming manner. He was unusual, not to say eccentric, and fascinated by Jordan's rural society. He made friends with the local Bedouin tribes whose customs and way of life he studied with avidity. He told me he had started out as an anthropologist, introduced me to new concepts and took me to visit the Bedouin where we once stayed the night. None of the other lecturers at the university was remotely like him, and I found him refreshing and original. He was French-educated and told me he had spent several years in Paris where he studied at the Sorbonne, all of which added to his charm.

It did not take long for us to get together. I enjoyed his company and on Fridays, our 'weekend', we would drive off in his battered old Mercedes to visit historic sites in Jordan I had never seen before. And when we returned in the evening I started to invite him to my flat on campus, though such behaviour was not considered proper for unmarried people and we had to keep it a secret. Most of the teaching staff were foreigners, and we were housed on campus in basic, prefabricated huts, freezing in winter and stiflingly hot in summer, in a wilderness of unpaved paths and rough ground where wildlife, including snakes and insects, was never far away. My flat was plagued by mice; to get rid of them I once borrowed a cat belonging to an American academic couple living in the unit next to mine. Unlike the run of Middle Eastern cats that would have made short work of any rodent within a mile, this cat was well-fed, had no interest in hunting the mice and spent the night sleeping on my sofa.

Abd al-Rahman was light-hearted and companionable, very different from my fellow Palestinians, who tended to be too serious and intense. He invited me back to his flat also, and our visits to each other became a regular habit. We socialised with some of the other academics, a variety of odd people from different countries, who became our friends. When I was taken off to be interrogated by the *Mukhabarat*, the Jordanian intelligence services, they were all scandalised.

It was a strange incident and happened in the wake of student protests at the university not long after I arrived. I was not sure what the protests were about, but the students were demanding to meet the president of the university and the demonstration was boisterous but peaceful. It was reminiscent of such student action in England, and I was immediately sympathetic.

I heard that several of the protestors were members of the Popular Front for the Liberation of Palestine, and under surveillance by intelligence officers. I found the whole thing interesting and, unaware of the risks, I made a point of talking to several of them about the PFLP and its current activities in

Jordan. Political activism in the cause of Palestine was not welcomed by the Jordanian authorities. Such activists and their sympathisers were automatically suspect, and there was many a frightening story of summary arrests and detentions without trial by the intelligence services. It was said that torture of suspects was routine, and some prisoners were incarcerated indefinitely. Whatever the truth, the Mukhabarat had an evil reputation and everyone feared them.

To my dismay, I was asked to report to the president the day following the demonstrations. Adnan Badran was a courteous, likeable man with a gentle manner. He told me apologetically that I would have to report to the intelligence services in Amman and that he could do nothing to prevent it. He did not know the reason for the summons, but tried to reassure me that it was unlikely to be serious. The next day was a Friday, clearly not a day of rest for the Mukhabarat, and he arranged for a car to take me there and bring me to his house in Amman for breakfast afterwards. I was in no doubt that there was a security file on me, which would need to have been cleared before I could be appointed at the university. This was a customary practice in Jordan, and especially for Palestinian nationalists like me. One could be denied an entry visa on those grounds alone. I had been stopped once before, in 1976, when travelling to Amman to attend a conference. My passport was confiscated at the airport without explanation and sent to the Mukhabarat, where it was kept overnight.

The intelligence agency headquarters was in those days an innocuous-looking, blue-painted building some way down from Shmeisani. People referred to it by various euphemisms, like 'the Palestine hotel' or 'the hospital for political diseases'. An expressionless official met me inside and led me through a labyrinth of silent corridors with closed doors on either side. I neither saw nor heard anything, but had an image of terrified men cowering inside the closed rooms. True to its reputation, the place evinced a menacing air, the harsh neon lights in the ceiling making it a house of perpetual night. I was finally admitted into an anteroom where several men were standing around, and through into a spacious office in which the head of the agency was expecting me.

This was during the time of Ahmad Obeidat, a well-dressed, dark-haired man with a smooth, impassive face that gave nothing away. Various subordinates were fussing sycophantically around him, but no one said anything. Obeidat greeted me courteously and kept me for about an hour. His manner was pleasantly conversational and relaxed. He asked me about my work and who I knew in Jordan. But for the place we were in, I might have liked him. His questions betrayed no clue as to why I was there, but he wanted to know what I did in London and why I had decided to come to Jordan. He then inquired about my political activities and what I thought of the situation in the region. Did I know any of the students who were demonstrating, and what did I think of them? It was all general information, which he could probably have obtained without detaining me and putting me through that opaque interview.

When he finally released me and the university car took me off to the president's residence, I had a sense of enormous relief, as if I had been guilty of some crime of which I had just been acquitted. When Dr Badran met me at the front door, he started at seeing me.

'My God! How pale you are. Come in and have something to eat.'

Only then did I realise how frightened I had been by that ordeal. And only when I puzzled over the whole incident afterwards did I understand what it had been about: intimidation, and a warning to stick to the lecturer's job I had come for if I wanted to stay out of trouble. My real 'crime', in fact, and that of many of the wretches in those cells, was that we were Palestinians, that we had a cause and that we would not give it up.

*　　*　　*

The affair with Abd al-Rahman was going well. We were closer than ever, visiting each other nearly every day and going about together. In such circumstances, keeping our relationship secret to avoid people's censure, or even an outright intervention by the university authorities, was becoming difficult. Despite the foreign staff and the benign administration of Dr Badran, Yarmouk was a conservative place and staff were expected to conduct themselves with propriety. I doubt Abd al-Rahman and I would have married had it not been for that, and I suspect we would have just carried on with our affair to see where it might lead. But yet, having made the decision, there was something thrilling about it. It was reckless and crazy and all about letting go. I had never done such an impulsive thing before, had always been too serious and inclined to pessimism, struggling to make a career and constantly afraid I would fall behind. Marrying Abd al-Rahman was the antithesis of all that and somehow in keeping with the eccentricity that had first drawn me to him.

We married at the beginning of 1980. In accordance with Jordanian law, the marriage took place in a shari'a court, and, as with all Islamic marriages, it was a brief, unsentimental and legal affair without fanfare or celebration. Once the marriage contract was drawn up, we became a married couple and could live together straight away. But it was the custom for Arab newlyweds to postpone this until after they had had a wedding party. These were often as elaborate and lavish as the groom's family, which was responsible for the costs, could afford to make them.

Abd al-Rahman and I dispensed with that, since we had no family in Irbid and our academic colleagues were more acquaintances than close friends. I had written to my father and had his and my mother's consent to the marriage; they said they had no reason to disapprove my choice of groom, and my siblings were also informed. That evening we had an intimate supper for two with candles and flowers in my flat, which was larger than his. It felt clandestine and exciting.

After the wedding I took Abd al-Rahman to meet my sister, who was then living in Damascus with her husband and children. She had done the conventional thing: married a Palestinian engineer while in her twenties, had four children and lived in a nice house. She fitted well into the society around her and was close to my uncle Abu Salma, the poet, and his wife. There were no discernible problems of adjustment or identity, no conflict between the years she spent in England and the life she had made in Damascus, and she appeared contented and at home in her milieu.

Everyone seemed to like Abd al-Rahman, especially my uncle, whom Abd al-Rahman greatly admired. The two of them soon became engrossed in a literary discussion and it seemed that all was well. We stayed overnight at my sister's house, and when we left to go back to Jordan she and her husband reiterated their invitation to come again.

In the event we never did. I fell pregnant soon after we married, only to discover it was the last thing Abd al-Rahman wanted. He was adamant that the pregnancy would have to be terminated if we were to remain together. He had a troubled relationship with a daughter from his previous marriage to a Frenchwoman about whom he felt great guilt and had promised her he would have no other child. I could see he felt strongly, but nothing would have deflected me from having the baby. I was not young, had not expected it to happen so quickly, and judged, not unrealistically, that it would be my last chance. If I did not have this baby, there would be no other. It might mean the end of the marriage, but I hoped it would not and that Abd al-Rahman would be won over. All my previous indifference to childbearing had gone, but not the desire to have it happen within a loving relationship. I could not see myself going through those nine months, with all their fears and excitements, experiencing the moment of birth, hearing that first cry and holding a small body in my arms, all without a partner. I was wretched at the thought.

But that was exactly what happened. I returned to England for an obstetric check-up. It was supposed to be a temporary visit, and I left all my belongings behind in my flat at Yarmouk. The break-up with Abd al-Rahman was not then final, but as we said goodbye at Amman airport, I remember having a sudden cold premonition that I would not see him again. Once in London I went to stay with my parents, fortunately still there and able to help me. The check-up in hospital and the amniocentesis, a test to detect genetic abnormalities that also revealed the gender of the child I was carrying, went well. Knowing I was to have a daughter I went out and bought the prettiest little dresses I could find, diminutive frocks in floral patterns with embroidered bodices and I tried to visualise my little girl inside them.

I chose a name for her, picked from a list my father had put together from his fine collection of Arabic literary works. But a few weeks before she was born, my uncle Abu Salma died, and I settled on Salma in memory of him. I added 'Lalla' for her Tunisian father; it was a title used in North Africa to mean 'Lady' or 'Princess'.

'When you're a big girl, you might become a writer or an artist,' my father told her when she asked about her name. 'And then you can be called simply Lalla Salma, and everyone will know you.'

I went through the later stages of pregnancy without any complications and gave birth in hospital. My parents did their duty by me throughout that difficult time, but I was aware that they thought what had befallen me was less bad luck than poor judgement: I should have known better; I should not have been so rash; I should have been more discerning. And they were right, but not for those reasons. Many years before,

I had transgressed the rules by marrying a man who was not a Muslim or an Arab. That was in the 1960s, when unions between Muslim women and non-Muslim men were uncommon, though not the other way around. My husband was an Englishman, a fellow student in my year at medical school. Had he been an Arab he would no doubt have been considered a suitable match, a decent young man with a promising professional future. But he was not an Arab, and though he converted to Islam in order to please the family, it made no difference. My mother, not so soft-hearted in those days, angrily rejected him and cut me out of her life as soon as we were married. I had broken a taboo and could not be forgiven. It took many months of begging and pleading to bring her round, and when the marriage inevitably broke down, unable to withstand the pressures of my guilt over what I had done to the family, she rejoiced openly.

And now here I was, many years later bringing a baby into my parents' gloomy house, the same house where I grew up after our arrival in England in 1949. Salma's entry into their old lives brought them great joy and, having known her from the moment of her birth, they felt that she belonged to them in a way their other grandchildren did not. They and I shared her between us and, daunted as I was by being a single mother, I accepted it and was grateful not to be alone. Motherhood did not come naturally to me, as it had not to my mother either, and I lacked a model for how to do it. I was frightened and uncertain, but concealed it beneath a tough exterior. I doubt anyone had the slightest idea of how lost I was, how big a blow that rapid succession of events, from marriage to pregnancy to divorce, had been for me to absorb.

We moved out after about nine months into a flat I owned that had been let out until then, and when Salma was four I sold it to buy a little house within walking distance of my parents. I was back living in Golders Green, which I had not done since going to university in Bristol to study medicine. It was still known as a Jewish area, but an influx of religious Jews and the departure of German Jews, so numerous during my childhood, had altered it. Other national groups had moved in as well, especially Japanese and Indian families. Yet my parents hung on in the same old, uncomfortable house, unwilling to move anywhere else. And because of that it was I who moved to be near them.

I went back to practising medicine, which I had put behind me hoping it would be for good. It had never been my choice to become a doctor; left to myself I would have studied history or literature, but my father, whose influence over me was immense, had insisted and I forced myself to study a subject I had no interest in. Now, finding myself in need of financial support after moving from my parents' house, I had no recourse but to return to the craft I had been trained in. I took up public health, a tedious, dead-end specialty in the 1980s, mostly concerned with committee work and report-writing. But it involved no clinical practice and no medical emergency cover, and as such it was a suitable occupation for the mother of a young child.

I registered with an au pair agency and found a girl to move in with us. These au pairs were usually from European countries who came to learn English and lived with families while they did so in return for helping with the housework and childcare. They normally stayed for one year, but might leave sooner. Most of ours stayed the whole year and became part of the family. I kept in touch with a few of them long after they had left us. How that arrangement affected Salma, who no sooner got used to one girl than another took her place, I dared not think about. It was but one of the consequences of single parenthood, and there were more to come.

On the face of it, I had pulled my life together again, started a new career and had the care of my child in hand. The tough, businesslike exterior I projected reinforced that impression. But it was nothing more than a facade to convince the world, and chiefly myself, that all was well. Behind it I concealed my real feelings as I had done throughout my life. It was how I had dealt with the numbing loss of Jerusalem all those years before and the terrifying dislocation that followed, moving to a foreign country that was like nothing I had ever known. But though my hard shell served as an effective defence against that sort of intolerable grief and fear, it was ultimately self-defeating. People took me at face value, assumed I could cope on my own whatever happened and had no need of the help or sympathy that I was in fact desperate for.

I kept my fears and uncertainties to myself and somehow soldiered on. I could see no escape from my life, working at a job I disliked, alone and responsible for a helpless little human being totally dependent on me. Although my parents were nearby, I was still in ultimate charge of her. Nothing like that had ever happened to me before and I was floundering.

Was I not a monster to feel like that, with a child as beautiful and bright as Salma, truly a gift from the gods? Not to find compensation for past unhappiness in the new life that was developing before me? Not to rejoice that I had attained what I longed for, a child of my own? Were other lone mothers as ungrateful, as depressed as I was? I was ashamed and filled with guilt.

Yet none of it affected my feelings for my daughter. I loved Salma with all my being, was overwhelmed by her presence in my life. My compassion for her was boundless and I was determined to make our situation as normal as possible, to create a new reality for her that would make up for the one we had. I took her to playgroups, sought out everyone I knew who had children, invited them over and went to visit them, cultivated the mothers of her kindergarten playmates – though I was far older and had nothing in common with them – and contacted my old friends whose children were grown up but who made a fuss of Salma. Each au pair was welcomed as one of us, and when Salma was about to turn five, we acquired a black kitten for her to bring up, which my father named Sambo, ignoring the political correctness that was fashionable in England at the time. When he grew past kittenhood, Sambo would regularly join us for dinner, sitting in the fourth seat at the table and looking over our food with interest.

Caught up in my domestic life, I stopped following political events in the Middle East. What had been for years an all-consuming involvement in everything that happened in and around Palestine faded into the background, and I lost touch. The 1980s, Salma's first decade of life, were dramatic for the Palestinians. Their situation in Lebanon underwent a catastrophic reversal. In the summer of 1982 Beirut was put under a merciless siege by the Israelis, and in September of that year the Israeli army presided over the grisly massacres at the Sabra and Shatila refugee camps. The PLO, long established in Lebanon and almost a state within a state, was routed and its leaders forced into exile. In 1987, when Salma was six, the first Intifada erupted in Gaza and then spread to the West Bank. A year after that the defeated PLO capitulated, definitively gave up its previous aim of Palestine's total liberation and recognised Israel's existence on four-fifths of the homeland. The organisation declared the 'State of Palestine' on the rump that remained.

All this passed me by as I struggled with my life. I wished fervently I had a partner to share it with, someone to care for me and my daughter and make our lives more normal. If only I had left it at that, as no more than a wistful desire, and desisted from finding such a man. Whatever he gave Salma of fatherly affection – and there was no doubt that he loved and cared about her – was more than offset by the harm I felt I had done her in choosing him, and then in hanging on to him when it was obvious the relationship was unsuccessful.

I met him when Salma was seven, in the same year that my parents decided to move to Jordan and end their lives there. This would be a severe blow to her, for whom they were the backbone of her life. She spent much time with them and frequently stayed overnight, in the small bedroom that had been my brother's many years before and was now hers. My mother used to rise early, wake Salma and take her half-asleep downstairs to keep her company, ignoring my father's pleas to leave her alone. She stuffed her all day long with her favourite foods, sweets and chips and fizzy drinks, and my father took her for walks and taught her about the places they passed. On one such outing, they went to the park near the house and sat down on a bench. He lifted her out of her pushchair and let her run about on the grass. An old man sitting at the end of the bench watching them, leant over and said,

'Your granddaughter?' My father nodded. 'She must be very special to you.'

'She is,' replied my father. 'The most special little girl in the world!'

Gerald, the new man in my life, was a freelance writer and semi-academic, half English and half Austrian, and he fascinated me. I was seduced by his intelligence and subtlety of mind, his wide knowledge and cultivated tastes. The psychologists would no doubt say he was a stand-in for my father, whose intellect I had always admired even if I also resented his aloofness. Gerald came into my household in 1989, the year my parents left London; he rented out his handsome flat in Highbury, a desirable area of north London, and arrived with his two cats to join us and the horrified Sambo.

In that tortured relationship I made all the classic mistakes that many a foolish woman in thrall to a man has made before me. In my passionate efforts to secure his affections, which I was unsure of, my daughter took a back seat. As I was getting to know him I would arrange for her to be out of the way as much as possible so as to concentrate on developing my relationship with him. He was in my thoughts day and night. Not surprisingly, Salma strongly rejected his arrival in our household and announced that she hated him and wanted him to go away. But in the end she learnt to accept him and grew accustomed to his company.

Close up, Gerald was a complicated man and I was out of my depth trying to understand him. He was a baffling mixture of warmth and detachment, and I sensed a great unhappiness inside him which he buried beneath a heavy schedule of incessant work, reading and writing, travelling to conferences and giving lectures. The intimate relationship, loving support and warm companionship I had longed for could not happen with a man like him, and we nearly separated several times. I wanted us to be a couple, and he wanted to go on being a bachelor. He shut himself up in the small room I gave him for a study and had no concept of family life. He was unused to children, had never had any, and did not know how to relate to Salma. But in his own way he loved her and taught her many new things, and by the end she was quite attached to him.

We stuck together for years, mainly because I could not let him go. I believed I could reform him, change him into the loving husband he could never have been. I persisted with the illusion that he was capable of it if only he could just allow himself to let go his fear of intimacy. In unguarded moments, his natural affection came through and we would spend happy times together. But they never lasted and we quarrelled frequently. At such times he went into terrifying sulks, his way of reacting to situations he could not deal with. He would spend weeks refusing to talk or interact and I was always the one to crack first. Both of us strove to keep Salma out of the stress and tension between us, but it was impossible. The only way to have done that was to have pushed him out of my life, and that I could not bear to do.

After it was over, I would look back in despair at my weakness and stubborn refusal to accept defeat and leave him. When at last it happened, over ten years had passed of my life that I bitterly regretted.

'In time to come,' said my father, 'you and your daughter

will have each other, living happily and peacefully together. You need nothing more.'

It was after I had broken up with Gerald and had come to visit him with Salma in Amman. I had felt an urge to confide in him and told him of my anxiety at having to be alone once more. The thought of joining that sad army of women without men, who dressed up only for each other, who were reduced to talking about men and never meeting any, terrified me. If I had thought for a moment that my father had any word of comfort for me, I was rudely disabused.

'What? Are you condemning me to a lifetime of loneliness as from now?'

'Why not?' He shrugged in a matter-of-fact sort of way. 'You've always been lonely. But now you've got a companion who'll always be with you.'

I was dismayed by his bluntness, and thought to myself, if he had always known that about me, why had he not been kinder to me through the many difficult times in my life?

Salma grew up, joined the legal profession and was much liked and admired. People told me what a credit she was to her mother, how much they envied me having such a daughter. Hearing that always gladdened and surprised me as if I did not deserve it, for I was only too aware of the mistakes I had made and how much better I should have been at caring for her. Perhaps all mothers feel something of the same, but a memory of her childhood always haunted me. It was while she was at primary school, which normally ended at 3.30 in the afternoon. Mothers collected their children at that time, chatting at the school gates while they waited. Since I was always at work then, either my father or the au pair would meet her, or one of the other mothers would take her home with her own children for me to collect her afterwards. In the way that adults are insensitive to children's needs, I had thought this a satisfactory arrangement.

On that afternoon, she had come out into the school yard to see a woman standing behind the school gates whom she took to be me. She ran towards her eagerly, but when the woman turned, it was someone else.

CHAPTER 17

The Conference

There was a power cut at the ministry, not at Dr Sabah's decrepit old building as might have been expected, but at the bright modern presidential compound housing Dr Farid's offices. No lights or computers were working and we were all packing our briefcaces again to go home. Such cuts were fairly frequent in the Occupied Territories, though not in Israel, and everyone accepted them philosophically. However, it was not clear if this power cut was another one of those or due to some local problem, and we were asked to wait. A team of electricians had arrived to investigate and they were in the basement and on the ground floor, where our offices were, shouting out at each other. Various theories as to what had happened were being voiced and tests carried out.

Not long after, another team of electricians turned up to make the same investigations. No one was sure who had called them in, but they also tried to go to the basement where the fuse boxes were. On seeing them, members of the first team immediately stopped working. They began to pack up their tools and prepared to leave.

'Wait!' said a distraught Adel. 'Please wait. We need to sort this out. I didn't mean to offend anyone. Please.' It was Adel who, afraid that the first electricians might not turn up before Dr Farid's arrival at the ministry, had asked the second group as a precaution. But the men were adamant.

'If you think that our work isn't good enough,' said their foreman, clearly offended, 'that's no problem. We've always served the ministry with never any complaints. But that's all right, you have our brothers here who you called in. They'll do the work just as well and no harm done.' The harm was all too obvious in the angry expressions and long faces of the group.

It took the intervention of all the ministry staff to mollify them. The second team was asked to leave, which they disgtuntedly prepared to do, and wanted to charge for their time. In the end, everyone made up and both teams were invited to sit down amicably together and have a coffee, which delayed the repairs even more. Power was not restored after all that and we went home anyway.

I had been steeling myself for a return to the fray over the conference, and had decided to be firm with Dr Farid and give him a piece of my mind if necessary. He was more determined than ever to make the conference, which he was now calling a 'seminar', a huge success and had appointed a new assistant, as he described him, to work on it – a young man called Jamal who had been living in Munich before returning to Ramallah. We were told that he was an expert in public relations and would be invaluable for promoting the seminar.

Jamal turned out to be an obnoxious young man with an arrogant manner, and I doubt he had any expertise in anything except to know how to curry favour with Dr Farid. He belonged to an ambitious, apolitical type of young Palestinian I was becoming familiar with, looking for a niche in the political structure from which to make as good a living as possible. The ideals of the revolution meant little to such people, although they brandished them whenever it was expedient. I did not like him, but could not condemn him for what the circumstances had made of him. When Dr Farid called the next meeting, he was the first to go to his office and make himself comfortable.

It was a large gathering; everyone who had worked on the seminar was there, Aref, the media group, Ilan Halevi, Amin, Adel, Firyal and several men I had not seen before. Dr Farid was not his usual urbane self; he looked slightly stressed and did not make any jokes.

'Well, Doctora,' he addressed me solemnly. I imagined he was annoyed by my lack of enthusiasm for his project which I had never been able to disguise. 'Where have we got to with the programme and workshops? Please bring us up to date.' I was conscious of Jamal's slightly sardonic expression as he looked at me. I turned towards Ilan and Amin, since they were also supposed to be working on the seminar. But they were staring expressionlessly ahead. It was left to me to give a summary of the preparations I had made and to pass round copies of the workshop papers and the draft programme I had drawn up. People turned the pages dutifully, but as they were in English, hardly anyone understood them.

Dr Farid looked impatient. He glanced at the papers I had given him and handed them on to Adel.

'Yes, yes, but have you sent out all the invitations to our friends abroad?' I looked at Amin who was giving an effective impression of not being there. He looked back at me and did not answer.

Ilan said vaguely that a number had gone out.

'A number?' demanded Dr Farid, as close to being angry as I had ever seen him. 'Not all? We've got barely three weeks to the seminar. How do you think busy people are going to be available at such short notice? I've been saying this for months.' He turned to Amin. 'I hope that Dr Khalil at least has been invited.' This was a Palestinian academic living in the US and an old friend of Dr Farid's, whom he had been anxious to bring over as a keynote speaker. I remembered that several weeks before I had asked Amin if this man's invitation had gone out. 'I'm not a secretary!' he had snapped angrily, and I doubted if anything had been done about it.

From our expressions as we stared back at him, Dr Farid suspected the worst. He looked at us in dismay and told Adel curtly to hand him his phone from the desk behind him. Silently we watched him make a call and waited while he put the phone to his ear. Someone answered at the other end, and by Dr Farid's suddenly affable manner we gathered this must have been his colleague. We heard Dr Farid explain about the seminar and invite him pleadingly, telling him his presence was essential.

'Business class?' he said into the phone. 'No other way, you say?' And after a pause as the other man said something, 'OK, don't worry, my friend, I'll arrange it.' When the phone call ended, Dr Farid looked more relaxed.

'Says he doesn't normally travel long distances except business class. Ah well, I can understand that at our age!' He smiled for the first time. 'Adel, please see about the ticket.'

One of the men I did not know had the temerity to ask how much that would cost. Dr Farid looked at Adel, who consulted his computer.

'$2, 200,' he said.

Everyone shifted about in their seats. Dr Farid, whose good humour had returned, smiled at us. 'Don't worry,' he said, as if delivering some really good news. 'The money will be found.'

'Now, Doctora Ghada,' he continued, looking towards me. 'I saw the workshop papers you've just passed round when you sent them to me before. I'm bound to tell you they're still not detailed enough. We need more political context, more explanation for why the topic is important.'

'But I've included all that if you look.'

Jamal chipped in, addressing Dr Farid. 'When we used to do these workshops in Germany, we always included maps and figures. I have such things on slides if you want me to show them at the seminar.' He clearly wished to be a participant. Dr Farid nodded. 'That's a good idea. Can you look at Jamal's slides, Doctora? Perhaps you can work on them together?'

Later that day, Dr Farid telephoned to remind me again about the workshop papers. Jamal, meanwhile, had taken over my computer in the office while I was at lunch, saying he had not been provided with one of his own. After an angry altercation between us I retrieved it from him, at which he got up and stormed out of the office, heading down the corridor towards Dr Farid's room.

'Oh Annetta, it's so awful,' I burst out when I saw her that evening. She was busy organising an art exhibition with Maher whose collection was to be used for it. The night before, they had been at the Cultural Palace for a concert conducted by Daniel Barenboim. I learnt afterwards that it was attended by Dr Farid, many other ministers and all the upper crust of Ramallah society. Barenboim, an Israeli citizen originally from Argentina and a lifelong Zionist, had unexpectedly taken up the Palestinian cause, much to the ire of his fellow Israelis. With Edward Said, the Palestinian intellectual, he had established a youth orchestra with Arab and Israeli musicians playing together as a symbol of how music could create harmony between warring peoples. The orchestra, named the East-West Divan, was enthusiastically received by Western liberal circles, although not everyone on the Arab side welcomed it. I remembered attending one of Barenboim's Divan concerts with a rapt audience in London, listening to Mozart as Israeli bombs were falling on Gaza, and wondering how this civilised exercise in bridging the political divide would help those poor people.

'What else can you do except go along with it?' asked Annetta. 'Your Dr Farid is not going to give up his pet project. God knows what battles he's trying to win over his rivals through putting on this showy seminar. Why not see it like that and do whatever he asks?'

The next day we all met again in Dr Farid's office. He was in an expansive mood this time, and held forth at length about the significance of the seminar in developing a greater consciousness amongst Palestinians of their responsibility to present their case more effectively to the world and beat the Zionists at their own game. He pointedly addressed his remarks to Ilan and Aref and the others, barely glanced at me, and gave instructions to several people at the end, avoiding me. I wondered what had happened and it made me a little anxious. But I assumed that he wanted to send out a message to anyone who did not share his view of the seminar and its importance.

'Don't worry about it,' Zeina reassured me afterwards. 'Dr Farid's one of the nicest people here. I like him. He's not small-minded like the others, but for some reason he's set his heart on this conference. Just humour him and he'll come round pretty quickly.' I was seeing her after another bizarre day of contrasts when I had gone to Jerusalem in the company of Barhoum Odeh, a Ramallah businessman with a Jerusalem ID. I had deliberately taken a break from the petty concerns of the seminar and the happenings at the ministry that threatened to overwhelm me. It was always a danger in Ramallah, as I had discovered, for the larger picture to be submerged by the daily small frustrations and anxieties of that enclosed, abnormal life.

When we reached the Qalandia crossing, Odeh veered to the right instead of taking the road to Jerusalem and drove along the smooth modern highway that led to the settlement of Atarot, which I could never resist calling 'Utter Rot' in my mind every time I saw the road sign to it. But for him, I would not have dreamed of going anywhere near it. It was a huge Israeli industrial park, built on the site of an older Zionist settlement first established in the early twentieth century and developed under the British Mandate before 1948. It changed hands at that time and was taken over by Jordan until 1967, when Israel took it back again and annexed it to the Jerusalem municipality. It became the largest industrial estate in the area, housing over 150 factories and industries and employing thousands of people.

Odeh apologised for making this detour, but said he had to visit Atarot and it would not take us too much out of our way. I did not know Odeh beyond the fact that he was an entrepreneur who frequently went to Jerusalem and was prepared to give me a lift there and back when I asked. As we entered the settlement he seemed very much at home and quickly drove down one of the streets to park in front of a grey building, indistinguishable from the others around it. The whole place was a soulless maze of roads, factories and industrial units. Its atmosphere was dour and businesslike, a purpose-built complex devoted to manufacturing and with no pretensions to be anything else.

'This won't take long,' said Odeh as we got out of the car, 'but I promised I'd drop in on my partner.'

To my surprise, his partner turned out to be an Israeli man called Gideon Cohen. His office was on the first floor of the building, and as soon as he saw Odeh he jumped up and embraced him warmly. He welcomed us into his office and without more ado the two of them got down to their business, poring over some documents. In the adjoining room I saw two men sitting at their desks and working on computers. They looked like Arabs, but Cohen spoke to them in Hebrew as we passed them on our way out.

'Are they Arab?' I asked Odeh afterwards. He nodded. 'Why are they working here? I don't understand.'

'Most of the people employed at Atarot are Arabs, either from Jerusalem or the West Bank. It's been like that for years, didn't you know?'

I shook my head, and, seeing my expression, he asked, 'Is there a problem?'

I was at a loss to answer, but I felt like saying: No problem at all. Any more than the wealthy Palestinians working with Israeli businessmen were a problem, or, come to that, the Palestinian builders helping to construct Israeli settlements on Palestinian land.

The next few days did not go well at Dr Farid's office. Jamal remained a negative presence, Amin worked reluctantly, laboriously dragging out every task, and Ilan popped in to make suggestions without doing anything. We all fell out with each other in frustration, while Dr Farid kept up a constant stream of instructions about the seminar through Adel or by phone from wherever he was. I dealt with his requests by email to spare myself from having to meet or talk to him. I sent him expanded versions of the workshop background papers as he had requested, adjusted the schedule of sessions and added an updated list of chairpersons for each. It did not help matters, and he started to communicate only with Ilan, the latter passing on his instructions to me and to Amin. The situation was becoming intolerable, and in the end I decided to take matters into my own hands and speak to Dr Farid directly.

If I could keep calm, I saw this as a diplomatic move to re-establish amicable relations. I still felt uncomfortable at the change of atmosphere between us and, despite what I thought his unreasonable demands and his absurd pursuit of what was an inconsequential project, I felt obscurely responsible for the stand-off between us and wanted to make amends. As soon as it was lunchtime on the next day and I had the office to myself, I phoned him. He sounded as if he were expecting me, and after a few pleasantries, he launched into questions about the introductory document to the conference. This was separate from the workshop papers I had been writing, and he had never raised any objection to it before. I had the feeling that he was casting about for a way to criticise me. And at the thought something exploded inside my head.

'Dr Farid, I have done everything you asked and more. I have written and re-written the papers, but apparently it's still not good enough. As you know I never agreed with the whole idea from the start. It was always my view that the time and effort, and the money, spent on this seminar should have been used on something more worthwhile. But you were keen to do it, and in spite of my reservations, I went along with you and did my best to comply with what was required. But I must tell you I've had enough and I don't feel inclined to do any more.'

He did not immediately react, and merely said we would talk further when he was back in the office. As I put the phone down I felt slightly worried. Had I overdone it? Should I have been less forthright, not quite so candid? I was unsure, but I also had an enormous sense of release and was glad to be rid of the whole thing. When I walked home later that afternoon, I felt lighter and more carefree than I had done in weeks. Nearing the Gemzo Suites, I turned into the road I usually took to get there, but it was blocked by a street wedding. Rows of chairs were set out on a red carpet spread over the road, and men and women, most of whom were wearing traditional Palestinian embroidered *thobes*, were beginning to arrive. These events were quite common amongst people who could not afford to hold weddings in a hired hall or a hotel. The street on the other hand was free of charge and, with a bit of imagination, could be transformed into a festive place full of jollity and fun.

The wedding chimed with my mood, and I complimented one of the women on her *thobe*. She responded in the typical Arab way by offering it to me. 'Take it, my sister! It is yours.' I wished her well and walked on home. My cheerful mood lasted into the evening, but then began to fade. What had I really accomplished? The seminar was still on course to take place, but after my outburst my position was unclear. Having announced that I would no longer be working on the seminar, did that mean I would have to leave my appointment at the ministry altogether, or what? I did not know, and avoided going into the office the next day. But to my surprise Dr Farid telephoned me in the evening. He sounded slightly strained, but otherwise behaved as if nothing had happened. He asked for the total number of speakers invited and indicated that I should see him in the office the next day.

In that time, nineteen people in Gaza were killed in Israeli air strikes. There was a state of emergency in the Strip, and pictures of distraught relatives appeared on all the TV screens.

But at the ministry people were more taken up with their internal concerns. The seminar was only a few days away, and there was a heightened state of tension among the staff. Everyone was rushing around, visibly agitated, and I went to Dr Farid's office in some dread. He had called a meeting to discuss the final details of the seminar, and when we all sat down he welcomed us in a calm, serious voice. To my amazement, Amin presented him with a list of additional invitees and topics. How, at this late stage, more changes could have been contemplated was extraordinary, and I wondered who had agreed to it. But Dr Farid did not seem overly concerned and made various comments about the new additions.

'Well, now,' he said looking round at everyone, 'I want to arrange the introduction to the seminar. I will open the proceedings with some general remarks and then I would like to ask some of you to say a few words, starting with you, Doctora Ghada. You've been here with us giving us the benefit of your valuable experience with the media and it is only right to invite you to say something.'

Was he being sarcastic, I wondered? I had not expected this after our telephone conversation of the evening before.

'Thank you, Dr Farid,' I replied after a moment. 'However, you know my feelings about the seminar, and in the circumstances I do not think it would be appropriate for me to say anything.'

Dr Farid's expression did not change. 'Very well,' he said casually, 'as you like. We will not call on you to speak.' Without further comment he moved on to the others to invite one or two of them to participate. No one passed any remark about what I had said, and when the meeting ended they all went back to work. Dr Farid did not ask to speak to me afterwards or attempt to dissuade me from my decision, as I half-expected him to, and it somehow felt like an anti-climax. It was a measure of my confusion and loss of bearings in that strange closed world that, despite the logic of my position, I ended up feeling left out and still uncertain that I had done the right thing.

The seminar took place at one of Ramallah's more modest hotels on the main road a little way down from the Muqata'a, the PA headquarters, made famous when Yasser Arafat chose it for his presidential base after 1996 and the place where world leaders and foreign diplomats visited him until his death. Little of it was left standing after the Israelis bombed and besieged it in 2002. They kept Arafat a prisoner inside its ruins right up to his departure to France for treatment of his last illness, widely believed by Palestinians to have been the result of poisoning at Israel's hands. After his death the Muqata'a was rebuilt and, Israel having refused Arafat's last wish to be buried in Jerusalem, a part of it was specially constructed to house his mausoleum.

The first day of the seminar went well. Dr Farid had managed to bring together nearly every public personality in Ramallah. Neither Dr Sabah nor any of his staff were present, since they had not been consulted or invited to participate in the preparations. The conference hall was quite full and there were many journalists covering the event. Dr Farid was clearly elated, his broad smile and expansive manner back, greeting colleagues with kisses and embraces, and directing proceedings with humour and charm. He chaired each session throughout the day himself, ignoring the carefully selected list of chairpersons in the programme I had drawn up. As he had announced to us a few days earlier, he opened the seminar with a summary of its purpose and how it was organised. None of the staff he had said would be asked to speak did so, and after his speech he ceded the lectern to one dignitary after another.

Each of them spoke dutifully of the importance of the topic, and some added personal experiences of their work in the same field. As soon as they had spoken they made their apologies to Dr Farid and hastened out of the hall, giving an

impression of having to resume more important business elsewhere. The speeches were not overly long, but there were too
many of them. I could see people tiring and leaving the hall to
chat outside. By the afternoon, there were more outside than
inside the hall, talking loudly and distracting those still trying
to listen to the speakers. This was a common hazard of Arab
conferences, where the audience was apt to treat the speakers
as background noise to their own conversations, rather like
the piped music that streamed out in shopping centres. Those
who went out to smoke or gossip rarely returned, the hall
progressively emptying as time went on.

Even so, I felt sure that from Dr Farid's point of view the
day had been a success. I wondered whether I should bother
to come back, but I was unwilling to miss the rest of a conference that I had done so much to organise. As I had told
Dr Farid, I would not be speaking and I had maintained my
silence on the first day, not that there were many opportunities to interject during the succession of lofty speeches we
were treated to. It would be different the next day, with more
specific working sessions and a variety of topics I had selected.
Far from declining, as often happened at conferences, audience nmbers actually increased. Many younger people had
joined us, some of them from Gaza, and were busy network-
ing with one another. Dr Khalil, looking jet-lagged, was also
there, and several other researchers and media specialists.

I settled down to attend the morning session, but it was
nothing like the one featured in the programme. Dr Farid, who
was once again in the chair, started off the proceeding. Instead
of introducing the speakers, he launched into a long speech
of his own about his dealings with the media which he illus-
trated by examples from his personal experiences. When he
had finished, he did not return to the programme but instead
introduced Jamal, another unscheduled speaker, who showed
a series of slides – presumably the ones he had mentioned in
Dr Farid's office, but not especially related to the topic of the

seminar. I was seated near the front staring at him and, on seeing me, he flashed a look of triumph in my direction.

I saw that the morning programme had in effect been hijacked; many sessions I had drawn up, and for which I wrote the background papers Dr Farid affected to find so important, had been scrapped at a moment's notice. Looking around me at the audience in dismay, I suddenly spotted the Israeli journalist, Amira Hass.

'I didn't want to come,' she told me afterwards. 'I know what these seminars are like. They're all the same and they're all a waste of time. But Farid invited me and was so insistent, I didn't want to upset him.'

Amira worked for the liberal Israeli daily newspaper, *Haaretz*, and was one of the few Israeli journalists prepared to portray Palestinian tribulations under Israel's occupation. She wrote of these sympathetically and unflinchingly, and had earned the admiration of many Palestinians and others for her courage and integrity. She spoke Arabic and was the only Israeli I knew, aside from Ilan Halevi, living in Ramallah and with an intimate knowledge of Palestinian life. Dr Farid saw her at the same moment and called out.

'Amira! Welcome!' He spoke in English. 'That's our good friend, Amira Hass,' he explained to the audience in Arabic. 'Please come up on to the platform.'

She shook her head. 'No? I can't persuade you?' he wheedled. 'Well, at least tell us what you think of the seminar so far, and of the Palestinian situation in general. Everyone would love to hear from you.'

She stared back at him. And then she said, 'Do you want me to be honest?'

'Of course!' exclaimed Dr Farid heartily.

'OK, I'll tell you what I think. I think you should not be wasting your time doing this seminar, and you and the rest of the Palestinian Authority leadership should not be behaving as if you were a government of a state. There is no state. You are under occupation and your proper role is to be the leadership of a people under occupation.' She spoke earnestly and without a smile.

I was impressed by her forthrightness and courage to speak as she did in such a place. But Dr Farid did not seem at all put out. He smiled at her as genially as before, and I wondered whether he had actually heard what she said.

'Thank you, Amira.' He nodded at her and then resumed directing the remaining sessions. I was eager to talk to her about her observations, but she left straight after lunch, saying she had a deadline to meet for her newspaper, and we agreed to see each other at another time. I never heard Dr Farid subsequently ever discuss what she had said, or refer to her attendance at the seminar.

The climax of the two-day event came in the middle of the afternoon session. Dr Farid stood up and announced the arrival of the president of the Palestinian Authority, Mahmoud Abbas, guest of honour at the seminar. I was sitting in the aisle of the conference hall, and as Abbas and his entourage walked in I stepped out to greet him. We had first known each other in the mid-1970s, when he was a prominent member of Fateh based in Damascus. I remembered him as a good-looking man with an interesting, sophisticated approach to the Palestinian struggle. He believed in studying Israel and Zionism and advocated that Palestinians learn Hebrew, which he himself had done, as the best way to understand Israelis and know how to deal with them. He was highly educated, with a degree in law from Damascus University and a doctorate from a Moscow academy on the controversial subject of the collaboration between the Zionists and the Nazis during the Second World War.

I had found him agreeable and charming, but not a leader of men, and everyone else at the time thought the same. He was not remotely in the same league as, let alone a substitute for, Yasser Arafat, as later happened. Nevertheless, in 2003,

Arafat reluctantly appointed him the PA's first prime minister because the Israelis refused to deal with Arafat and preferred the milder Abbas. He was a man in the right place at the right time, and when Arafat died he was the obvious candidate to replace him, all other potential Palestinian leaders having been imprisoned or liquidated by Israel.

His rejection of the armed struggle and what was described as his moderate stance on politics appealed to the West. He made friendly overtures to Israeli leaders and believed in a negotiated solution to the conflict. That position inevitably led him to crack down on all forms of Palestinian violence against Israel, which he did not accept as legitimate resistance, and to oversee the expansion of the Palestinian security services into a force that worked closely with the Israelis to police his own citizens. People accused him of doing Israel's dirty work, of acting to protect its interest at the expense of his fellow Palestinians and filling Palestinian jails with resistance fighters. They also said he was lining his pockets and those of his sons with Palestinian aid money.

Nonetheless, he was elected Palestinian president in 2005 and from that position continued to advocate for a solution through peaceful means. Seeing him after all those years, he came across in the irreverent English phrase as nothing more than a harmless old buffer. His hair and moustache were all white and his face had filled out to give him a benign, grandfatherly appearance behind his large-framed glasses. The accusations against such a kindly looking elderly man seemed implausible. He said he remembered me, and after a warm exchange of greetings he invited me to visit him at his office. However, our conversation was soon cut short by Dr Farid who walked down to receive him and lead him up to the platform.

When he addressed the gathering it was in vernacular Arabic, to my surprise, since formal or public speeches were usually expressed in literary Arabic. But it made him more approachable.[1] He said little about the seminar except to thank Dr Farid for organising such an important event, and restated his view that there was no way forward but the way of peace. This meant, he went on, the total abandonment of all forms of military action and violence on the part of Palestinians. He believed that such action had only harmed them in the past and set back the cause of peaceful resolution. His words were met by stony silence among the younger people in the hall and a few half-hearted handclaps from the rest.

'Where has all this peacefulness got us?' one young man called out to murmurs of agreement. Were they thinking, I wondered, of the freeing of Gaza from Israel's army and its settlers that had brought no freedom, or of the settlements ringing Ramallah that went on expanding, or of the army incursions and arbitrary arrests that happened daily in every Palestinian city?

Abbas did not look at the questioner. His eyes were fixed on a point at the back of the hall and he seemed reluctant to answer. After a pause he said, 'We must all be patient. We took a wrong course and we're suffering the consequences. But we're changing that and it will bring results, you will see.'

A youngish woman took up the same theme. 'Israel just thinks we're weak if we try to be peaceful. We go on peaceful demonstrations against the Wall every week, but it's not made any difference. They go on building it.'

Encouraged, several others put up their hands to speak. But they were ignored and Abbas, still not looking directly at anyone, said in a final sort of way,

'My position is clear. We go the way of peace. No violence. No force. It's our only course. I am a man of peace and will not discuss anything else.' And with that he raised his hand in

---

1 Modern Standard, or literary, Arabic is the universal medium of writing, journalism and formal speech. The form used in everyday interactions is colloquial or vernacular Arabic, which differs from country to country in the Arab world.

farewell and slowly stepped down from the platform, Dr Farid and his assistants beside him. As he started to walk along the aisle, an earnest-looking young man with two or three others behind him stepped into his path.

'Abu Mazen,' he said, using the title by which Abbas was familiarly known, after his eldest son, Mazen, who had died some years before. 'What should we do if the Israelis don't respond to our being peaceful and go on attacking and killing us just the same? Shouldn't there be a point where we change course?' He was clearly desperate for guidance.

One of Abbas's guards tried to push him out of the way, but the young man shook him off.

'I've said all there is to say,' Abbas replied. 'My way is the way of peace. I do not change.'

'But if your way doesn't work, what then?'

Abbas smiled and said, 'You heard me. I do not change.' This time his guard succeeded in moving the young man aside. I looked after Abbas as he walked on and wondered if the peaceful strategy he espoused was anything other than an admission of weakness in the face of Israel's might. I remembered the vigorous, creative young revolutionary he had been and could hardly believe that this defeated, submissive creature was the same man.

After Abu Mazen's departure, Dr Farid assembled everyone for the final session of the conference. The hall gradually filled up and all the chatterers outside were urged to go in. A panel of speakers presented a summary of their views on the topic and answered questions from the audience. It was a short session, and Dr Farid concluded the proceedings with several resolutions for future work that had been passed by a sub-committee earlier. This was a popular practice in such conferences. People worked hard to draw up worthy resolutions that no one ever implemented or even read afterwards. He thanked the speakers and the audience for its attendance, and then paid fulsome tribute to all those who had helped in the organisation of the conference. He mentioned by name every staff member at the ministry, followed by Ilan Halevi, Jamal, Aref, the Bir Zeit university media group, his personal assistants Adel and Firyal, and he thanked even the lowliest workers at the ministry. But in all that long list he did not once mention my name.

I was stunned. He had ignored me throughout the two days of the seminar, but even so, I had not expected this. I felt snubbed and demeaned. Several people who knew of my work on the conference, including Ilan and Adel, looked round at me questioningly. But Dr Farid seemed not to notice; he beamed his approval at the panel and shook hands with several of them before turning to the audience again and bidding them farewell. The gathering broke up and everyone started talking. I put my papers together and, not speaking to anyone, walked towards the front of the hotel to leave. There was a conference dinner that evening for some of the participants; to which I had been invited. Although I had initially accepted, I now decided to decline and went back to the Gemzo Suites.

I felt wretched. The events leading up to the last two days, all those agonised preparations and recurrent frustrations I had endured for weeks, went through my mind. The seminar papers I drew up and the programme I put together so pains-takingly might just as well never have been written. I had not been able to find the courage, either to turn down my part in a project that I despised right from the start, or to play along with it like the others and do nothing. In the end, Dr Farid had his way and it was I who was left ignored and belittled.

I last saw Dr Farid the day after the seminar, when I forced myself to go into the ministry and say goodbye to him with the others. I was told he was off to Norway, probably to one of the international conferences he so loved to attend. We shook hands in farewell, but his manner was cold, and I wondered what he would say about me in the UNDP evaluation report that all ministries with assigned consultants were required to fill in. Likewise, I had been asked to provide a final media strategy for the ministry before I left.

I found out later that Dr Farid had passed on my evaluation report for Adel to complete, which the latter duly did, making up the answers as he went along. On the other hand I took care over the strategy report that I submitted to UNDP and to Dr Farid. It did the Ministry of Media and Communications no favours and I spared no effort in laying bare the facts as comprehensively as I could in the best manner of the similar reports I used to draw up for the NHS. Despite its critical nature, it was genuinely meant to be a helpful guide for policy-makers in the future. I described the damaging division between the two ministries, the wasteful duplication, the lack of staff oversight and poor use of the available resources. I ended with a list of recommendations for future action, although I had no hope that either Dr Farid or anyone at the ministry would ever read the report. However, a British NGO which part-funded the Ministry of Media and Communications came across it after I left and got in touch with me, much alarmed by some of its findings.

Why on earth did I ever come to this place, I asked myself again? What had made me imagine that there was anything here for someone like me? I looked back on my whole assignment in 'Palestine' and realised that I had achieved none of my aims because it would never have been possible in the Palestine that I found. I had travelled to the land of my birth with a sense of return, but it was a return to the past, to the Palestine of distant memory, not to the place that it is now. The people who lived in this Palestine were nothing to do with the past I was seeking, nor were they a part of some historical tableau frozen in time that I could reconnect with. This Palestinian world I had briefly joined was different: a new-old place, whose people had moved on from where I had them fixed in my memory, had made of their lives what they could, and found ways to deal with the enemy who ruled them.

That struggle had its own logic and priorities, its own strategy for managing the situation they were in. It had produced an impressive edifice of institutions, public services and a civic structure, all the features that convincingly mimicked those of a small state. In reality, they were ways for an occupied people to survive and maintain some integrity against a force that unceasingly tried to rob them of it; even the antics of Dr Farid and his PA colleagues were attempts at wresting some sense of purpose for their existence out of the subordination Israel imposed on them.

It was a life-and-death struggle, and it would continue until the end. There was no other choice, except abject surrender, which none was prepared to contemplate. What the outcome of this struggle would be no one could know, but it was certain that out of it a new reality would emerge, and it was they, the people on the ground, who would be its heirs. Not those like me who no longer belonged here, who lost out in 1948 and were scattered all over the world, never to return. The gap in time of over fifty years in our collective history since then had made us different people, with new lives and new identities. How was it possible after so much disruption to bring us all together again as if nothing had happened? And had Israel finally succeeded in fragmenting us beyond recall?

As this thought struck me, I felt a shiver of alarm. Ever since we left Jerusalem and throughout my life I had held on to our cause as that of a nation which was dispossessed, and must one day return to its country. It was the underlying theme of all my writings, my lectures and my political work for Palestine. I could not accept for that national cause to be whittled down to one of local occupation after 1967. Nor did I share the political fashion for what was called 'pragmatism' in dealing with the right of return, shorthand for selling the refugees down the river.

For me, return was at the heart of the issue. Without it, the injustice that had blighted our lives for generations would never cease. One day, when my sister and I had been discussing our fragmented family and how dispersed we were, how no one lived close to the other, each alone in the world, and how unnatural it all was, she said bitterly, 'If we had never left our country none of this would ever have happened. We would have been amongst our kin, growing up together, helping each other, none of us living or dying alone.' And looking up to heaven, she raised her hands, palms upward in supplication, and exclaimed with quiet vehemence, 'I pray to Almighty God that he may wreck their lives as they have wrecked ours!'

I knew there were formidable practical difficulties in the way of our return, an aim that seemed ever more unattainable with the passage of time. But I was determined that Israel should never be allowed to get away with what it had done. Despite the resignation and defeatism of the Palestinian official stance and the indifference and cynicism I saw amongst many Palestinians around me, I never once doubted the rightness of my position, or that the crime committed against us in 1948 would somehow be redressed. I could not have lived with myself if I had thought differently. Such an injustice could not be allowed to stand for good, and the perpetrators would sooner or later have to give up their gains. The Palestinian refugee camps which still stood after more than half a century, not one of them ever closed down, bore eloquent testimony to an unfinished business that would have to find its proper conclusion.

But now, for the first time, my core belief in that certainty began to falter. I thought about the exiled Palestinian communities long settled in Britain, Europe, America and elsewhere. They were well established, and although they still remained devoted to what they called the cause of Palestine, and many of their children too, they went on entrenching themselves ever more deeply in their adopted countries. Many had found a workable accommodation for their commitment to the cause in the form of various activities and charitable works. These would not bring Palestine back, but it was a comfortable compromise that satisfied the demands of conscience and did not upset the tenor of everyday life.

I could see this situation continuing for good. What cause did such exiles really adhere to, and how likely was it that any of them, so comfortably settled, would truly strive for the right of return? Could the refugees trapped in their camps, helpless and still dreaming of return, make anything happen? Would those whose primary concern was not the right of return, but the struggle against Israel's occupation and how to end it? Had Israel kept us out of our homeland for so long that we were forced to make alternative lives and thus suspend indefinitely our right of return? And in such circumstances, would any of us ever go back? The thought was unendurable. Even to contemplate it sickened me.

What my time in Palestine had really shown me was that the two fundamentals I had always lived by were transformed out of all recognition. There was no national cause any more, and no unified struggle for return. What future we all had lay with those who lived here, in the West Bank, Gaza and Jerusalem under Israel's occupation, at the mercy of their success or failure to rebuild our cause. And if ever we went back, it would be through them, and no one else.

Epilogue

Amman, May 2007

My father lingered on through April. His condition did not improve; the nasal tube was back in place, but the amount of nourishment that reached him through it was paltry, despite Margo's loving preparations of liquid food for him. I stayed in Amman as long as I could. My sister was living with him at that stage, and he was in the care of male nurses who changed from time to time. Salma came to visit him during that period, and if anyone could have roused him from his semi-coma, it was she. She would sit by his bed and hold his hand, saying,

'Hello, *Jiddo*' – Arabic for granddad – 'it's me, Salma. How are you?' And it seemed that he half-smiled at hearing her voice and gave a slight nod.

I had not visited him as often after leaving Ramallah in 2005 as during my period there. Before his final illness set in, he had remained keenly interested in my experiences in the Palestinian territories. When I went to Amman to stay with him in October 2005, a week after my assignment at the Ministry of Media and Communications ended, I told him about the seminar and its aftermath, and relived the details of that depressing time in the telling.

I could not hide from him the sense of disillusionment I had been left with, although I did not know what I expected from him who had suffered disappointments and regrets to dwarf mine. He listened to me quietly and just shook his head. I wondered whether he might have wanted me to say something else, perhaps to point to a way other than that of despair. How I wished at the time I could have seen a ray of light or a chink of hope in the bleakness of the Palestinian plight, the promise of a new beginning rather than the certainty of an end.

He died on 5 May 2007. I was not with him when it happened, but, as well as the faithful Margo, my sister and a cousin of ours – the same who used to read the Quran to him when he was in hospital – were there in another room. The provisional diagnosis was of a massive heart attack, but everyone said it was a wonder he had lingered on for so long. Although I knew it was inevitable, his death was still a shock, somehow unreal, as if I might suddenly hear that it had all been a mistake and he was alive after all. I suppose I felt all the usual things people conventionally go through at such times, the unfamiliarity of life after the last parent has gone, the loss of personal definition, the unwelcome awareness of being the next in line for death, and the end of all he represented for us.

He was buried according to Islamic custom. His body was taken away on the night that he died for the ritual washing the next day, and my nephew Omar came over from Ramallah to be present at the washing. Salma, who was the most affected of us all by his death, was in the middle of her law examinations and could not come.

My father's body, wrapped in its white shroud and placed in a temporary coffin (by Islamic custom, the dead are not buried in a coffin but only in their shrouds), was taken to the mosque for the ritual prayers. He was then driven to a cemetery outside Amman for burial in a grave distant from my mother's, not by design but in accordance with the way the cemetery authorities assigned burial plots. A large number of men but no women, as was traditional, attended the funeral. Three days of formal mourning followed, the men received in a specially erected marquee outside what had been my father's home and the women inside. I flew in from London and arrived for the second day of mourning.

Margo served the bitter coffee and dates that were normally offered at such times, but no one thought to ask how she felt about my father's death, or how she feared for her future. After it was all over, my sister, who continued to live in my father's flat, kept her on for a while, but then returned her to Sri Lanka, giving her the generous sum of money my father had left her. When she reached her home town she found that her only son, to whom she had sent all her wages over the years to build a family house for them, had squandered the money and never completed the building of it. There was nowhere for her to live and she had to fend for herself.

My father's death was marked by obituaries in the Arabic press, the London *Guardian* and *Independent* newspapers, and the BBC Arabic Service. They somehow made his death more real, and I thought: my poor father, who had not expected to die ever, was truly dead. When I looked back at his long life I was unutterably saddened that it had all been spent in the shadow of strife and loss. He had lived for more than a century, as if holding out for some resolution to take place before he died, giving providence a chance again and again to make it happen. By rights, he and all Palestinians should have been rewarded for their patience with the ending of the conflict, a life of normality and the restitution of what had been lost. Instead he, and my mother before him, left the stage with the drama still running, and they would never know how it ended.

Was that to be my fate too, and my daughter's and all of us? Despite my gut-wrenching despair, I was determined that it would not.

On the Typeface

This book is set in Sabon, a narrow Garamond-style book face designed in 1968 by the German typographer Jan Tschichold. Tschichold had been a leading voice of sans-serif modernist typography, particularly after the publication of his *Die neue Typographie* in 1928. As a result, the Nazis charged him with 'cultural Bolshevism' and forced him to flee Germany for Switzerland.

Tschichold soon renounced modernism – comparing its stringent tenets to the 'teachings of National Socialism and fascism' – and extolled the qualities of classical typography, exemplified in his design for Sabon, which he based on the Romain S. Augustin de Garamond in the 1592 Egenolff-Berner specimen sheet.

Sabon is named after the sixteenth-century French typefounder Jacques Sabon, a pupil of Claude Garamond and proprietor of the Egenolff foundry.

.